Classic Motorcycles

WORLD FAMOUS
A.J.S. PORCUPINE
500 cc
1947
NOWN SURVIVOR WITH
ONTAL ENGINE

Classic Motorcycles

The complete book of
motorcycles and their riders

ROLAND BROWN

HH
HERMES
HOUSE

🏍 ACKNOWLEDGEMENTS

The Publishers would like to thank the following for their kind permission to reproduce their photographs:

Martyn Barnwell/EMAP and EMAP Archives 10 (all), 11tr, 12tr, 15bl/br, 18b, 19tl, 28b, 37tl/m, 44 (all), 67tl/tr, 68t, 86t, 88t, 92t, 93ml, 95, 96, 102t/b, 120t/b, 122t, 130 (all), 131b, 138b, 147ml/mr, 157bl, 158t, 159t, 160 (all), 193 (all), 195tr, 198t, 200m, 207t, 213m, 216t, 217tl, 218 (all), 219tl/ml, 220 (all), 222 (all), 214ml, 216t, 222 (all), 224t, 228t, 238m, 247tmr/br 248t, 249t/r 3 down. **British Film Institute** 29b, 30 (all), 31t/b, 36lm. **Roland Brown** 19tr/bl, 21b, 22b, 23m, 27b, 33tr, 46b, 53tl/b, 56tr, 57t, 63tmr/tr/b, 78t, 89br, 93mr, 98t, 99b, 109tl, 113t, 115tl/br/bl, 125tl, 127bl, 133b, 134b, 136m/b, 141t, 144t, 151 (all), 152t, 161t/ml/mr, 165tr, 167ml, 173bl, 183br/bm, 186 (all), 194 (all), 200t, 210b, 216m/b, 219tr, 221t, 223br, 231bl, 232 (all), 233tr, 241m, 245tl/b, 250m, 251m. **Roland Brown/Graeme Bell** 157t. **Roland Brown/Jack Burnicle** 104t/m, 132t/b, 133tl. **Roland Brown/Gold & Goose** 63tl, 99tl, 108t/b, 124 (all), 125tr, 126b, 134t, 135tr, 143t, 195l 2 down/bl, 217b, 243b. **Roland Brown/Phil Masters**

46t, 71tr, 103b, 107b, 109b, 112t/m, 167r, 171mr/b, 195l 3 down, 204b, 205tl, 225b, 240t, 244b. **Roland Brown/Mac McDiarmid** 22m, 45b, 201b, 203b, 210t. **Roland Brown/ Oli Tennent** 15t, 19br, 24-5, 27tl, 33b, 59tl, 60b, 61t, 63tltml/tmr, 94, 105b, 106-7t, 113b, 127br, 135br, 137t/ml/b, 148-9b, 163tml, 164 (all), 165tl, 178m/b, 179b, 180 (all), 181tl, 182 (all), 183t/bl, 184t, 185tr/ tl/m, 197b, 203tl/m, 202 (all), 208t, 227 3 down, 235tl/tr, 242 (all), 245tr /m, 250t/b. **Jack Burnicle** jacket front flap, 82 (all), 83 (all), 84b, 85t, 104b, 145bl, 162b. **Jason Critchell** 192m/ b. **Kel Edge** 6, 23b, 42-3, 61m, 62, 63m, 77ml, 78b, 81 (all), 109m, 128t, 155tl/b, 159tl, 171tl, 174t, 185bl, 189ml/mr, 192t, 205tr, 217ml, 229b, 235m 3 down, 237b, 241bl, 254b, 255bl. **John Freeman/(c) Anness Publishing** jacket back flap top, 36m/tr/b, 37tr. **Gold & Goose** 18t, 20t/b, 21t, 48b, 49tr, 52b, 53tl/m, 64-5, 67ml, 72t, 73b, 74-5b, 79t, 99tr, 114, 126t, 135bl, 168b, 169tl, 170b, 172, 175tl/tr, 177b, 184b, 187bl, 188-9b, 189t, 231t/m, 253tl. **Hulton Deutsch Collection** 12tl/b, 16t, 29tl/tr, 45tr, 66 (all), 67b. **Imperial War Museum** 50 (all), 51tl/tr/b. **Phil Masters** back jacket bottom, 20m, 21m, 34b, 35t/b, 47tr, 54-5, 60t, 61b, 69b,106-7b,

115tr, 117t, 129m, 153b, 157m, 166 (all), 204t, 233b, 236t, 244t, 251b, 252, 253b. **Mac McDiarmid** front jacket, back flap bottom, 1, 2, 5, 17t/m, 22t, 32b, 37br, 38 (all), 39 (all), 40, 41t/b, 45tl, 48m, 57b, 59tr, 60m, 70b, 71tm, 87t/m, 88b, 89tl/tr/bl, 90t, 98b, 103tl/tr, 115m, 116 (all), 117bl/br, 120m, 122m/b, 128b, 129mt/mb, 131tr, 144b, 154 (all), 155tr, 159m, 161b, 162t, 169b, 190-1b, 191l, 197tr, 199tl/tr, 201m, 209tl/tr, 215b, 223l, 226t, 227 2 down, 230m/b, 235b, 238t, 239tl/b, 241tl/tr, 246 (all), 248m/b. **Don Morley** back jacket top left and right, 3, 8-9, 11tl/m/b, 12m, 13t/b, 14, 16b, 26t, 27tr, 31tl, 32t, 33tl, 34t, 48t, 49tl/b, 51bl, 52t, 53tr, 58tl/tr, 59b, 67mr, 68t, 69tl/tr, 70t, 71tl, 72b, 73tl/tr/m, 75tr, 76t/b, 77tl, 79m/b, 84t, 85b, 86b, 87b, 90b, 91tr, 92b, 93t/b, 95, 97 (all), 99m, 100 (all), 101t/b, 103 (all), 105t, 107m, 109tr, 110, 111 (all), 112b, 118 (all), 119 (all), 121 (all), 122t, 123 (all), 125m/bl, 127tl/tr, 129tl/tr/2 down, 133tr/m, 135tl, 136t, 137mr, 138t/m, 139, 140 (all), 141ml/mr/b, 142m/b, 143bl/br, 145m/br, 147t/b, 149t/bl, 155m, 156t, 157br, 158b, 159b, 161mr, 163tr/m, 165bl/br, 167tl 169tr, 170t, 173tl/tr/m/br, 174m/b, 175m/bl/br, 176t, 179tl, 181tr/b, 187br, 190t, 191tr/mr, 195br, 196

(all), 197tl/m, 198b, 199m/bl/br, 200b, 201t, 205bl, 206 (all), 207m/b, 208b, 209m/b, 211tl/mr/b, 212 (all), 213 tl/tr/b, 214 (all), 215t/ml/mr, 217tr, 219mr, 221tl/ml/mr, 223t, 224b, 225t, 226b, 227t/b, 228b, 229t/m, 231br, 233tl, 236b, 237tl/tr/ml, 238b, 239tr, 240b, 243t/ml/mr, 247t/ml/lmr, 249tl/r 2 down/b, 251tr, 254t, 255t/bm/br. **Nick Nicholls** 71b, 74t, 75tl, 76m, 77tr/b, 145t, 211m, 219b, 251tl. **John Nutting** 171tr, 187t, 195tl, 205br, 211tr, 234 (all) 253tr/tm. **Dick Parnham** 91tl/b. **Garry Stuart** 26b, 28t/m, 46m, 47tl/mr/b, 148t, 149m/br, 150 (all), 152b, 153t/m, 156b, 176b, 177t/m, 178t, 179tr, 221b. **Phillip Tooth** 146. **Oli Tennent** back jacket top middle, 80, 142t, 168t, 188t, 235m 2 down. Thanks also to the PR departments of BMW, Ducati, Honda, Moto Guzzi, Kawasaki, Suzuki and Yamaha for their help in supplying photographs, and to Frontiers Motorcycles Ltd, 0181 540 7774, for the loan of clothing on p36.

t=top b=bottom l=left r=right
m=middle tr= top right tl=top left
ml=middle left mr=middle right
bl=bottom left br=bottom right
lm=left middle tmr=top middle right tml=top middle left

This edition published by Hermes House
27 West 20th Street, New York, NY 10011

A CIP catalogue record for this book is available from the British Library

ISBN 1 84038 000 4

Publisher Joanna Lorenz
Project Editor Joanne Rippin
Designer Michael Morey
Illustrator Stephen Sweet

Also published as *The Encyclopedia of Motocycles*

Printed and bound in China

© Anness Publishing Limited 1996, 1999, 2000, 2001
Updated © 2002
1 3 5 7 9 10 8 6 4 2

CONTENTS

SECTION ONE

THE WORLD OF MOTORCYCLING

Two wheels and an engine. The basic ingredients of the motorcycle are so simple; but its attraction, stronger than ever after 110 years of relentless development, is so hard to explain. Part of the reason for this is that motorcyling means so many things to so many different people. More than merely a form of transport, it incorporates everything from an ancient Scott roadster to Aprilia's modern 250cc Grand Prix racer, from a booming Velocette single to Honda's futuristic EXP-2 desert racer.

This section of the book takes a winding ride from the first ever motorcycle – Gottlieb Daimler's Einspur – to the fastest ever – Dave Campos's 322mph (518kph) Harley-Davidson – via Chelsea Bridge, Hollywood and the Nürburgring. But if it is the machines that form the outline of the motorcycling picture, then it's the people who design, build, modify, pose, commute or tour on, race, crash, repair, fight or save lives on them who add the colour.

The World of Motorcycling is their story: from Mick Doohan pulling a wheelie on his Honda NSR500 to Marlon Brando leaning on his Triumph Thunderbird; from a medical worker delivering supplies in the African Bush to a Sunday-morning superbiker cranking a Ducati 916 through a turn. Different people, on different motorcycles, and in very different situations, united by a shared appreciation of two wheels and an engine.

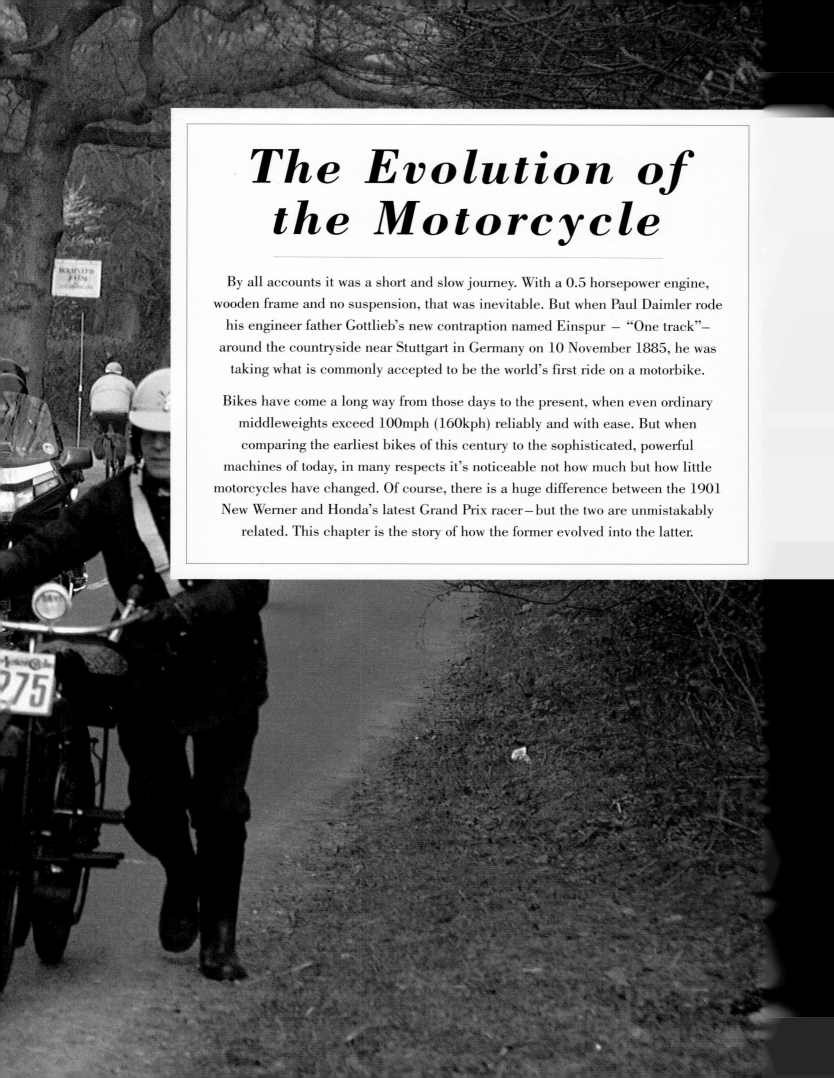

The Evolution of the Motorcycle

By all accounts it was a short and slow journey. With a 0.5 horsepower engine, wooden frame and no suspension, that was inevitable. But when Paul Daimler rode his engineer father Gottlieb's new contraption named Einspur — "One track"— around the countryside near Stuttgart in Germany on 10 November 1885, he was taking what is commonly accepted to be the world's first ride on a motorbike.

Bikes have come a long way from those days to the present, when even ordinary middleweights exceed 100mph (160kph) reliably and with ease. But when comparing the earliest bikes of this century to the sophisticated, powerful machines of today, in many respects it's noticeable not how much but how little motorcycles have changed. Of course, there is a huge difference between the 1901 New Werner and Honda's latest Grand Prix racer — but the two are unmistakably related. This chapter is the story of how the former evolved into the latter.

EARLY DAYS

Gottlieb Daimler wasn't much of a motorcycle man, and soon after producing Einspur in 1885 he gave up bikes to make his name in the newly-developed car industry. But Daimler had made a major breakthrough. Although steam-powered railways and ships were already well established by the 1880s, steam was ill-suited to smaller vehicles. With Einspur's 265cc internal combustion engine, Daimler, who had previously worked as an assistant to Dr Nikolaus Otto, inventor of the four-stoke engine, had shown the way forward for personal transport.

Steam-powered bikes had been tried before, notably the Michaux-Perreaux velocipede built in France in 1869, but they were gradually abandoned as petrol-burning engines gained

■ LEFT *The Werner brothers of Paris sold several hundred of their light and practical 1898 model "motocyclette" which had its engine mounted above the front wheel.*

■ BELOW *In 1901, the French firm patented the New Werner layout, with engine positioned between the wheels for improved handling, which motorcycles have used ever since.*

■ ABOVE *It is said that the first ever bike race took place when two motorcyclists met on the road for the first time — these two road riders certainly look to be enjoying a bit of friendly competition in 1903.*

■ TOP *The De Dion Bouton tricycle, powered by the same firm's reliable four-stroke single engine, was raced very successfully in the final years of the last century.*

■ ABOVE *Indian's single, with its engine inclined to the rear in American fashion, was very successful in 1902 – over 100 were built and there was a reported 17-year waiting list.*

■ RIGHT *Such was the pace of change in motorcycling's early years that Daimler's Einspur, with its huge wooden frame, was totally outclassed by bikes of 15 years later.*

popularity. Among the earliest converts were the German brothers Hildebrand, who with their partner Wolfmüller produced the world's first production motorcycle in 1894. The Hildebrand & Wolfmüller held a watercooled, 1500cc twin-cylinder four-stroke engine in a specially made steel frame. Among other high-tech features, it benefited from John Boyd Dunlop's recently invented pneumatic tyres. Its top speed of about 25mph (40kph) was quite fast enough considering the rear emergency brake consisted of a simple metal bar that dragged on the ground.

The next big step in motorcycling's development came soon afterwards when two Frenchmen, Count Albert De Dion and Georges Bouton, produced a single-cylinder, four-stroke engine of about 125cc. The De Dion unit was rated at 0.5bhp but in reality produced more, revved reliably to 1800rpm, and was very compact. It was originally used to power the De Dion tricycle, which was raced successfully in the late 1890s. Frustratingly for its manufacturers, the design was blatantly copied by

numerous other firms as motorcycle production spread across Europe.

Few of the new firms could agree on the best place to locate the engine until the Paris-based Werner brothers, whose original bike used a De Dion-style unit above the front wheel, revised their design in 1901. The New Werner's engine was placed low, between the wheels, in a steel frame, and drove the rear wheel via a leather belt. With its bicycle-style saddle, wheel-rim brakes, and improved handling due to its lower centre of gravity, the New Werner set the pattern for 20th-century motorcycle design.

■ LEFT *The Wall Autowheel, pictured here in 1910, was an engine and auxiliary wheel that clamped to a bicycle — very useful for well-laden bikes.*

■ BELOW *Lawrence of Arabia was the most famous rider of the fast and sophisticated Brough Superior V-twin of the 1920s.*

Development from that point was rapid, as enthusiasm for bike production spread across Europe and America. In that same year of 1901, Americans George Hendee and Oskar Hedstrom produced the first Indian motorbike. Three years later, as Indian was pioneering the twistgrip method of throttle control and planning its first twin-cylinder model, the firm gained a new rival named Harley-Davidson. During the next ten years, Indian, Harley and other firms including Excelsior adopted the V-twin engine layout that remains America's favourite to this day.

American firms Indian and Pierce both launched four-cylinder models as early as 1909, but by then the ultra-sophisticated four from Belgian manufacturer FN had already been on the market for four years. Benefiting from an aircooled, 363cc in-line four engine with shaft final drive, the FN was a remarkably smooth and classy device – undoubtedly an early superbike! During two decades of FN production the four's engine capacity was increased to 750cc, and further refinements including a clutch, gearbox and leading-link forks were added to the original design.

Elsewhere, too, technology was leaping ahead. By 1910 the British-built Scott featured not only a watercooled, two-stroke twin engine

■ LEFT *The world's first kick-start, situated alongside the rear wheel, was just one of the features pioneered by Yorkshire firm Scott on its two-stroke parallel twin in 1910.*

■ RIGHT *Despite some faults, Ariel's smooth Square Four of 1937 represented the pinnacle of two-wheeled sophistication before the Second World War.*

but also a kick-start, chain final drive and telescopic front forks. Early four-stroke advances included Harley's use of all-mechanically operated valves, in place of the early inlet-over-exhaust (IOE) design whereby the inlet valve was simply sucked open by the piston. In 1913, another American firm, Cyclone, produced a big V-twin roadster with overhead camshafts. Only a year later, French firm Peugeot had a vertical-twin racebike with twin cams and four-valve cylinder heads.

The American motorcycle industry suffered badly in the years after the First World War, partly due to competition from Henry Ford's ultra-cheap Model T motor car, but in Europe the bike business boomed in the 1920s. English firms such as Matchless, Triumph and Velocette, German marques BMW (whose first flat-twin, the 493cc R32, appeared in 1923) and Zündapp, and Italian manufacturers

■ BELOW *Early BMW flat-twins, such as this 482cc R52 from 1928, established a reputation for cleanliness and reliability that the firm would benefit from for many years.*

Benelli and Moto Guzzi all produced a variety of increasingly sophisticated bikes.

By the late 1930s, motorcycles had evolved into reasonably fast, reliable and easily ridden machines. At the top end of the market was Ariel's Square Four, a luxurious 1000cc tourer. Triumph's 500cc Speed Twin had been launched in 1937, with a parallel twin engine layout that would serve for over 50 years. Glamorous, large-capacity V-twins were being produced by Brough and Vincent in Britain, and by Harley and Indian in America. Barely half a century after Einspur's first faltering trip, motorcycling had well and truly arrived.

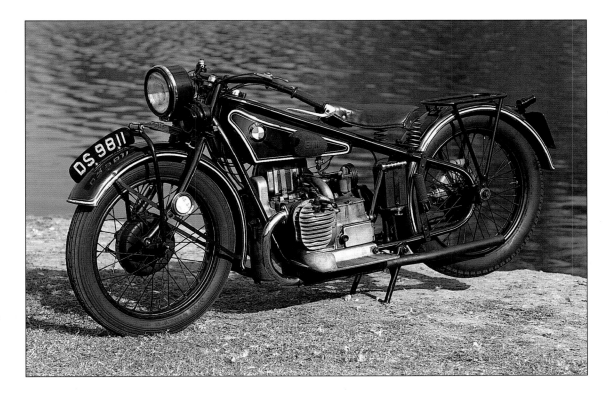

■ OPPOSITE *Several decades of progress are clear in this 1935 London Motorcycle Show publicity shot of a 500cc New Imperial with an 1897 Holden, the world's first four-cylinder bike.*

THE GOLDEN AGE

Motorcycling's rate of progress slowed considerably in the decades following the end of the Second World War. In contrast to those inventive early years, the period spanning the 1940s, 1950s and early 1960s was characterized by numerous singles and twins from the dominant British industry.

In those days, machines like the Norton Dominator, BSA Gold Star, Triumph Thunderbird and Velocette Venom ruled the road. Now these names are enough to arouse misty-eyed nostalgia for an era of blood-and-thunder biking, when traffic was light, noise regulations and speed limits were much less rigorously enforced than today's, and

motorcycling was an all-year-round pursuit whose benefits included social alienation and ingrained dirt under the fingernails.

For all the lack of revolutionary change, there was nevertheless a gradual refinement in two-wheeled design. A typical roadster of the late 1940s had no rear suspension, crude girder front forks, a bicycle-style single saddle, a manual ignition advance-retard lever, and a sluggish, low-compression engine that had been designed to run on low-octane wartime fuel. Paint finish was dull, frequently army-surplus camouflage green. Items such as a speedometer, brake light and pillion footrests were still optional extras.

■ BELOW *The Brough Superior's image and reputation for performance lived on through the 1940s and 1950s, long after production of models such as the SS100S had come to an end.*

■ RIGHT *Indian ceased production of its Chief V-twin in 1953, but the firm's subsequent attempt to produce British-style parallel twins was unsuccessful.*

Throughout the 1950s that format was modified through the adoption of brighter colours, telescopic forks, plunger and swing-arm rear suspension, speedos, dual-seats and more sophisticated electrics. Four-stroke engines adopted shorter-stroke dimensions, higher compression and aluminium barrels for added performance and reduced weight. A mid-1950s Triumph or BSA 650cc twin was good for a genuine 100mph (160kph), and handled reasonably well besides.

Britain's bike industry went from strength to strength in the 1950s, with domestic sales rising to a peak of 330,000 in 1959. The Brits

also made a big impression in America, where the home industry – suffering from poor direction and lack of small-capacity models – was in serious decline. Of the last two great American manufacturers, Indian built its final big V-twin in 1953, and Harley sold fewer than 10,000 bikes in 1955.

■ RIGHT *This 750cc Norton, shown being given as the prize in a raffle organized by the London-based 59 Club, was a typical British parallel twin of the mid-1960s.*

■ FAR RIGHT *Motorcycling clergyman the Reverend Bill Shergold, pictured here buying a new Triumph, founded the 59 Club and was a prominent figure during British biking's heyday in the 1960s.*

■ **LEFT** *These riders, far from causing trouble, are setting off from London's Trafalgar Square to deliver posters during Christian Aid week in the 1960s.*

■ **OPPOSITE MIDDLE** *Triumph's 650cc Bonneville was the most famous British twin.*

■ **OPPOSITE BELOW** *Soichiro Honda, pictured (left) with co-founder Takeo Fujisawa, led Japan's assault on British dominance of the motorcycle market.*

The British firms, however, had more competition from Europe, where German firms BMW and NSU made rapid post-war recoveries. Italian manufacturers including Ducati, Gilera and MV Agusta built rapid 100 and 125cc sportsbikes that were raced in road events such as the Milano-Taranto and Giro d'Italia. Scooters also became increasingly popular, the modest performance of the Vespas and Lambrettas being offset by the advantages of weather protection and, more subjectively, style. By comparison, British small-capacity rivals, mostly powered by two-stroke Villiers engines, were considered terribly dull.

■ **RIGHT** *Triumph's "bathtub" full rear enclosure, introduced on this 350cc Model 21 in 1957, was later used on bigger twins but was unpopular.*

■ **LEFT** *Velocette's 500cc Venom carried the British single-cylinder tradition into the 1960s.*

In 1965 Honda launched the CB450 twin, which competed almost head-on with Britain's traditional parallel twins. Following hard on Honda's heels Kawasaki, Suzuki and Yamaha would soon release big motorcycles of their own – and there was nothing the British firms could do to stop the erosion of their market lead.

Italy also spearheaded the attack on British dominance on the racetrack following the introduction of the world championship series in 1949. AJS, Norton and Velocette, successful in the first few seasons, gave way to fours from Gilera and MV Agusta; in the smaller classes Moto Guzzi and Mondial battled with Germany's NSU. On the street Britain was still in the lead in the mid-1950s, but disaster was looming for firms whose complacency had led to a lack of investment and innovation.

As the 1960s arrived, it was the growing challenge from Japan that held the real danger to Britain's long-dominant industry. In 1960, Triumph boss Edward Turner made a now famous visit to several factories in Japan, returning to warn – to little avail – of what he termed as the somewhat frightening spectacle of its hugely promising and fast-growing motorcycle firms. By then Honda had already made a successful first trip to compete in the Isle of Man TT.

In the showrooms, an expanding range of well-built and sophisticated small-capacity motorcycles had been enhanced by the 50cc C100 scooter, whose famous "You meet the nicest people on a Honda" slogan would help attract annual sales of over half a million for years. Despite what many in the European industry vainly continued to believe, the Japanese would not remain content to build small bikes for long.

THE MODERN ERA

When Honda introduced the CB750 in 1969, it was not just the Japanese machine's four-cylinder, overhead-cam engine and 120mph (193kph) top speed that heralded the start of motorcycling's modern age. Equally important was the Honda's lavish specification, including an electric starter and front disc brake, and its general air of sophistication. Ironically, Triumph's three-cylinder, 750cc Trident T150, which was launched at the same time, handled at least as well and was slightly faster. But the British bike's pushrod engine, kick-start and drum brakes – plus its dubious reliability and need for frequent maintenance – marked the Triumph as a machine from an earlier era.

Japan had shown the way forward, and the 1970s would belong not just to Honda but to Kawasaki, Suzuki and Yamaha too. Kawasaki

■ LEFT *Ducati's 750 Super Sport (left) and its successor the 900SS, both singleminded race-replicas, were among the fastest and best Italian superbikes of the mid-1970s.*

■ LEFT *Honda's sophisticated CB750 four caused a sensation when it was revealed at the Tokyo Show in late 1968, and again when it was displayed at the Brighton Show shortly afterwards.*

■ ABOVE *Britain's crumbling hold on the bike market came under further attack in the 1970s when Triumph's Bonneville (left) was faced by Yamaha's XS650.*

■ BELOW LEFT *The Japanese firms' race to build bigger and more powerful superbikes climaxed in 1979 with the massive, six-cylinder Kawasaki Z1300.*

■ BELOW RIGHT *Moto Guzzi's 850 Le Mans Mk.1 V-twin (left) and Kawasaki's 900cc Z1 four offered contrasting brands of 1970s superbiking.*

raised the stakes again in 1973 with the launch of the 900cc Z1, whose muscular twin-cam engine gave 130mph (209kph) top speed with unburstable reliability. The bike they nicknamed the King and its descendants would dominate superbiking for much of the decade.

Not that the Japanese had it all their own way. Britain's industry might have been dying but Italy, in particular, had much to offer. Ducati and Moto Guzzi, each with a distinctive brand of V-twin engine, and Laverda, with powerful 1000cc triples headed by the legendary Jota, all produced memorable mid-1970s superbikes. The Italian bikes' biggest advantage was in handling, for the Japanese firms found chassis harder to perfect than engines. Not until the Suzuki GS1000 appeared in 1978 did Japan build a superbike

that could hold its own in the bends – and even then poor wet-weather performance remained.

Japanese manufacturers also had a "bigger is better" fixation that reached a peak in 1979 with Kawasaki's massive Z1300 six. But there were some excellent small bikes too, including Yamaha's long-running RD series of middleweight two-stroke twins. Smelly strokers fell foul of emission regulations in America, but thrived elsewhere throughout the 1980s. That decade saw Japanese aircooled fours take over the large and medium capacity market to such an extent that the term UJM – Universal Japanese Motorcycle – was coined to describe them. But there were more imaginative designs, too – notably the turbocharged models tried and then abandoned by each of what, by now, were termed as the Big Four.

■ LEFT *Ducati's 916 V-twin and Honda's 750cc V-four, the RC45, updated the two firms' traditional formats to produce stunning mid-1990s superbikes.*

■ BELOW LEFT *Kawasaki's ZZ-R1100 — the ZX-11 in America — was the world's fastest production bike for five years following its launch in 1990.*

More successful 1980s' developments included the increasing fitment of fairings (and luggage systems for tourers), and the adoption of chassis features such as single-shock rear suspension and radial tyres. Aluminium became frequently used in frame construction, following the dynamic arrival of Suzuki's ultra-light GSX-R750 race-replica in 1985.

By 1990 the Japanese had almost universally adopted liquid-cooling for engines, partly to satisfy tightening emission laws. Kawasaki's awesome new ZZ-R1100 had a 16-valve engine producing over 140bhp, a twin-beam aluminium frame, a top speed of 175mph (281kph) and levels of handling, roadholding and

■ BELOW *Naked, large-capacity "retro bikes" proved popular with 1990s' riders, and Yamaha's XJR1200 was arguably the pick of the Japanese bunch.*

braking that would have been unthinkable ten years earlier. The best bikes' all-round excellence meant that developments were less dramatic than before, but outstanding machines continued to appear. Honda's CBR900RR of 1992 combined superbike power with light weight. Kawasaki's 1995-model ZX-6R challenged Honda's long-standing middleweight champion, the CBR600F, with a 160mph (257kph) top speed that few open-class bikes could better.

But not every rider simply wanted speed. From Honda's mighty Gold Wing tourer – introduced as a basic 1000cc flat-four in 1976, now a lavishly equipped 1500cc six – to scooters via sports-tourers, trail-bikes and cruisers, the Japanese built something for almost everyone. As bikes were increasingly used for leisure rather than mere transport, and the average age of riders rose to above 30 in many countries, what some bikers wanted was an unfaired retro-style machine whose appeal was based on simplicity and nostalgia.

One thing most riders seemingly did not want was technology at a premium price.

■ BELOW RIGHT *Trail bikes such as BMW's giant R1100GS have proven popular with many riders. Although most have traditionally been ridden mainly on the street, advances in technology have made trail bikes increasingly capable of handling difficult off-road terrain.*

■ BELOW *Rock star Paul Young's custom Harley-Davidson, pictured in London's King's Road, epitomizes the American machines' shift in image from outlaw hog to fashionable accessory.*

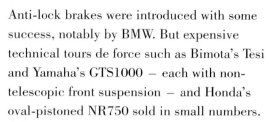

Anti-lock brakes were introduced with some success, notably by BMW. But expensive technical tours de force such as Bimota's Tesi and Yamaha's GTS1000 – each with non-telescopic front suspension – and Honda's oval-pistoned NR750 sold in small numbers.

By the mid-1990s there were increasing signs that motorcycling's balance of power was

shifting again. Japanese firms had been hard hit by the strength of the yen, which made their bikes increasingly expensive in most markets. Although the Japanese firms' engineering was stronger than ever, many models showed a lack of new ideas.

By contrast, Harley and several European manufacturers, having succeeded in matching Japanese quality, were enjoying huge success. Harley's retro-styled V-twin cruisers, BMW's sophisticated yet traditional flat-twins, reborn Triumph's classy triples and Ducati's racy V-twin sportsters offered all-important character to an increasingly image-conscious market.

INTO THE FUTURE

■ BELOW *Honda's EXP-2 could be the forerunner of future clean-burning and environmentally friendly two-stroke roadsters.*

Futuristic concept machines appear at all the major international bike shows. With names like Morpho or Nuda, they attempt to point the way forward for motorcycle design. But while some concept-bike features do eventually make it into real life, predicting the future of the powered two-wheeler is a risky business.

In the immediate future, bikes are likely to incorporate many of the features already seen in limited numbers. Catalytic converters, fuel-injection, variable valve timing and even programmable, smart-card engine-management systems, as seen on Honda's 1994 Japanese market NSR250 race-replica, have already hit the street and seem likely to become more and more common.

Electric power has already been used for several small bikes, most promisingly by Piaggio's recent Zip & Zip scooter, which combines a petrol engine for open roads and batteries for use in town. But current batteries are heavy, inefficient and give limited performance which would indicate that their widespread adoption in larger motorcycles is still many years away — despite the sleek,

■ ABOVE *The power characteristics of this Honda NSR250 could instantly be varied by putting a different memory card, which also acted as the ignition key, into the slot in its dashboard.*

■ LEFT *Yamaha's Morpho concept bike, pictured at the Cologne Show in 1990, had futuristic features including forkless front suspension — which was introduced on the GTS1000 two years later.*

■ LEFT *Bimota abandoned plans to compete in Grands Prix with its 500cc V-twin two-stroke, but continued to develop the engine for road-going use.*

■ BELOW LEFT *"Showdown" was Spanish student Cesar Muntada's award-winning idea of what a Harley-Davidson roadster might look like in 2020.*

Granada-Dakar Rally, Honda successfully unveiled an experimental two-stroke racer called the EXP-2, whose 402cc environment-friendly single-cylinder engine could soon be seen in a road-going form.

Bimota had earlier made headlines with the forkless Tesi, although the sales failure of this and Yamaha's GTS1000 suggests that most motorcycles' chassis will remain relatively conventional for some time. Possible chassis developments in the early 21st century include active suspension, which reacts to bumps using a computer instead of springs, a system which had already been used in the car world.

Further into the future may come hydraulic steering, tried unsuccessfully in early Tesi prototypes, two-wheel steering and two-wheel drive, which has been used with some success by off-road machines. But despite that, motorcycling's immediate future is likely to be based on more down-to-earth factors such as lightness, simplicity and individuality.

hydrogen battery-powered ES21 concept bike shown by Honda at the Tokyo Show in 1993.

More promising is the direct-injection two-stroke engine, which dramatically cuts emissions by injecting fuel directly into the combustion chamber after the exhaust port has closed, instead of allowing large amounts of unburned fuel to escape, like a conventional two-stroke. Ford has produced a prototype direct-injection car, developed in collaboration with Australian specialists Orbital, which has shown much promise.

Bimota, the small Italian firm best known for chassis engineering, produced a prototype 500cc V-twin two-stroke with direct injection in 1992, and at the time of writing finally looked set to put it into production. In the 1995

■ ABOVE *The weight and performance of batteries has so far limited their two-wheeled use, but the 1994 special "Violent Violet" was fast.*

The Rider's View

There is a lot more to motorcycling than simply riding a bike. Owning and using a motorcycle gives a different perspective on life to that of the average pedestrian or car driver. Depending on the rider, the machine and the moment, you are an individual – free, rebellious, fast-moving, glamorous, somehow above the dull troubles of the normal world. You're also mistrusted, maybe persecuted, even pitied, always vulnerable.

Those shared emotions produce a bond between motorcyclists that can sometimes bridge the huge gaps between the many different types of rider. Many's the time that the owner of a superbike has pulled up to help a novice with a broken moped. But within the overall two-wheeled scene is a vast number of diverse subgroups and cultures, reflecting the variety of experience that motorcycling has to offer.

■ BELOW *Highlight of the year for the British Motorcyclists Federation is the rally in Peterborough, which attracts tens of thousands of riders.*

■ BOTTOM *If you forget exactly where you parked your Harley-Davidson at Sturgis in August, you can expect to take a long time trying to find it.*

JOIN THE CLUB

Riding a motorcycle is essentially a solitary pursuit. You sit there gripping the handlebars, peering intently ahead through visor or goggles, ears full of noise from wind and engine, mind concentrating on the road ahead. On a bike there is rarely either the time or the opportunity for conversation.

Yet motorcycling can also be a most sociable hobby. Wherever in the world there are bikes, there are riders who congregate to compare machines, modifications and cornering lines; to swap information, spare parts and tall stories. From the regulars at the Rock Store café near Los Angeles, famous weekend haunt of Harley-riding Hollywood stars including Stallone and

Schwarzenegger, and at Box Hill in Surrey, England, to Japan's Tougekozo (the "peak to peak kids"), who race their sportsbikes on mountain roads, there's a group of bikers meeting somewhere every day, and that's just the informal gatherings. There are also hundreds of official motorcycling clubs and organizations. Some are political pressure groups, notably the Brussels-based Federation of European Motorcyclists, which incorporates individual groups in over a dozen countries. Motorcycling has long been a tempting target for legislators – and riders are increasingly well organized to fight back.

Bike sport is generally run through clubs, some of which have a thriving social section. Specialist road-riding groups include Christian Bikers, Gay Bikers and Women on Wheels. Many clubs are simply locally-based organizations with a wide variety of members. One-make clubs exist for manufacturers ranging from Messerschmitt to MV Agusta. The bigger marques have national clubs in numerous countries, plus an international umbrella organization.

There are also groups for many individual models as diverse as the BSA Bantam, Honda CBX1000 and DKW rotary. Few branches of motorcycling are too obscure to have their own organization – ask the stalwarts of the Post Office Vehicle Club, or the Raleigh Safety Seven and Early Reliant Owners' Club.

■ ABOVE LEFT *Sportsbikes and Harleys gather every Sunday morning at the Rock Store, California's best-known bikers' meeting place.*

■ ABOVE RIGHT *One-make organizations such as the Norton Owners' Club offer members social events and technical assistance.*

■ BELOW *Members of Britain's all-party Parliamentary Motorcycle Group line up outside London's Houses of Parliament.*

Honda's Gold Wing alone supports two vast organizations in America, each with branches all over the United States, plus groups in many other countries.

The one-make club with the highest profile is the Harley Owners' Group, which has more than 250,000 members worldwide in almost 800 branches, over 500 of them in America alone. Annual gatherings at Daytona in Florida and Sturgis in South Dakota attract vast crowds, the majority on Harleys, though many of the more upwardly-mobile bikes arrive on the back of pick-up trucks these days. In many respects Harley-Davidson's claim of selling not just a motorcycle, but the lifestyle to match as well, is not an exaggeration.

MODS, ROCKERS & ANGELS

The bad boy image has been an integral part of motorcycling for years, and probably always will be. Bikes are a potent symbol of speed, rebellion and youthful aggression. And despite the ever-increasing numbers of respectable, leisure-time riders, many people still view motorcyclists as undesirable and outside the law.

In the 1960s the main cause of the bad reputation, particularly in Britain, were the Rockers. Generally dressed in studded black leather jackets, jeans and black boots, they met at cafés such as the Ace, in north London, and Johnsons, near Brands Hatch circuit in Kent, to drink tea, talk bikes and go street-racing. Favoured machinery included BSA Gold Stars,

■ LEFT *Probationary patch-club members have to earn the right to wear full colours on their backs.*

■ BELOW *The Ace Café in north London was the famous meeting-place of café racers and Rockers in the 1960s.*

Triumph Bonnevilles, Norton Dominators and the legendary Triumph/Norton hybrid the Triton, generally with tuned motors, lightened chassis and turned-down Ace handlebars.

When the Ace regulars were not racing against each other or outrunning a Daimler V-eight police car, a popular trick was to put an Elvis or Eddie Cochran single on the jukebox, then run out to the bike and attempt to complete a pre-set road circuit before the disc ended. Despite plenty of brushes with the law, the Rockers were more into bikes than violence. Even so, their bank-holiday seafront battles with their rivals the Mods – scooter riders dressed smartly in suits and anoraks – made national news regularly in the 1960s.

The Hell's Angels, whose notoriety peaked at about the same time, were a different and much more dangerous proposition. Formed in 1950 in San Bernardino, California, but later best known through the chapter based in Oakland, near San Francisco, the Angels were by far the biggest and most powerful of the many American outlaw bike groups that included Satan's

■ RIGHT *Most British café racers of the 1960s wore open-face helmets and leather jackets, and rode singles or parallel twins with low "Ace" handlebars.*

■ BELOW *A leather-jacketed Rocker is led away by a policeman after a clash with scooter-riding Mods at Margate, on England's south coast, in 1964.*

■ OPPOSITE
America's veterans of the Vietnam War have their own motorcycle club, complete with Angel-style colours and regalia.

Slaves, Gypsy Jokers and Commancheros.

Angel fever spread worldwide, and numerous chapters still exist in Europe and elsewhere. But their profile is much lower than it was in the 1960s when the Angels, famously dirty, wearing their ever-present colours – the winged-and-helmeted skull symbol – and

riding chopped Harley-Davidsons, became a feared force through clashes with police and civilians. They were immortalized in films including *Hell's Angels on Wheels* and *Hell's Angels '69*, both of which starred genuine members of the Oakland Angels, and in Hunter S Thompson's memorable book *Hell's Angels*.

■ RIGHT *The film* Hell's Angels '69 *starred members of the Oakland Angels, the most powerful and best-known of California's numerous groups, or "chapters".*

MOTORCYCLES IN THE MOVIES

There's no more vivid way of charting motor-cycling's changing image than through its portrayal on film. Bikes have starred in the movies since the likes of *No Limit*, improbably featuring ukulele-playing George Formby at the Isle of Man TT, and *Motorcycle Squad*, about a bike cop who joins a gang of criminals, were released in the 1930s.

The most famous bike film is *The Wild One*, Stanley Kramer's 1953 classic starring Marlon Brando and Lee Marvin. Triumph-riding Brando and Harley-mounted Marvin played rival bike-gang leaders in a film loosely based on the events that occurred in 1947 at Hollister, California, where a minority of motorcyclists at a big rally caused trouble. The film was controversial enough to be banned in Britain for 15 years. It inspired teenagers, horrified their parents and formed attitudes that last to this day.

Later films featuring dubious biking characters include *The Leather Boys*, a British period piece from the 1960s, and *Girl On A*

■ LEFT *The 1930s' film* No Limit *starred George Formby as "Speed Demon" George Shuttleworth, riding his streamlined Shuttleworth Snap at the TT races.*

Motorcycle, starring Marianne Faithful. The 1960s also produced *Easy Rider*. The story featured Peter Fonda, Dennis Hopper and Jack Nicholson riding across America on a pair of chopped Harleys, complete with drugs, rednecks and music by Steppenwolf and others, and remains a classic biker film.

Another of the better efforts is the 1974 Australian production *Stone*, which features excellent street-race footage as well as outlaw gang fights. *Mad Max*, the Australian film that shot Mel Gibson to stardom in 1979, also has

■ LEFT *Jack Nicholson (left) and Peter Fonda rode a Harley across America with Dennis Hopper in* Easy Rider, *the ultimate 1960s' bike movie.*

■ ABOVE *Marianne Faithful turned plenty of heads in the 1968 film* Girl on a Motorcycle, *also released with the title* Naked Under Leather.

■ ABOVE *Marlon Brando, here with co-star Mary Murphy and his 650cc Triumph Thunderbird, caused outrage as bike-club leader Johnny in* The Wild One.

■ RIGHT *Silver Dream Racer combined a couple of songs from lead star David Essex with road-race action footage shot at Brands Hatch and Donington Park in Britain.*

its share of bike action. Other big names in films with two-wheeled interest include Mickey Rourke and Don Johnson, stars of *Harley-Davidson and the Marlboro Man*. A Harley also makes the title of the 1973 movie *Electra Glide in Blue*, which stars Richard Blake as a bike cop with an attitude problem.

Films about bike sport are headed by *On Any Sunday*, which stars Steve McQueen, already the veteran of a bike chase in *The Great Escape*, plus racers Malcolm Smith and Mert Lawwill, and conveys the thrill of dirt-track and desert racing. Robert Redford makes a fair off-road racer in *Little Fauss and Big Halsy*. Motorcycling has no road-race movies to compare with four-wheel epics such as *Grand Prix* and *Le Mans*. But both *Silver Dream Racer*, the 1979 British film starring David Essex, and *Race For Glory*, its 1989 American equivalent, include some reasonable action footage.

RIDING THE CLASSICS

Of all the two-wheeled trends of recent years, the growth of classic biking is perhaps the most dramatic. For most of the motorcycle's life, the classic concept has barely existed. To most riders, old bikes have simply been that: old bikes. Interesting and useful to a degree, but generally less desirable than the superior machines of the day.

That attitude began to change in the 1970s, as Japanese bikes took over the motorcycle market and an increasing number of enthusiasts became nostalgic for the old-fashioned, mainly British, machines of the past. The launch of *Classic Bike* magazine in 1979 reflected a growing demand, although at that time few people could have imagined the way in which interest would snowball.

These days classics are a major part of the motorcycling scene, above all in the UK. There is a wide choice of specialist magazines, each full of advertisements from firms who sell, maintain, restore, make bits for or insure classic machinery. Complete Nortons – Manx racers and Commandos – are built from new parts. Many European dealers specialize in importing British and Japanese bikes from

■ ABOVE *Veteran machines from motorcycling's earliest years set off on the annual Pioneer Run, from London to Brighton on England's south coast.*

■ LEFT *The annual Classic Bike Show at Stafford, England has become a huge event, with club and trade stands, an autojumble, auction and concourse contest.*

■ **ABOVE LEFT** *Some modern-day classic riders prefer to dress in period fashion, although old-style headgear offers little protection from injury or the law.*

■ **ABOVE RIGHT** *Recreations of long-distance classic events such as Italy's Milano-Taranto give owners of old machines a perfect opportunity for a run.*

American states where the combination of consistently high sales figures and a kind climate has left clean old machines in abundance.

And there is a huge choice of events for classic bikes, too, from club runs and race meetings to shows and concourse contests. At the latter, fanatical officials dock points for a restoration that uses over-polished alloy or slightly the wrong shade of maroon on a side-panel. Bikes restored to factory standard – or, better still, with a verifiably interesting history – are highly desirable and change hands for vast sums of money.

The question of how to define a classic bike causes much heated discussion. To some hard-liners only British bikes qualify; others accept American and European machines too. One of the fastest-growing organizations of all is the Vintage Japanese Motorcycle Club, which caters for owners of Japanese bikes over 15 years old and has more than 4,000 members.

Things are more precisely defined for really old bikes, for which long-running organizations such as the Vintage Motor Cycle Club have established rules. Veteran bikes are defined by the VMCC as those built before 1915; vintage as made between 1915 and 1930; and post-vintage as between 1931 and 1945.

At the other end of the scale are those riders who prefer their classics straight out of a crate. Most current Harley-Davidson models, the glut of Japanese retro-bikes and Triumph's 1995-model Thunderbird – complete with traditional mouth-organ tank badge and peashooter silencers – combine the advantages of modern engineering with the look and at least some of the nostalgic appeal of the originals.

■ **RIGHT** *Demand for classics such as this Indian Chief has led to the emergence of many firms specializing in the restoration of bikes and production of spares.*

LEARNING TO RIDE

For many motorcyclists, learning to ride a bike involved wobbling off on a two-wheeler for the first time, possibly on a private training-ground with a road-safety instructor on hand to impart the basics of throttle and brake control. But these days, with bikes ever-faster and roads increasingly crowded, more advanced forms of two-wheeled tuition have become popular.

■ BELOW *Many sports-bike riders take advantage of the advanced courses that help reveal the secrets of Germany's uniquely demanding Nürburgring circuit.*

Some of these take place on the road, in the form of expert-level instruction along the lines of that given to police motorcyclists. The course run by the London-based Metropolitan Police combines vital safety tuition with spirited road riding and is considerably more exciting – and probably more beneficial – than the more conventional advanced driving courses.

But it is the racetrack where the majority of motorcyclists go to learn how to ride fast and safely – or simply for an excuse to blast round at high speed with no fear of police radar traps, or of traffic coming in the opposite direction. Road-racing schools take place at circuits as far apart at Laguna Seca in California, Donington Park in England and Germany's Nürburgring, often with a fleet of identical, race-prepared bikes available for use by the students.

Best-known of the American set-ups is the California Superbike School run by Keith Code, a former national-level racer who counts among his former students Grand Prix stars Eddie Lawson, Wayne Rainey and Doug Chandler. Keith Code's analytical approach to controlling a motorcycle at speed, outlined in videos and books including *A Twist of the Wrist*,

■ OPPOSITE *In many countries professional training is now compulsory before a novice motorcyclist takes to the road for the first time.*

has helped many motorcyclists to ride at high speeds more safely.

Germany's famous old Nürburgring course, with its 72 bends in 13 miles (20 kilometres) of snaking, armco-lined tarmac, presents a very different challenge. For much of the year the Ring is a public road, which any vehicle can use on payment of a few Deutschmarks. But the circuit also hosts intensive riding courses, some lasting for several days, at which track experts pass on their hard-won knowledge.

The final part of a typical three-day course is a single assessment lap for each pupil, marked by a team of instructors who hide in the bushes at key points around the track. Pass that exam with a perfect score, and on Ring open days you might stand a chance of keeping up with the Porsche factory testers or even the locals who also make frequent use of the circuit.

■ ABOVE *Few pupils have the time or energy to admire the scenery during off-road riding schools such as the one held in Wales by enduro star Geraint Jones.*

■ LEFT *Many road-race schools, including the Yamaha-sponsored one at Donington Park, provide bikes and clothing as well as expert tuition from leading riders.*

THE GEAR

Modern motorcycle clothing is almost as sophisticated as the bikes themselves. These days a serious rider wears a full-face helmet made from lightweight composite materials, and brightly-coloured, one-piece protective leathers. The well-dressed motorcyclist is likely to draw some suspicious looks if found wandering around on foot.

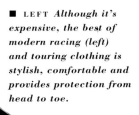

■ LEFT *Although it's expensive, the best of modern racing (left) and touring clothing is stylish, comfortable and provides protection from head to toe.*

■ ABOVE *Marlon Brando's role in the controversial movie* The Wild One *stamped the image of a tough biker in jeans and black leather jacket on the public consciousness.*

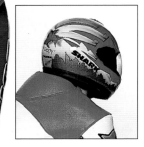

■ ABOVE *This leather suit's neck hump, designed to smooth the air-flow, gives a tiny speed increase to a 125cc racer but is of dubious benefit for road use.*

■ ABOVE *A two-piece touring suit usually has a zip to hold jacket and trousers together, reducing draughts and increasing protection.*

Riding gear was very different in biking's early years, when motorcyclists wore cloth caps and tweed jackets, just as they had for riding the bicycles from which many early machines were developed. Before the Second World War many riders' kit comprised nothing more specialized than a back-to-front cap and pair of goggles. Others would wear a leather flying helmet, and maybe a leather trenchcoat, heavy leather gauntlets and thick boots.

After the War, motorcyclists began to adopt a uniform of ex-airforce flying jackets and boots, with various items of army-surplus clothing being used for bad-weather gear. Crash

■ RIGHT *Modern off-road and bad-weather riding gear makes use of man-made fabrics such as Goretex and Kevlar to provide strength and weather protection.*

■ BOTTOM *The black leather jacket is the classic biker uniform — often customized with badges, patches, lettering and studs.*

■ ABOVE *Geoff Duke was among the first of the racers to wear wind-cheating one-piece leathers in the 1950s.*

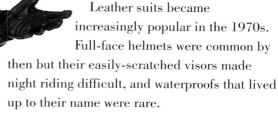

Leather suits became increasingly popular in the 1970s. Full-face helmets were common by then but their easily-scratched visors made night riding difficult, and waterproofs that lived up to their name were rare.

By the 1990s full leathers were commonplace among serious riders, with many firms offering wide ranges of colourful one- and two-piece designs. Many modern suits incorporate sophisticated body armour; racers and some road riders wear spine-protectors too. Helmets feature sophisticated air vents and long-lasting anti-scratch visors.

Bad-weather clothing ranges from simple unlined waterproofs to elaborate suits, made from breathable, man-made fibres, featuring high-visibility reflective patches, detachable linings and padding of their own. In cold weather riders can switch on electrically heated gloves, vests or full suits. Modern motorcycling gear isn't cheap, but the best of it is extremely effective.

■ ABOVE *Before the Second World War bike riders usually wore goggles, a cap, a coat, leather gauntlets and a pair of stout shoes.*

helmets, which had been used for racing since the 1930s, became more common among road riders, and the early leather-sided pudding-basin design was gradually superseded by a more protective open-face style.

Black leather jackets were popular with American motorcyclists by the early 1950s, and hit the big time with the release of *The Wild One* in 1953. Marlon Brando's character Johnny, in his turned-up jeans and double-breasted Schott jacket, epitomised this classic style along with James Dean, Elvis and others. Over the years the basic item has been added to and modified with various tassels, patches, badges and metal studs, but its essential appeal – and attitude – remains.

TOURING

Motorcycle touring means different things to different people. From a gentle weekend trip to an epic journey around the world; from a professionally planned expedition involving dozens of riders, to the result of one person's sudden urge simply to get on a motorbike and ride. The beauty of touring by motorbike is that the journey itself is as much a part of the experience as the stops.

■ BELOW *Big cruisers are not the most comfortable or practical way to travel, but they can cover long distances enjoyably if you don't mind taking your time.*

With its unique ability to cover reasonably large distances while immersing its rider in his or her surroundings, the motorcycle is perfect for explorers. Ted Simon, author of *Jupiter's Travels*, the best-selling story of a four-year trans-world ride on a 500cc Triumph twin in the 1970s, wrote of his gut feelings about how he wanted to travel. He instinctively knew his transport had to be a motorcycle, even though he had neither bike nor licence before planning his trip.

Simon chose the Triumph Tiger partly out of patriotism and partly because it was fairly light while relatively simple and solid – a positive boon when it came to repairs. Similar thinking has led many more recent two-wheeled explorers to use single-cylinder trail bikes such as Honda's XL600 and Yamaha's XT600 Ténéré. Others accept the extra weight of BMW's long-running boxer twins, notably the dual-purpose R80 and R100GS models, to gain the benefits of increased comfort and shaft final drive. Husband and wife team Richard and Mopsa English also opted for an old

■ ABOVE *Many riders' favourite touring mount is a big BMW fitted with fairing, top-box and panniers.*

■ RIGHT *Norway provides tourers with some excellent roads, and breathtaking views.*

■ BELOW *Ireland's charm makes it a great country for touring, and a big slow-revving Moto Guzzi California is an ideal bike on which to travel.*

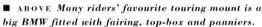

Triumph twin for the round-the-world trip described in their book *Full Circle*, but they added a large sidecar too.

Choosing the basic motorcycle is merely the first step in preparing for a very long tour, particularly one through difficult terrain. Any bike will require modification, notably to enable it to carry the large amount of luggage necessary. Solid fibreglass or preferably aluminium panniers may be fitted, in conjunction with soft luggage of leather, plastic or canvas. Many riders fit home-made metal racks that hold cans for spare fuel and water. Other common modifications include large-capacity fuel tanks, oil-coolers and protective engine bash-plates, extra fuel filters and heavy duty wheel-rims and spokes.

■ ABOVE *Many riders would argue that America's wealth of magnificent scenery is best appreciated from the saddle of a well-laden Harley-Davidson.*

Purpose-built tourers such as Honda's Gold Wing, Yamaha's Venture or Harley's Electra Glide make life easier with fairings, big seats and easily detachable luggage facilities, and often provide accessories such as stereos, electrical sockets, cruise control and footboards. But small and apparently unsuitable bikes can be used successfully – provided factors such as route, daily distances and luggage are chosen accordingly.

Riders wishing to venture further afield without the time and expense of buying, preparing and possibly transporting a bike can turn to a growing number of specialist firms. Some offer just bike hire, but many provide complete motorcycling package tours for which the cost usually includes a local guide, food and accommodation, plus a following vehicle to carry excess luggage and deal with problems. Whether you want to ride a BMW in the Alps, a Harley-Davidson across America or an Enfield Bullet through India, there is a firm that can arrange it.

Several manufacturers have seen the potential for organized excursions, too. Honda's Transalp Rallies provided a good excuse for European owners to test their XL600Vs' dual-purpose ability, and Honda has also arranged longer, more road-oriented trips for the ST1100 sports-tourer. Harley-Davidson tours have included an 80-strong excursion to Norway's Nordkapp, deep inside the Arctic Circle. Best of all were the series of Spirit of Adventure trips organized by Yamaha for owners of Ténéré and Super Ténéré trail-bikes. These were demanding treks, in Egypt, Mexico, America and Australia, which gave owners the opportunity to ride through harsh and often beautiful terrain, with organization, riding gear, machinery and back-up – including a medical helicopter – taken care of.

None of those things is necessary for an average bike tourer, whose trip maybe lasts for two weeks in Europe or America and is all on tarmac roads. Most medium or large-capacity bikes can be pressed into service for an annual touring holiday, merely with the addition of a tank-bag, a set of throw-over panniers and perhaps a rucksack either worn by the pillion passenger or strapped to the empty seat.

■ RIGHT *A tank-bag and pair of throw-over panniers can transform even a simple unfaired roadster such as Triumph's Trident 900 into a capable tourer.*

■ BELOW *Yamaha's series of Spirit of Adventure trips gave owners of the firm's trail bikes the opportunity to ride them in remote places such as central Australia.*

Motorcycles and their Anatomy

Few motorcyclists are prepared simply to ride their bikes and leave them alone the rest of the time. Most riders are enthusiasts, far more knowledgeable about their machines than the average car driver. The majority positively enjoy maintaining, tuning, customizing or adapting their bikes in some way, whether to improve performance, enhance looks or to make theirs different from everyone else's.

In the early years regular work was absolutely unavoidable, as bikes were mostly used as a cheap form of transport, and needed frequent maintenance that in most cases only the rider was able to provide. As bikes improved, and basic servicing was increasingly carried out by professionals, keen owners could always think of ways to improve their machines. Even now, with standard bikes better and more reliable than ever before, the opportunity to spend large amounts of time and money on them is undiminished.

CAFÉ RACERS AND SPECIALS

Specials are arguably the most exciting and glamorous bikes of all. The term essentially means something hand-built, either a one-off or a small series of similar machines. Some are notable mainly for their unusual design – bikes with two engines or radical suspension, some created as much for the engineering challenge as for pure performance. But most specials are built for speed, and that certainly goes for café racers. The tuned-up sportsbike with low handlebars and a single seat remains one of motorcycling's most vivid images.

BSA's Gold Star Clubman of the late 1950s and early 60s was arguably the first café racer, although the legendary 500cc single was not

■ ABOVE *In 1974, when superbike riders wore open-faced helmets and flared jeans, Dunstall's Honda and Kawasaki fours were among the ultimate café racers.*

■ LEFT *The most successful 1960s special was the Triton, a fast and fine-handling blend of Triumph parallel twin engine and Norton Featherbed frame.*

■ BELOW *Some specials,*
such as this four-cylinder
Triumph powered by a
side-by-side pair of
750cc Bonneville
engines, are built more
for show than for go.

■ RIGHT *BSA's 500cc*
Gold Star, complete
with "Ace" handlebars
and filterless Amal
carburettor, had few
rivals as a café racer
during the early 1960s.

■ BELOW *The*
handsome red special
built by German firm
AMC was among the
best of many recent
sportsbikes powered by
Harley-Davidson's
V-twin engine.

actually a special but a standard factory-built model. Twins from BSA, Norton and Triumph took over in the 1960s, and were frequently modified with clip-on handlebars, rear-set footrests, alloy fuel tanks and free-breathing exhaust systems. Many parts were provided by engineers such as Paul Dunstall, whose Norton-powered Dunstall Dominator was a 1960s classic.

The archetypal café racer was the Triton, the blend of Triumph engine and Norton Featherbed frame that gave the best of British power and handling. Some riders combined Triumph motor and BSA chassis to form a Tribsa, or housed a Vincent V-twin engine in a Featherbed frame to produce the exotic Norvin.

The era of the café-race special continued when Japanese bikes took over in the 1970s. Honda's CB750 and then Kawasaki's Z900 and Z1000 provided seemingly endless four-cylinder horsepower, but early models were let down by their handling. Established British chassis specialists such as Dresda and Dunstall, plus others including Rickman, Harris, Fritz Egli from Switzerland, Bimota of Italy and Georges Martin from France, developed racy chassis kits for the big fours.

Engine tuning also featured highly in the café-racer cult over the years. State-of-the-art motors progressed from Bonneville lumps with ported heads and open-mouthed Amal carbs, via Yoshimura-tuned GS1000 Suzukis to modern turbocharged Kawasaki ZZ-R1100s. Harley-Davidson's long-standing lack of a sportsbike led to dozens of firms building V-twin sportsters of their own in a variety of styles.

■ BELOW *By far the most popular custom bike powerplant is Harley-Davidson's V-twin, here used to good effect by Dutch chassis specialist Nico Bakker.*

CUSTOM CYCLES

To some riders, the way a bike looks is far more important than the way it rides. A motorcycle can be an art form – a sculpture on two wheels – a chrome-plated, custom-painted, elaborately engraved celebration of style and individuality that may be difficult to control due to over-long forks, a hard-tail rear end, a massively wide rear tyre or a combination of all three.

The best custom bikes, built by visionaries such as California-based legend Arlen Ness, challenge existing concepts with intricate engineering and new images. Their influence can be seen in the thousands of less radical customized bikes at Daytona Beach or Sturgis, each sporting aftermarket parts chosen to make a machine stand out from the crowd.

Ironically, the custom movement began in America in the 1940s and 1950s when Harley riders began to strip their bikes of unnecessary accessories, mainly in search of improved performance, to produce machines known as bobbers. Modifying the chassis by kicking out the front forks for extra stability became popular, and in the 1960s this was increasingly taken to extremes with longer and longer forks,

■ BELOW *By far the most popular custom bike powerplant is Harley-Davidson's V-twin, here used to good effect by Dutch chassis specialist Nico Bakker.*

■ RIGHT *Much of a custom bike's appeal is in the quality of its finish, and paintwork is often done by experts such as Californian Jeff McCann.*

■ BELOW *The Harley ridden by Peter Fonda in* Easy Rider, *with its ape-hanger bars, long forks and lack of front brake, summed-up the late 1960s custom style.*

often holding a bicycle-thin front wheel with no brake. The classic late 1960s custom was the chopped Harley with high, pull-back handlebars, massively extended forks and hard-tail (ie, unsprung) rear end, as ridden by Peter Fonda's character, Captain America, in the film *Easy Rider*.

In the mid-1970s Ness, who had progressed from painting bikes to building complete machines, was central in popularizing a new custom look, with lower handlebars, short forks and a long, low-slung chassis reminiscent of a drag-racer's. Ness's Bay Area style (his shop was in San Leandro, near San Francisco)

■ LEFT *Arlen Ness has become known as the master Harley customizer, having repeatedly introduced new styles with a string of imaginative machines.*

■ BELOW *Sometimes custom bikes are treated as art, as when British customizer Uncle Bunt's Yamaha formed part of a Birmingham exhibition in 1994.*

■ ABOVE *Harley-Davidsons are frequently referred to as hogs, but this customized V-twin looks as though it would be more at home in a cattle market.*

■ BELOW *For those who don't like fancy paint and shiny chrome, building a ratbike provides the perfect opportunity to let the imagination run wild.*

normally centred on a tuned Harley V-twin engine with open-mouthed carburettors, intricate exhaust pipes and names like Kwik Silver, Accel Bike and Strictly Business. Harleys have always been the most popular bikes for customizing, with Honda's CB750 making an impression in the 1970s and Triumph twins retaining a loyal following.

That remains true today, as Harley-Davidson itself has recognized in recent years with a wide variety of niche models and an array of factory accessories. Specialist customizing shops have thrived, too, offering everything from chrome-plated footpegs to hard-tail frames and complete machines. And although most modern custom bikes are merely Harleys with a few bolt-on parts, there will always be individuals dedicated to building motorcycles with a radical and eye-catching look.

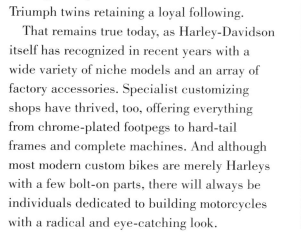

SIDECARS AND TRIKES

Many modern motorcyclists regard sidecars as strange contraptions that lack both the motorbike's advantages of mobility and performance, and the car's benefits of comfort and convenience. In these days of relatively cheap cars, it certainly is difficult to make a logical argument for three-wheeled travel. But both sidecars and three-wheelers are still popular – albeit with a minority – not for practical reasons but simply because they are different and fun.

The three-wheeler's attraction has traditionally been more down-to-earth. Very early examples included Edward Butler's pioneering Petrol-Cycle of 1888. In the 1920s, three-

transport was a big single-cylinder Panther bike weighed down by an enormous double-adult unit alongside, loaded with children. The same decade saw the bubble cars, tiny enclosed three-wheelers made by firms including German aircraft manufacturers

wheelers such as the Morgan and Coventry Victor, generally with two wheels up front and one behind, offered good performance at a low price and even led some observers to predict that they would take over from bikes altogether. In the 1930s the opposite layout became more popular in America, where Indian's Despatch Tow and Harley's Servicar – basically a 45ci model with a large box between two rear wheels – served as small-scale pick-up trucks.

In Britain the sidecar's popularity peaked in the 1950s, when the typical mode of family

■ BELOW *Custom trikes powered by big V-eight car engines are a frequent sight at gatherings such as Daytona — for some owners, the bigger the better.*

■ ABOVE *The Californian-made Flexit sidecar, here fitted to a Triumph Trophy 1200, featured a linkage system that allowed it to lean with the bike in bends.*

Heinkel and Messerschmitt. Cheap cars spelt the beginning of the end for three-wheeled travel by the 1960s. But machines such as the Bond Bug and Reliant Robin, increasingly car-like in looks if not stability, were produced for some years afterwards.

These days the only three-wheelers still in production are enthusiasts' machines, such as the Triking, whose transverse V-twin Moto Guzzi engine, exposed between two front wheels, gives the look of an early Morgan. Other idiosyncratic offerings along similar lines are the JZR, powered by Honda's CX500 V-twin, and the Lomax, which uses the engine, chassis and suspension from Citroen's 2CV car. More upmarket is the sporty Grinnall Scorpion, whose four-cylinder BMW K1100 engine gives a top speed of 130mph (208kph).

True sidecars remain popular in Continental Europe, especially Germany, where fully-enclosed and often lavishly equipped modern devices can be seen alongside colour-matched superbikes such as Honda's CBR1000 or Yamaha's FJ1200. Among the most exotic is the Krauser Domani, a futuristic and expensive BMW-powered device that resembles a Grand

Prix kneeling sidecar. Perhaps the most unlikely – and exciting – is the Flexit, a Californian creation whose linkage system allows bike and sidecar to lean in parallel through corners, in similar fashion to the Flxicar racers of the 1920s.

BELOW *In the 1920s, when it was not done for a young lady to ride pillion, a chap's best hope was to fit his Triumph with a Gloria sidecar.*

ARMY BIKES

The motorcycle's speed and manoeuvrability has made it an important tool in wartime, and the "iron horse" has been used to good effect from the First World War to recent times. Bikes of many types and nationalities have been converted for fighting use with camouflage paint schemes, modifications for extra strength and reliability, and even fitment of machine-guns – sometimes in a sidecar alongside, sometimes on a solo for use by the rider alone.

British forces in the First World War used a variety of bikes, mainly for reconnaissance and communications work. Triumph supplied the Army with 30,000 units of its three-speed Model H; Douglas built almost as many of its sturdy horizontal twin; and P&M supplied the Royal Flying Corps with its 3.5bhp, two-speed single. German forces also used bikes, notably after production of the four-cylinder Belgian

FN had been taken over by the occupying German Army.

Germany's best-known bike in the Second World War was the BMW R75, which normally came fitted with a sidecar and later starred in many war films. Moto Guzzi also produced several military models such as the Alce and

■ ABOVE *A Canadian rider and his Harley WLC are the centre of youthful interest in 1941, in the grounds of an English country house used as a Brigade headquarters.*

■ LEFT *These British Army riders, splashing their single-cylinder machines through a ford, are taking part in a training exercise in Essex in 1941.*

■ LEFT *This captured Second World War BMW flat-twin and sidecar gave three British RAF mechanics the chance of a ride at Sidi Rezegh, Libya in 1942.*

■ RIGHT *BSA's M20 was useful for delivering copies of an Army newspaper to South African troops based in a remote part of the Western Desert in 1942.*

■ LEFT *A military bike enthusiast poses in suitable attire with his neatly restored Triumph Model C, built in 1914 and a veteran of the First World War.*

Airone, which were flat-singles of 500 and 250cc. The bigger bike often dragged a sidecar, and was also made as a three-wheeler called the Trialce. An early predecessor of Guzzi's current transverse V-twin engine was used to power a small armoured car.

Most of the bikes produced for the Second World War were simple 350cc singles from Matchless, Norton and Triumph, but the best-known Allied bikes were the American-made V-twins: Indian's 500cc Model 741 Military Scout and Harley's 750cc WLA 45. The Harley, in particular, was churned out in huge numbers – at one point in 1942 the Milwaukee factory was building 750 a week, for use by Russian and Chinese armies as well as by the Americans, Canadians and British. After the war many ex-army 45s were converted to civilian use, and did much to increase Harley's worldwide popularity.

Even in these days of ultra-sophisticated weaponry, many forces still have a role for the

■ BELOW *French Army troops, waiting for embarkation orders at a British port in June 1944, on Harleys with rifles mounted alongside the front wheel.*

humble motorbike. Harley-Davidson's 350cc military machine, powered by a single-cylinder Rotax two-stroke engine, is exported to forces including the British Army. Basically a sturdy trail bike with panniers around its front wheel and a rifle rack on the back, the Harley is mainly used for reconnaissance work and convoy duties. Its predecessor, the 500cc Armstrong, played a role in the Gulf War, as did Italian-made Cagivas and Husqvarnas.

THE MOTORCYCLE AT WORK

For many riders motorcycling is not just a hobby but a job. Bikes are used for a variety of work – in most cases because their combination of open-road speed and ability to cut through traffic is unmatched by any other form of transport. The attraction of being paid to ride a bike draws many enthusiastic motorcyclists to try despatch riding, although for many the reality of riding all day in all weathers fails to match the dream. Some riders in cities around the world have found alternative employment as a two-wheeled taxi service whose journey times beat those of any conventional cab.

Police motorcyclists are some of the most visible two-wheeled workers, and use a huge variety of specially adapted bikes. Best known is the Harley-Davidson V-twin, as used by American forces for many years, including in a lead role in the film *Electra Glide in Blue*.

■ LEFT *The comfort, performance and reliability of BMW's boxer twins helped make them popular with police forces in many countries for years.*

■ LEFT *American forces, such as the California Highway Patrol, have traditionally used Harleys, although Kawasaki fours were popular in the 1980s.*

■ ABOVE LEFT *Grand Prix stars and Riders for Health charity workers Randy Mamola (hidden, left) and Kevin Schwantz (right) visit Lesotho in 1992.*

■ ABOVE RIGHT *Many national organizations such as Britain's Post Office run fleets of small-capacity bikes, like Honda's single-cylinder RS250, for city-centre use.*

■ FAR RIGHT *Despatch riders are a familiar sight on many city streets, normally loaded with luggage and carving through the traffic with practised ease and confidence.*

■ RIGHT *Motorcycling paramedics can reach emergencies quickly on machines such as this Norton rotary, fitted with a variety of life-saving equipment.*

Traditionally a large-capacity road model converted with a single seat, radio equipment, extra identification lights, first-aid kit, fire extinguisher and weather protection, the police bike often ends up being rather heavy – although small bikes are commonly used for urban duties.

Almost every major manufacturer produces at least one model aimed at the lucrative police force market. Among the most common have been the Triumph Saint 650cc parallel twin of the 1960s; the Kawasaki Z1000 four that was popular in America in the 1980s and featured in the popular *CHiPs* television series about the California Highway Patrol; and the BMW flat-twin, which in various guises has been in police use, in Germany and other countries, for many decades.

Other two-wheeled workers include those from the motoring rescue services, whose first response to a breakdown call is often by bike, and the organizations that transport blood and other urgently needed medical supplies to hospitals. Motorcycling paramedics, carrying a wide range of life-saving equipment, can often reach road-crash or heart-attack victims before an ambulance – sometimes with life-saving results. It has been known for local midwives to find mopeds or motorcyles to be the quickest and most efficient way to travel.

Motorcycles also perform a vital service in less developed countries, where they provide otherwise impossible mobility to health workers and teachers. Riders For Health, the motorcycling charity backed by leading Grand Prix racers including Randy Mamola, works in African countries teaching local riders how to use and maintain their machines so that they can reach remote areas whenever needed.

ANATOMY OF A MOTORCYCLE

A motorcycle's essential ingredients may simply be two wheels and an engine, but its design can go in any direction from there. Bikes vary from the latest Grand Prix missile to the earliest roadster; from a high-tech sports-tourer to a humble commuter machine. Over the years motorcycles have been powered by batteries, by rockets, even by the sun. They have used vastly different frames, bodywork, suspension, seating and engine positions.

But that's only a tiny minority, and most motorbikes are essentially very similar. Since the New Werner in 1901, the predominant layout of motor and riding position has been unchanged. Piston engines, in both two-stroke and four-stroke form, have powered the vast majority of bikes since even before then. A handful of basic systems has been adapted and updated over the years to provide suspension, braking, roadholding, and sometimes weather-protection or luggage-carrying ability.

The days when all motorcyclists needed to be knowledgeable about the workings of their temperamental machines are gone. Modern technology and production efficiency ensures that most modern bikes are reliable, oil-tight and require minimal maintenance. They increasingly feature sophisticated electronics, engine-management systems and parts requiring specialist tools—so it's not surprising that many modern riders rely on a professional for all but the most simple mechanical work. But beneath the neon-coloured plastic and the manufacturers' publicity claims, most bikes work in much the same way they have for years.

Ducati's World Superbike racing championships have played a big part in the firm's recent sales success

Removing the cover reveals a pillion seat — and unusually for a sports-bike, the 900SS has a passenger grab-rail too

Ducati's tubular steel ladder frame uses the engine to add rigidity

Like the front forks, the single shock absorber is made by Japanese specialist Showa, and is adjustable for spring preload plus both compression and rebound damping

The cantilever style aluminium swing-arm operates the shock unit directly, rather than via a rising-rate linkage as used by many modern bikes

Twin silencers are large to meet strict noise limits — although the 900SS retains Ducati's traditional V-twin exhaust note

A small single brake disc is adequate at the rear, as forward weight transfer under hard braking makes the back wheel lock up very easily

Tyres are both low-profile radials, the rear being much wider than the front to cope with the forces of acceleration

■ BELOW *Ducati's 900SS, here with the lower part of its fairing removed, combines the Italian marque's traditional V-twin engine and tubular steel frame with many features typical of a modern sportsbike.*

Handlebars are set low to give a wind-cheating riding position

Fairing and screen protect the rider from the elements, and help give a top speed of over 135mph (216kph) despite the engine's fairly modest 80bhp output

A large airbox is crucial to engine performance, with the result that much of what looks like a large fuel tank contains only air

Twin Mikuni carburettors are situated in the crook of the engine's Vee

The Ducati's fork angle, or rake, is 25 degrees — fairly steep, to give quick and light steering, but not dramatically so by modern sportsbike standards

Front forks are the "upside-down" type currently fitted to most sports machines, with the thicker and more rigid outer section at the top

Twin discs are large at 320mm in diameter, can "float" on their mountings to allow for expansion when hot, and are gripped by four-piston calipers whose large pad area provides maximum braking power

An oil-cooler helps control the temperature of the engine, which is cooled by a mixture of air and oil

Drive to the desmodromic engine's single overhead camshaft is by toothed rubber belt

The longitudinal V-twin engine's cylinders are spaced at 90 degrees, with the front "pot" angled almost horizontally to aid cooling

The 900SS's cylinder heads have two valves each, instead of the four-valves-per-cylinder layout more common on high performance bikes, and feature Ducati's desmodromic system of positive valve closure

Like most sportsbikes' front wheels, the Ducati's is made from cast aluminium and is 17 inches in diameter

Anatomy of a Motorcycle

SUCK-SQUEEZE-BANG-BLOW

The four-stroke engine is named after its four basic operations: induction, compression, combustion and exhaust. Invented by Dr Nikolaus Otto and also known as the Otto Cycle, the four-stroke principle has been motorcycling's mainstay throughout this century. While such elements as valve train

■ RIGHT *This four-cylinder, 16-valve cylinder head from BMW's K1 is disassembled to show its twin camshafts and valves, their springs and the "buckets" operated by the camshaft lobes.*

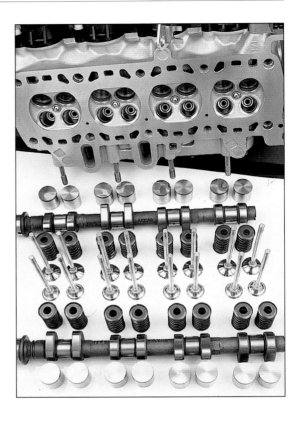

THE FOUR-STROKE CYCLE

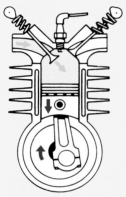

1 INDUCTION (SUCK)
As the piston descends, the inlet valve opens, allowing fuel/air mixture to be drawn into the cylinder

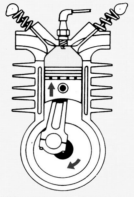

2 COMPRESSION (SQUEEZE)
The inlet valve then closes and the piston travels upwards, compressing the mixture

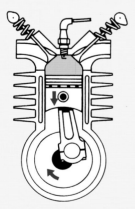

3 COMBUSTION (BANG)
Just before the piston reaches the top of its stroke (known as Top Dead Centre), the spark plug ignites the compressed fuel/air mixture, forcing the piston down on its power stroke

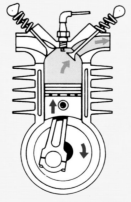

4 EXHAUST (BLOW)
As the piston rises again the exhaust valve opens, allowing the burnt gases to be released through the exhaust port

design and materials used have changed greatly since early motors that produced just a few horsepower, the basic suck-squeeze-bang-blow sequence remains the same.

Road-going four-stroke multis now run reliably to as high as 15,000rpm, and provide phenomenal performance. The best Japanese four-cylinder 600cc engines deliver 100bhp, more than most car units, while the biggest bikes are so powerful that in many countries their 140bhp-plus motors have to be restricted for legal purposes.

■ TYPES OF FOUR-STROKE ENGINE

The earliest and simplest four-stroke layout, the single, dominated in the 1950s and is still used for various motorcycles ranging from mopeds to racebikes. In spite of increasingly

■ RIGHT *On this cut-away of Honda's CBR600F it is possible to follow how air travels from the duct above the front wheel to the airbox, through the air-filter and carburettors to the engine, and then out via the exhaust system. Note also the cross-section of the steel frame beams visible at the steering head.*

sophisticated balancing arrangements, its practical limit remains about 650cc. Parallel twins took over in the 1960s, and can be used in either 360-degree – both pistons rising together – or 180-degree layouts. BMW's classic flat-twin, or boxer, layout is generally smoother and ideal for cooling, if not for ground-clearance. V-twins vary in the angle of their cylinders, and can be longitudinal, like the 45-degree Harley and 90-degree Ducati, or transverse, as favoured by Moto Guzzi.

Three-cylinder engines can be arranged either across the frame, as with Triumphs and Laverdas, or along the line of the bike like BMW's K75. Likewise with in-line fours, where BMW's K series follows the old Henderson/Indian longitudinal layout, but with horizontal instead of vertical cylinders. Many modern bikes use the familiar Japanese transverse format popularized in 1969 by Honda's CB750.

Honda fours also include the V-four of the VFR750 and the flat-four of the earlier Gold Wing models. Ariel's legendary Square Four was named after its unusual engine layout.

Five-cylinder bikes are rare, the most original being the amazing 1922 Megola,

■ RIGHT *Different approaches to four-stroke valve design are highlighted by pistons from (clockwise from top left): a two-valves-per-cylinder Moto Guzzi; a two-valve Harley-Davidson; a four-valve Suzuki GSX-R; and a five-valve Yamaha FZ750.*

whose 640cc five-pot engine was arranged radially inside the front wheel. The modern 1500cc Gold Wing is a watercooled flat-six; other six-cylinder designs include the straight-six Honda CBX1000, Kawasaki Z1300 and Benelli 750 of the 1970s.

Laverda raced a V6 in 1978, and fellow Italian firm Morbidelli has produced an exotic 850cc V-eight to power a prototype sports-tourer. Meanwhile the mighty Boss Hoss makes do with the V-eight Chevy unit commonly found in American cars.

Anatomy of a Motorcycle

TWO-STROKES AND ROTARIES

Two-stroke motors are lighter and potentially more powerful than four-strokes of similar capacity, which is why they are used for Grand Prix racebikes. They are also mechanically simpler and generally cheaper to produce, which is why they are popular for small commuter bikes. But the two-stroke's workings are more complex. Instead of having mechanical valves, a two-stroke uses the underneath of the piston to force the incoming mixture of fuel and air into the combustion chamber, via the crankcase and connecting transfer ports.

This allows the engine to fire with every rotation of the crankshaft (ie, every two strokes), rather than every two rotations (or four strokes), which gives the "stroker" its power advantage. But it means that lubricating oil cannot sit in the crankcases, and must be carried in the fuel/air mixture and burnt,

■ ABOVE *Suzuki's RG500 features rotary disc valve induction. Its carburettors are mounted on the side of the crankcase, and induction is controlled by slotted discs that spin with the crankshaft.*

■ ABOVE RIGHT *A piston-ported two-stroke such as Yamaha's TZ750 has a non-return reed valve between each carburettor and the engine. This allows mixture in, and prevents it from being blown back.*

adding to pollution. And despite the modern two-stroke tuner's skill in selecting the correctly shaped expansion chamber for the exhaust system, some of the mixture goes down the exhaust without being burnt – further increasing emissions. These problems are being addressed by the new wave of clean two-strokes under development.

■ **TYPES OF TWO-STROKE ENGINE**

Many of the best two-strokes have been parallel twins, from the Scott Squirrel of motorcycling's early years to Yamaha's recent RD350LC. Kawasaki's late 1970s KR250 and 350 Grand Prix racers were tandem twins, with one cylinder behind the other. Modern Grand Prix 250s are in-line V-twins, as are several roadsters including Aprilia's RS250. Two-stroke triples have included 1970s classics such as Kawasaki's aircooled 750cc H2 and 500cc H1, and Suzuki's watercooled GT750.

Freddie Spencer's 1983 world championship winning Honda NS500 was a V-triple, as was the NS400 roadster it subsequently spawned. Four-cylinder two-strokes have included

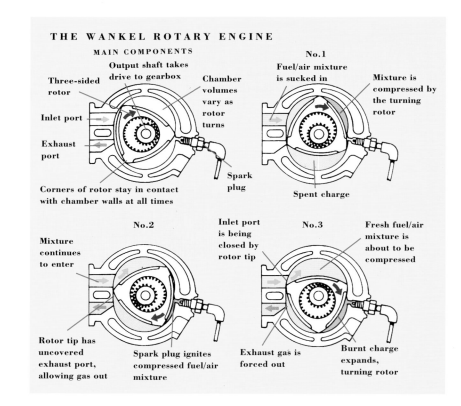

THE WANKEL ROTARY ENGINE

MAIN COMPONENTS

Output shaft takes drive to gearbox
Three-sided rotor
Chamber volumes vary as rotor turns
Inlet port
Exhaust port
Corners of rotor stay in contact with chamber walls at all times
Spark plug

No.1
Fuel/air mixture is sucked in
Mixture is compressed by the turning rotor
Spent charge

No.2
Mixture continues to enter
Rotor tip has uncovered exhaust port, allowing gas out
Spark plug ignites compressed fuel/air mixture

Inlet port is being closed by rotor tip

No.3
Fresh fuel/air mixture is about to be compressed
Exhaust gas is forced out
Burnt charge expands, turning rotor

■ BELOW LEFT *Kawasaki's 750cc H2 aircooled triple of the early 1970s was smelly, thirsty, noisy, inflexible — and very powerful indeed.*

■ BELOW RIGHT *Most two-strokes have followed Suzuki's GT750 triple in using watercooling for a more controlled operating temperature.*

THE TWO-STROKE CYCLE

A INDUCTION
As the piston rises, the fuel/air mixture in the cylinder is compressed, while fresh mixture is being drawn into the crankcase

B TRANSFER
As the piston descends on the power stroke, it first compresses the fuel/air mixture in the crankcase, and then uncovers the transfer port (on right of diagram) through which the mixture is forced into the cylinder

C COMPRESSION
The piston's upward movement compresses the charge in the combustion chamber

D COMBUSTION
As the piston nears the top of its stroke the mixture is ignited, after which the piston begins its downwards, or power, stroke

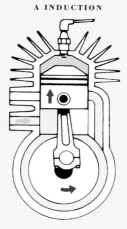
A INDUCTION

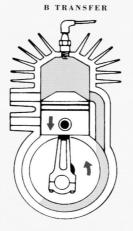
B TRANSFER

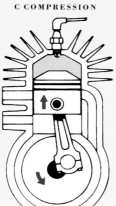
C COMPRESSION

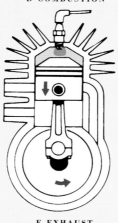
D COMBUSTION

E EXHAUST
Near the bottom of the power stroke, the piston uncovers the exhaust port. The burnt gases escape due to their own pressure and by being displaced by the fresh charge being forced through the transfer port. Despite two-stroke tuners' best efforts, some fresh mixture is inevitably lost through the exhaust port

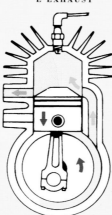
E EXHAUST

Yamaha's straight-four TZ750 racer and Suzuki's racing and road-going square-four RG500. Recent 500cc Grand Prix racers have been V-fours. Honda's NSR500 has a single crankshaft while Suzuki's and Yamaha's V-fours use two geared-together cranks.

■ **THE ROTARY ENGINE**
The smoothest engine of all is the Wankel rotary, named after its inventor, Felix Wankel. A figure-of-eight shaped chamber holds a three-sided rotor, which turns in such a way that its corners always remain in contact with the sides. The rotor's movement forms three compartments of varying volume, in which the suck-squeeze-bang-blow cycle takes place. The Wankel engine can be powerful, compact and light although fuel consumption is high. Rotary roadsters from DKW, Suzuki and Norton have not, however, been commercially successful.

■ ABOVE *Norton's Classic roadster proved that a rotary bike engine could be neat, reasonably powerful, and very smooth.*

Anatomy of a Motorcycle

FRAMES AND SUSPENSION

■ BELOW *Bimota's SB6 uses an ultra-rigid development of the aluminium twin-spar frame layout used by most modern sportsbikes.*

The motorcycle's basic layout may have changed little during this century but chassis performance has improved hugely – as a ride on most classic bikes, with their heavy, flexible frames and crude suspension, confirms. Handling depends on many variables, notably frame strength and geometry, weight distribution, suspension type and adjustment. All have been affected by advances in chassis technology, leading to modern machines that are stable, well-balanced and comfortable over a wide range of speeds and road conditions.

Until the 1950s, many bikes had thin steel frames and springer front forks with no damping or a simple friction arrangement. Rear suspension was provided by a crude plunger set-up or was non-existent leaving the rider cushioned only by the back tyre and a sprung saddle – not surprisingly this was known as a hard tail. Later models had sturdier frames, either of pressed steel or, in the case of the legendary Norton Featherbed, braced and often triangulated steel tubes designed to hold a pair of hydraulically damped rear shock absorbers. Sometimes, as with Honda's four-cylinder racers of the 1960s, the engine was an integral stressed member of the frame.

The increases in superbike engine's power and weight in the 1970s left many chassis

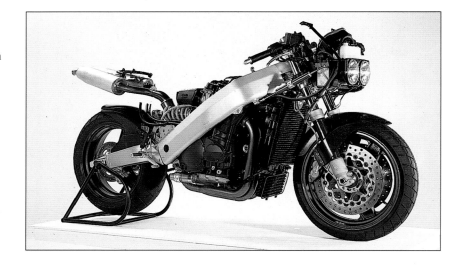

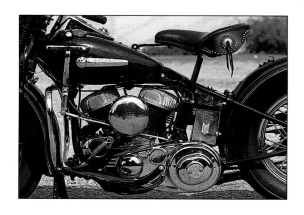

unable to cope – leading to wobbles and weaves – but technology has moved fast in recent years. A typical modern sportsbike has a rigid frame, particularly in the crucial link between steering head and swing-arm pivot. Frame design may incorporate a traditional tubular steel cradle, a large diameter main spine as used by Triumph, a space-frame or ladder of thinner tubes – a recognizable Ducati trademark – or the common sports and racing format of twin aluminium spars.

■ SUSPENSION DESIGN

Front forks and rear shock units work in essentially the same way. They absorb shocks with a coil spring, using a hydraulic damper – oil forced through holes of various sizes – to control the rate of its compression (bump or compression damping) and, more importantly, of its return (rebound damping). Suspension action produces heat, so many modern shock units have remote oil reservoirs, situated alongside or away from the main unit, to aid cooling.

The more sophisticated front and rear units are adjustable, both for spring preload – which controls the amount of weight needed to

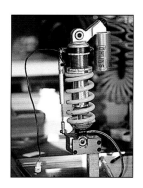

■ ABOVE *At the Öhlins factory in Sweden, shock units are developed and tested with the aid of sophisticated suspension dynamometers.*

■ LEFT *Many modern Harleys use hidden suspension units to give the look of a genuine hard-tail such as the 1949 model WL45.*

compress the unit further – and for compression and rebound damping. Multiple springs of different rates can be used to give a progressive effect. At the rear, rising rate suspension is more commonly provided by a mechanical linkage system at one end of the shock. This allows a light action for small bumps, and a firmer response nearer the end of the spring's travel to prevent bottoming out.

■ ALTERNATIVE FRONT SUSPENSION

Many engineers argue that telescopic forks are a poor solution – because they are affected by braking, and acted upon by forces in directions they are not designed for. Alternative hub-centre designs, in which the front wheel pivots on a bearing inside its hub, get over these problems and separate the processes of steering and braking. Bimota's Tesi and Yamaha's GTS1000 use different forkless systems to provide a high degree of stability, particularly under braking. But neither has proved commercially successful, partly because of high costs but mostly because modern front forks actually work very well indeed.

■ CHASSIS GEOMETRY

The way a bike handles is greatly affected by the geometry of its chassis. A modern racebike has a short wheelbase, steep front forks, very

little trail and plenty of weight over its front wheel for quick and light steering – often at the expense of marginal stability.

At the other extreme, a cruiser is set up for stability, with raked forks, lots of trail, a long wheelbase and more weight over the rear wheel. Most roadsters fall somewhere in-between, and some chassis can be fine-tuned using adjustable fork yokes to vary rake and trail, plus various methods to raise or lower the front or rear suspension.

■ RIGHT *Bimota's Yamaha-engined YB4 and YB6 were among the first sportsbikes to use the now-common alloy beam frame format.*

■ BELOW *Triumph's modular chassis is based around a large-diameter steel spine frame, with the engine used as a stressed member.*

Anatomy of a Motorcycle

WHEELS, TYRES AND BRAKES

The motorcycle's inherent instability makes its tyres and brakes all the more important, especially as the need to lean in corners means that even the biggest and most powerful bikes have tyres whose footprint is precariously narrow by car standards. Until the 1960s most bikes wore tubed front and rear tyres of crossply construction and roughly similar size. In contrast, modern sports machines achieve incredible cornering angles – well in excess of 45 degrees – due largely to the high levels of grip provided by their sticky, low-profile, tubeless radial tyres, the rear of which is much wider than the front to cope with high levels of power. Soft-compound superbike rear tyres are often worn out after less than 2000 miles (3218 kilometres) of hard road use.

Increasingly specialized demand has led to an extraordinary variety of tyre types, from treadless racing slicks designed to put down maximum surface area in dry conditions, but useless in the wet, to heavily treaded knobbly tyres for trials or motocross events. In-between come sports tyres which are lightly treaded (because tread flex increases heat build-up, thus reducing performance) and harder, more comprehensively patterned tyres for commuting or touring. Dual-purpose tyres, designed for trail bikes, are generally biased towards road riding and of limited use in heavy mud. Road-racing wet tyres, with block-pattern tread and ultra-soft compound, can wear out literally in minutes if used on a dry track.

The most notable advance in motorbike wheels has been the move from wire-spoked to cast-construction, something which happened gradually through the 1970s and 1980s. Cast wheels, normally made of aluminium but sometimes of lighter magnesium, are generally stronger and can accept modern tubeless tyres.

■ LEFT *This shows only part of the huge collection of wheels and tyres that Yamaha's 500cc Grand Prix team requires for each race.*

■ BELOW *The Manx Norton's combination of Roadholder forks, wire front wheel and twin-leading-shoe brake was impressive in the 1960s.*

■ BELOW *A front disc brake with single-piston caliper was a very sophisticated feature when Honda's CB750 four was released in 1969.*

■ BELOW *This Suzuki RGV500 racer is fitted with upside-down forks and huge carbon-fibre brake discs, gripped by four-piston calipers.*

■ BELOW *The rear end of Ducati's 916 features a single-sided swing arm and an ultra-wide, 190-section radial tyre for maximum roadholding.*

■ BELOW *BMW's single-shock R1100GS trail bike uses a system of rods to counter its shaft-drive motor's effect on handling.*

Wire wheels, however, are still fitted to some new bikes, mainly to emphasize their retro look. Sportsbike wheel diameter has become standardized at 17 inches front and rear, although notable exceptions include Honda's CBR900RR, which uses a 16-inch front. In the early 1980s the fashion was for 16-inch front wheels — led, as with much in roadster chassis design, by developments in Grand Prix racing.

■ **BRAKE DESIGN**

Until fairly recently most motorbikes were stopped by drum brakes, and some small bikes still are. This consists of a pair of semi-circular shoes which are forced open against the inside of the drum when the brake is applied. Some drums, such as those fitted to the otherwise magnificent Brough Superior, were notably poor, and prone to overheating and fading with hard use. Others, such as the big, ventilated four-leading-shoe Grimecas used by specials and racebikes in the 1960s, were very powerful although they required regular adjustment to give optimum performance.

Disc brakes began to take over the motorcycle world in the early 1970s, led by Honda's CB750. A simple system consists of a single steel disc gripped by the twin pads of a hydraulically operated caliper. Discs don't

■ BELOW *This Michelin rack in a roadrace paddock holds (from left) two front slicks; a wider rear slick; heavily treaded rear and front wets; a lightly treaded front intermediate; and two more front slicks.*

require adjustment for wear and tend to cope better with the heat generated by braking, but early systems worked very poorly in wet weather. Modern superbikes use twin front discs, with another at the rear, gripped by calipers each containing four or even six individual pistons for improved power and feel. Some bikes, including several Moto Guzzis and Honda's CBR1000F, use hydraulics to link front and rear brakes.

Several manufacturers have developed efficient anti-lock or ABS systems, but the complexity and expense is such that fitment is restricted to BMWs and sports-tourers such as Honda's ST1100 and Yamaha's GTS1000.

Sport on Two Wheels

The Olympic motto, *citius*, *altius*, *fortius*, meaning faster, higher, stronger can equally be applied to competition aboard motorcycles.

Almost as long as bikes have been built, people have been holding contests to see who could make them go quickest, last longest—even get to the top of the biggest hill.

Motorcycle competition does not have to be all about speed. The sport of trials, for example, produces champions as skilful as any on two wheels. Endurance often plays a part, whether in a 24-hour road-race or the three-week slog from Paris to Dakar. But mostly it's the thrill of high velocities that attracts riders and spectators to bike sport.

This is true wherever they are in the world, and on whatever surface they compete—from the steep, man-made banking at Daytona to the sand of the Baja desert; from frozen ice-race ovals to the unforgiving public roads of the Isle of Man.

EARLY RACERS

■ OPPOSITE *Top Texan racer Eddie Hasha poses in front of a steeply banked board-track, or motordrome, with Indian's new eight-valve V-twin in 1911. In the following year he and seven others died following a crash at Newark in New Jersey.*

When motorcycle racing began, at the end of the last century, riders had to contend not only with their rivals but with the fragility of their crude bikes and the often appalling condition of the roads. Many early racing machines were tricycles, some with engines as large as two litres. Riders competed in gruelling inter-city marathons on temperamental bikes with no suspension, typically wearing clothing no more protective than a woolly jumper, plus-fours, stout shoes and a peaked cap.

Continental Europe was the birthplace not just of the motorcycle but also of bike racing, with the first major event being held between Paris and Rouen in July 1894. The next year saw pioneering races in both Italy and America. Other, even longer, events around the turn of the century included Paris-Vienna and

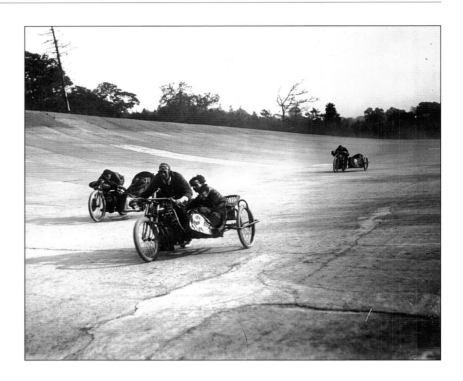

■ ABOVE *The width and banking of the concrete Brooklands track are clear in this shot of a Zenith outfit leading a race "for cycles and sidecars" in 1913.*

■ LEFT *The stopwatch is running as Sunbeam rider HR Davies gets under way at Caerphilly in Wales on a hill-climb, a popular early form of competition.*

■ RIGHT *Flying Merkel factory racer Maldwyn Jones won second place in a 300-mile (480 kilometre) race, at Savannah, Georgia in 1913.*

■ BELOW *These Indian V-twins hit 100mph (160 kph) with no suspension or brakes, and tyres prone to coming off the rims.*

Paris-Madrid. In the early 1900s short-circuit races became popular, often held on banked cycle tracks such as those at Lille and Paris's *Parc des Princes* in France, and at Plymouth and Crystal Palace in Britain.

The first big international race took place in France in 1904. The Coupe International was a 170-mile (273-kilometre) event in which a maximum of three bikes from each country was allowed. French rider Demester won on a Griffon, at an average speed of 45.1mph (72.5kph), but the race was declared void due to the dubious legality of the winning bikes, and after it became clear that tyres had been sabotaged by nails sprinkled by spectators.

The year 1907 was notable for two momentous events in Britain, one of which was the first-ever Tourist Trophy meeting in the Isle of Man. The other was the opening of Brooklands, the world's first artificially constructed race circuit. Surfaced with concrete and 2.8 miles (4.5 kilometres) in length, the egg-shaped Surrey track included two high and wide banked turns, remains of which are still visible today. Brooklands' layout allowed high speeds and attracted bike racers, record-breakers and testers until its closure at the start of the Second World War.

■ ABOVE RIGHT *Rem Fowler overcame mechanical problems to win the twin-cylinder class of the first TT in 1907 on this Peugeot-engined Norton.*

■ BELOW *Three competitors get under way side-by-side in this 1913 shot of the Brighton Speed Trials, an event that still takes place today.*

Banked tracks of a different kind became popular in America, where big V-twins from Indian, Thor and Flying Merkel thundered round narrow wooden circuits with sides as steep as 60 degrees. These were thrilling and highly dangerous events, at which professional racers with names like "Fearless" Balke and "Dare Devil" Derkum raced head-to-head, reaching speeds of 100mph (160kph), in front of crowds of 10,000 people. Board-racing's decline can be traced almost exactly to the day when two riders and six spectators were killed in a crash at Newark, New Jersey in 1912.

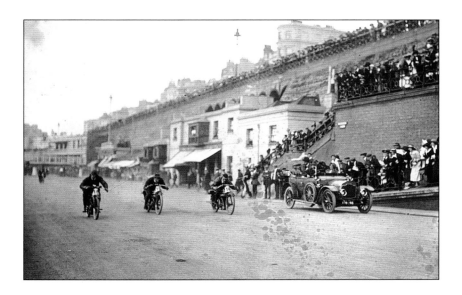

RACING ON THE ROADS

For many years the Isle of Man Tourist Trophy was the world's greatest motorcycle racing event. Even today there are those who maintain that the legendary 37.7-mile (60.6-kilometre) Mountain course makes the TT the supreme test of rider and machine. And although purpose-built circuits now dominate the sport from amateur to world championship level, pure road racing continues at places as far apart as Ireland, Belgium and New Zealand.

The TT's history dates back to 1907, when the Isle of Man was chosen as a race venue because competing on public roads was banned on mainland Britain. The event was known as the Tourist Trophy because machines had to be fitted with brakes, mudguards and a toolbox. Rem Fowler averaged just 36.2mph (58.2kph) when he won the twin-cylinder class on a Peugeot-engined Norton, pedalling up hills and stopping several times to repair punctures and broken drive-belts.

By the early 1920s, winning riders were averaging over 50mph (80kph) in gruelling

■ RIGHT *Charlie Collier, who ran the Matchless firm with his father and brother, won the single-cylinder class of the first TT in 1907, and won again three years later.*

■ BELOW *Mike Hailwood crashed his MV Agusta in the 1965 Senior TT, but got back on again to win with a bleeding nose, a broken fairing and flattened exhaust megaphones.*

races of five or more laps. On his TT debut in 1922, Stanley Woods had time to have his clothes catch fire while refuelling, stop to mend his engine and then crash and remount – yet still finish fifth. Woods went on to win a total of ten TTs between 1923 and 1939. Speeds had risen sharply by 1950, when Norton's Geoff Duke raised the lap record to 93.33mph (150.19kph) on the way to his first victory. Duke dominated the TT during the 1950s with six wins, but it was Bob McIntyre who set the first 100mph (160kph) lap – riding a four-cylinder Gilera in 1957.

Heroes in the 1960s included Giacomo Agostini, who scored ten wins, and Mike Hailwood, whose total of 14 victories included the 1967 Senior in which ":Mike the Bike" beat "Ago" in the race that many fans still consider to be the greatest TT of all time.

Hailwood's most famous win came in 1978 when he returned from retirement to take the Formula One race on a Ducati. By then the TT had lost its world championship status, and

■ BELOW Hailwood returned from retirement to ride a Ducati to an emotional Formula One TT win in 1978.

■ RIGHT Joey Dunlop's exploits at the TT and his native Ireland earned him the title "King of the Roads".

■ BELOW The beauty and danger of the TT circuit are clear as Scottish star Steve Hislop ignores the speed limit on the exit of Ginger Hall.

stars such as Barry Sheene and Kenny Roberts refused to risk the obvious dangers of racing at speed between stone walls.

But the TT continued to produce its own breed of heroes into the 1990s, when men like Joey Dunlop — who won a record nineteenth

TT in 1995 — and Steve Hislop lapped at average speeds of 120mph (193kph). Racing on the roads will never regain its former prestige, but events continue to take place at circuits including the TT, Ireland's North West 200 and Belgium's Chimay.

GRAND PRIX 500s

Grand Prix racing's 500cc class is the most prestigious in motorcycling. In the modern era, whoever has worn the 500cc crown has been entitled to call himself the best motorcycle racer in the world. As the most powerful and fastest bikes, the 500s have generally attracted the top riders, the biggest budgets, the greatest interest and the most publicity.

Modern 500 stars battle in a true world championship that in recent years has included rounds as far apart as Australia, America and Argentina. The situation was very different in 1949, when the world championship was first formed from the "Continental Circus" – the band of riders who, with their bikes and a few spares in small vans, followed a winding route around Europe from one race to the next. Britain's Les Graham won the 500cc title after six rounds, all of which were in Europe.

Graham won that first 500cc crown on a British twin, the AJS Porcupine, and Geoff Duke took the championship two years later on a single-cylinder Norton. But for the rest of the

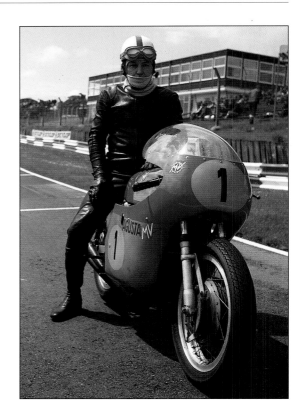

■ RIGHT *John Surtees began MV Agusta's domination of the 500cc world championship in 1956, with the first of his four titles for the Italian factory.*

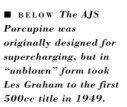

■ BELOW *The AJS Porcupine was originally designed for supercharging, but in "unblown" form took Les Graham to the first 500cc title in 1949.*

1950s, 1960s and early 1970s, racing's premier class was dominated by multi-cylinder Italian four-strokes, firstly from Gilera – whose six championships included a hat-trick from Duke between 1953 and 1955 – and then from MV Agusta.

MV's red and silver machines set records that will probably never be equalled, winning 17 consecutive world 500cc championships between 1958 and 1974 as well as a total of 38 riders' world titles and 37 manufacturers' championships. The so-called "Gallarate Fire Engines" reigned supreme in the 500cc class, winning the championship with John Surtees in 1956 and then, after a year's break, regaining it with Surtees, Gary Hocking and Mike Hailwood, who won four in a row.

Competition between numerous Italian factories was intense until the mid-1950s. But

■ BELOW *Giacomo Agostini's haul of eight 500cc and seven 350cc world championships makes him the most successful Grand Prix rider of all.*

■ LEFT *Gilera's DOHC four changed the face of 500cc Grand Prix racing, winning six titles and providing the ins-piration for MV Agusta's similar machines.*

■ BELOW *Guzzi withdrew from Grands Prix before the legendary 500cc V-eight, pictured in the factory museum, could prove its worth.*

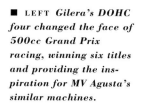

■ BELOW *The changing face of 500cc racing is summed-up in this 1975 shot of Barry Sheene, on a two-stroke Suzuki, coming up behind reigning world champion Phil Read riding the four-stroke MV Agusta.*

Mondial, Moto Guzzi and Gilera quit the arena in 1957, Guzzi without ever realizing the full potential of their exotic and super-fast V-eight. MV's next serious works challenge came from Mike Hailwood who left for Honda in 1966 and twice came desperately close to taking the title, with Agostini just beating him each time. Honda then quit racing, and Ago went on to take seven consecutive championships for MV.

Phil Read retained the 500cc title for MV in 1973 and 1974 but the Japanese two-stroke challenge was looming. Ironically though, it was Italian hero, Agostini, who in 1975 won the title for Yamaha, ending Agusta's glory years and confirming the two-stroke as the dominant force in 500cc Grand Prix racing.

GP 500s: The Two-stroke Era

Modern 500cc Grand Prix bikes are the purest, most highly developed motorbikes on the planet. On the straights their 185bhp two-stroke engines produce top speeds of up to 200mph (322kph). In the corners their light weight, ultra-rigid frames, sophisticated suspension and fat slick tyres allow incredible angles of lean. The factory 500s' performance is so violent and demanding that only a select band of talented and highly-paid professionals – men like past champions Eddie Lawson, Wayne Gardner, Wayne Rainey, Kevin Schwantz and Michael Doohan – can even come near to mastering them.

The two-stroke revolution began with Yamaha who, in the early 1970s, first built a 500cc four: basically two twins combined, with the cylinders set in line across the frame. With

■ LEFT *Factory honour is at stake as Shinichi Itoh (Honda, 7), Alexandre Barros (Suzuki, 6), Daryl Beattie (Yamaha, 3) and Doug Chandler (Cagiva, 10) battle in the 1994 Italian Grand Prix.*

■ BELOW *Kevin Schwantz, world champion in 1993, retired two years later after a Grand Prix career that contained many victories and almost as many injuries.*

■ LEFT *Honda's
Freddie Spencer and
Yamaha's Kenny
Roberts, here at the
Italian Grand Prix,
clashed many times
during the 1983 season.*

■ BELOW *The Suzuki
RG500s of Barry
Sheene and Dutch star
Wil Hartog lead Kenny
Roberts' Yamaha in the
French Grand Prix at
Nogaro in 1978.*

■ ABOVE *Freddie
Spencer won two 500cc
titles in the 1980s.*

■ BELOW *Australian
ace Michael Doohan
retained the champion's
No.1 plate in 1995.*

double the number of power strokes for a given
engine speed, a two-stroke should always
produce more power than an equivalent
capacity four-stroke, and Yamaha's format was
immediately a major success. Jarno Saarinen
won the French Grand Prix on the four's debut
in 1973. Although the Finnish star was killed
later that year, Yamaha's Giacomo Agostini
went on to win the Daytona 200 in 1974 and
the 500cc world title the following season.

Suzuki's more compact square-four RG500
took Barry Sheene to the championship in
1976 and 1977. Kenny Roberts then arrived on
the scene to win three consecutive titles on his
straight-four YZR Yamaha, redefining the art
of riding a 500cc Grand Prix bike with a

power-sliding style developed from American
dirt-track racing. Suzuki and the RG hit back,
with championships for Italians Marco
Lucchinelli and Franco Uncini, before Freddie
Spencer finally won Honda's first 500cc title in
1983 on the NS500 two-stroke triple.

Since then, the dominant 500cc engine
layout has been the V-four, with Honda's NSR,
Yamaha's YZR and Suzuki's RGV each taking
championships in recent years, and Cagiva's
V-four becoming competitive before the Italian
firm's withdrawal from Grand Prix racing at the
end of 1994.

The future of Grand Prix racing was then
unclear, although in many ways the 500cc class
had never been healthier. Teams had become
increasingly professional, worldwide television
coverage had brought the sport to millions,
grids were full and tracks had been made safer
than ever before. Serious accidents, like the
one that left triple-champion Wayne Rainey
paralysed in 1993, are a sad and inevitable
fact of motorcycle racing. But it was not such
events that threatened the health of Grand Prix
racing. The exotic, hugely expensive 500s were
under threat from the road-based Superbikes
that were regarded by some manufacturers as
more relevant to motorcycle sales.

THE SMALLER GP CLASSES

■ BELOW *Phil Read keeps his two-stroke Yamaha twin ahead of Jim Redman's Honda four-stroke twin in a 350cc race at Mallory Park in 1964.*

The smaller Grand Prix categories can't match the straight-line speed or the sheer glamour of the 500s – but they often more than make up for that with closer racing, more technical variety and a wider number of potential winners. The thrilling sight of six or more tiny 125s and riders slipstreaming each other down the straights and clashing fairings through bends for lap after lap has long been commonplace. In countries such as Spain, riders of the tiddlers, diminutive giants such as Angel Nieto and Jorge "Aspar" Martinez have traditionally been regarded as highly as big-bike champions.

In recent seasons, racing's rules have limited Grand Prix 125s to a single cylinder and 250s to two, with six gears apiece. But rules were less restrictive in the past, which inspired some remarkable bikes. The Suzuki RK66 on which Hans-Georg Anscheidt won the 50cc

world title in 1966, for example, had two cylinders, 14 gears and made 17.5bhp at 17,300rpm. Honda and MV Agusta built many multi-cylinder 250s and 350s in the 1960s. In 1964 the Japanese factory unveiled the

■ BELOW *Haruchika Aoki (No.12), one of several outstanding Japanese 125cc riders, screams his Honda into the lead in the 1995 Spanish Grand Prix.*

■ BELOW *Ever-stylish South African Kork Ballington rode to 250 and 350cc world titles for Kawasaki in both 1978 and 1979.*

■ ABOVE *Germany's Hans-Georg Anscheidt, a triple world champion in the 1960s, leaps Ballaugh Bridge on his 50cc, 14-speed Kreidler during the 1964 TT.*

legendary 250cc, six-cylinder RC166, which reached 150mph (241kph). The next season Honda's Luigi Taveri won the 125cc title on an exotic five-cylinder machine.

In recent years the Grand Prix solo classes have comprised just 500s, 250s and 125s, but in the past there have also been races for 350 and 50 or 80cc bikes. Riders commonly used to contest more than one class. In 1967 Mike Hailwood rode works Hondas in the 250, 350 and 500cc classes. At Assen, after winning his

third Dutch TT of the day, Hailwood almost fell off his motorcycle through sheer exhaustion. Riders often contested both 250 and 350cc championships until the larger class was dropped in 1983, and both Kork Ballington and Anton Mang scored double championship wins aboard Kawasaki's tandem twins.

One of racing's most spectacular achievements was Freddie Spencer's 250 and 500cc championship double for Honda in 1985. Since then the increasingly competitive nature of Grand Prix racing, together with the contrasting technique required to get the best from the 250cc twins and the almost doubly powerful 500cc V-fours, has kept riders to one class. High cornering speed has always been crucial on 125s and 250s, while the ultra-powerful 500s demanded the "slow in, fast out" style refined by Kenny Roberts. Even 250cc champions such as Christian Sarron and Sito Pons struggled to repeat their success after moving up to 500s, although evolving engine and tyre technology have made the transition slightly smoother in recent seasons.

SIDECAR RACING

■ OPPOSITE TOP LEFT
*Rolf Biland (centre left)
and passenger Kurt
Waltisperg celebrate
after winning the 1984
French Grand Prix.*

Racing sidecars are very different vehicles from the road-going motorcycle combinations to which they are related. Far from being a bike with a sidecar alongside, a modern racing outfit is a specialized structure whose aluminium one-piece chassis holds three small-diameter wheels, each wearing a fat, square-section tyre. These machines have more in common with a racing car than with a bike.

It was not always this way. When sidecar racing first became popular in the 1920s, outfits were indeed solos with a lightweight,

■ OPPOSITE FAR
RIGHT *Passenger
Freddy Henriksen used
a steering wheel to
adjust the angle of this
1970 grasstrack outfit,
which was later banned.*

■ LEFT *Driver Rolf
Biland takes a tight line
through a left-hander in
a 1990 Grand Prix.*

large-wheeled chair bolted on. In 1923 the first Isle of Man sidecar TT was won by Freddie Dixon, whose Douglas outfit featured a lever with which passenger Walter Perry made the machine bank through corners. Banking Flxicar sidecars were also successful in American dirt-track racing in the 1920s. By the time Britain's Eric Oliver won the first of his four sidecar world championships in 1949, the sidecar had become much lower so allowing the passenger, Denis Jenkinson, to lean out in left-hand bends.

■ LEFT *Fritz
Scheidegger and John
Robinson, here
attacking a Brands
Hatch right-hander, won
the world title with a
BMW flat-twin in 1965
and 1966.*

■ LEFT *Egbert Streuer
leads Rolf Biland, Steve
Webster and Markus
Eglof through Assen's
sweeping Strubben curve
at the 1988 Dutch TT.*

■ ABOVE *Alain Michel's passenger had no time for the view as their LCR outfit sped up the Mistral straight at Circuit Paul Ricard.*

■ BELOW *Owen Greenwood's Mini (No.7), ahead of world champion Scheidegger in this 1966 shot from Mallory Park.*

Switzerland and Germany have produced many of the world's best sidecar drivers and designers over the years. Germany's Max Deubel and Emil Horner won four consecutive championships on BMW flat-twins in the 1960s. Swiss Fritz Scheidegger won two titles and did much to advance technical thinking in sidecars. German Helmut Fath won the championship in 1960 with a BMW, and returned after a serious injury to win it again eight years later with the URS, whose four-cylinder four-stroke engine he built himself.

Two-strokes took over in the 1970s, initially with German Königs and then with Yamahas. The sidecar's chassis revolution came a few years later, led by the Swiss Seymaz, whose monocoque aluminium platform and car-style suspension and wheels gave a lower, lighter machine than the traditional steel frame and telescopic forks. The 1980s and early 1990s were dominated by the LCR chassis, designed by Swiss Louis Christen and a development of the theme.

The greatest driver of modern times is Switzerland's Rolf Biland, who in 1994 won a record seventh championship. Biland also helped develop the BRM V-four engine, which proved powerful but unreliable in 1995, and was intended for use in both sidecars and 500cc solos. But in other respects the gap between two and three-wheeled racing has widened. Although sidecars retain a following they have been excluded from many Grand Prix venues, and their future remains in doubt.

SUPERBIKES

Superbikes are the rising force of bike racing. Visually similar to, and directly derived from, road-going machines, the big four-strokes are strictly limited in the modifications allowed. That often makes for close racing. In recent seasons, booming Ducati V-twins and screaming four-cylinder Japanese 750s, backed by the major factories and ridden by top riders such as Scott Russell and Carl Fogarty, have provided some memorable racing battles.

Superbike racing began in America, where the tradition of competing on modified streetbikes dates back to the 1970s. Then riders such as Reg Pridmore, Wes Cooley and Steve McLaughlin locked high handlebars on BMW flat-twins and 1000cc fours from Suzuki and Kawasaki. In the early 1980s, rising stars Freddie Spencer (Honda) and Eddie Lawson (Kawasaki) clashed on big four-strokes before

moving into Grands Prix. Fellow future 500cc world champions Wayne Rainey and Kevin Schwantz also raced and won on superbikes. But in those days the class was a poor relation; the bikes disparagingly referred to as diesels by Grand Prix riders.

That attitude began to change in 1988, when the World Superbike Championship was established by McLaughlin, the former rider who earlier had been instrumental in starting the US series. Another flamboyant American,

■ ABOVE *The Ducatis of Carl Fogarty, champion Doug Polen and Frenchman Raymond Roche emphasize the Italian factory's Superbike strength at Donington Park in 1992.*

■ LEFT *Californian Fred Merkel, riding for an Italian-based team, won the first World Superbike championship on an RC30 fitted with factory race-kit parts.*

■ BELOW *Freddie Spencer, pictured at Daytona, 1980, rode a four-cylinder Honda Superbike before graduating to Grands Prix.*

■ BOTTOM *Steve McLaughlin won American national Superbike races on a Suzuki GS1000 in the late 1970s.*

"Flyin' Fred" Merkel, won the first two titles on a factory-backed Honda RC30, and the roadster-based series was an immediate success. Italy's Ducati then took over – aided by rules allowing twins a capacity and weight advantage over fours – with championship victories for Frenchman Raymond Roche in 1990 and America's Doug Polen in 1991 and 1992.

The subsequent sales success of Ducati's red race-replica V-twins highlighted the commercial potential to be gained from Superbike success, and the factories stepped up their involvement. Scott Russell won on a lime-green works Kawasaki ZXR750 before Carl Fogarty regained the crown for Ducati in 1994. Honda joined in again, initially unsuccessfully, with the V-four RC45.

By 1995 Yamaha had boosted its presence with a full works team, and Bimota had also joined the fray. Suzuki, Aprilia and Cagiva – the latter having quit Grands Prix in favour of Superbikes – waited in the wings.

Superbike racing's high level of competition, relatively low cost and big influence on roadster sales had raised the possibility, unthinkable just a few years earlier, that the four-stroke class would replace Grands Prix as bike racing's star attraction.

ENDURANCE RACING

Long-distance racing adds an extra dimension to the spectacle of high-speed motorcycling. Modern endurance events are run at a furious pace, and races of up to 24 hours contain fuel-stops, rider and tyre changes – all conducted in just a few seconds – and hours of hard riding through the night. For riders who crash or break down, the race can include a long push back to the pits, after which a team of well-drilled mechanics works flat-out to get a damaged bike back onto the track.

Things were less hectic but even more tiring when the Bol d'Or, the oldest and most famous 24-hour event, was first held on the outskirts of Paris in 1922. The winning rider – only one was allowed per machine – covered over 750 miles (1206 kilometres) on a 500cc Motosacoche. By 1930 the Bol, held on a different road circuit near Paris, was attracting over 50,000 spectators and had become an important showcase for manufacturers. Best and toughest of the early racers was Gustave Lefèvre, who had five solo wins on a 500cc Norton, and then two more after co-riders were allowed in 1954.

In the 1970s endurance became a demanding proving ground for large-capacity roadsters. BSA/Triumph triples won in 1970 and 1971, before big four-cylinder Hondas and Kawasakis took over. Bikes raced by legendary

■ BELOW *Riders run across the track to their bikes in the traditional Le Mans start, with fastest qualifiers on the left, as the famous 24-hour race gets under way at the French circuit in 1987.*

■ LEFT *The pit lane stays busy at night during the Spa 24-hour race in Belgium, as lap-scorers signal times to riders, and bikes arrive for refuelling or repair.*

■ RIGHT *French endurance ace Jean-Claude Chemarin won races for both Honda and Kawasaki, on whose 1000cc four he is pictured at the Bol d'Or in 1983.*

■ FAR RIGHT *Honda's factory 750cc V-four RVF dominated endurance racing in the mid-1980s, and formed the basis of the Japanese firm's RC30 roadster.*

■ RIGHT *Works endurance bikes can be refuelled and given fresh tyres in just a few seconds, and every moment can be vital — as Kawasaki's Scott Russell discovered when he lost the 1994 Suzuka eight-hour race to Honda by less than a third of a second.*

French pairings such as Godier/Genoud and Chemarin/Léon housed factory-tuned 1000cc motors in specially built chassis. Many innovative engineering solutions were tried and endurance trends were often copied on road-going superbikes.

In more recent years three riders have been allowed in 24-hour races, and bikes have been limited first to 750cc and then to Superbike format, reducing cost but also outlawing the technically interesting prototypes. Although endurance is unpopular in many countries, and has often failed to support a full-scale world championship, the French 24-hour classics at Le Mans and the Bol d'Or feature top-level factory teams and are unbeatable for atmosphere and drama. The Suzuka eight-hour in Japan, which regularly attracts over 100,000 spectators, is regarded by the Japanese factories as the year's most important race.

MOTOCROSS

Today, a top-level off-road race is almost as likely to take place in a covered arena as in its natural habitat of a dusty, sandy or muddy out-door track. The old sport of scrambling has developed into motocross and its descendent, supercross, which sees colourfully clad riders – astride tall, lightweight 125 or 250cc single-cylinder two-strokes with long-travel suspen-sion and knobbly tyres – fly over gravity-defying jumps on courses constructed in city stadia.

The link to racing a motorbike around a field remains, but the sport has seen more than the odd change of name since the first off-road meeting was organized in 1924. In that year, a group of riders from Surrey decided to run an adaptation of Yorkshire's Scott trial, excluding the observed sections where points could be lost. Without these the event couldn't be called a trial, and one competitor's comment that the

race would be a fair old scramble led to the new form of racing being called scrambling.

Scrambling's popularity spread from Britain to continental Europe in the 1940s, and in 1947 the first international Moto-Cross des Nations was contested between five-man teams from France, Belgium, the Netherlands and England. In the 1960s and 1970s the sport was dominated by Belgian and Scandinavian riders including Joël Robert, Roger De Coster and Heikki Mikkola.

The sport had become known as motocross but was otherwise essentially little changed when it reached America in the late 1960s. Americans had

■ ABOVE *Kurt Nicholl, leading Grand Prix star and British multiple motocross champion, takes a jump in typically effortless style on his factory Honda.*

■ LEFT *Greg Albertyn's 1994 world championship-winning Suzuki RM250 shows off the massive suspension travel it requires for landing from high jumps.*

■ RIGHT *Three-times former world champion Dave Thorpe kicks up the sand as he uses a berm, or bank, to get round a left-hand turn at maximum speed.*

other ideas, and in 1972 the Olympic Coliseum in Los Angeles was converted into an indoor motocross circuit with dramatic jumps.

Supercross had been born, and four years later it had grown into an eight-round national championship, was attracting huge crowds and was on the way to taking over as the most important branch of the sport in the States.

In the last two decades America has produced many spectacular riders including Bob Hannah, Rick Johnson and the most recent superstar, Jeremy McGrath. Americans have proved they can ride outdoors, too, winning every Motocross des Nations from 1981 to 1993. Meanwhile, supercross has in turn been adopted by countries as far apart as Scandinavia, Japan and France. Indoor races at venues such as Bercy in Paris provide an extravaganza of laser-shows, fireworks, huge leaps and wheel-to-wheel racing action.

■ LEFT *The French sport of supermoto, a combination of motocross and road-racing, demonstrated by Gilles Salvador at Paris's Circuit Carole.*

■ BELOW *The first turn of a top-level motocross race is no place for the faint-hearted, as a gang of snarling, dust-throwing motorcycles aims for the same piece of land.*

TRIALS, ENDUROS AND DESERT RACING

Trials bikes' light weight and knobbly, low-pressure tyres allow them to navigate terrain that looks impossible for a mountain goat, let alone a motorcycle. These range from sheer rock faces and deep gullies in conventional trials, to artificial hazards such as huge pipes or a series of tables in the increasingly popular indoor events. Riders often stop completely for several seconds and bounce their machines sideways, all without scoring penalty points by putting a foot on the ground or falling.

Modern courses test mainly the skill and balance of the riders within a time limit, but when the sport began after the turn of the century it was the bikes' reliability that was on trial. Among the most famous events is the Scottish Six Days Trial, which dates from 1910 and attracts a large number of riders ranging from club riders to top professionals, although it is not a world championship event. Another famous trial, the Scott, takes place on the Yorkshire Moors and began as a closed event for workers at the nearby Scott factory.

The most famous trials rider in the 1950s and 60s was Sammy Miller, the Irishman who won over 1000 events, including five Scottish Six Days, on bikes including his famous Ariel with its registration GOV132. In the mid-60s

Miller rode for the Spanish firm Bultaco and helped develop the two-stroke 250cc Sherpa that led the move away from four-stroke singles, known as thumpers. Spain has other leading marques in Gas-Gas and Montesa and has produced many outstanding riders, including multiple world champion Jordi Tarrés. Rivals include Honda, and the Italian firms Aprilia and Beta.

■ LEFT *Until the 1960s, trials were dominated by four-strokes such as the 250cc Greeves Anglian on which Bill Wilkinson won the Scottish Six Days Trial in 1969.*

■ LEFT *Solo and
sidecar enduro
competitors in typically
muddy action as they
tackle a bog during the
Welsh Two-Day event at
Llandrindod Wells.*

Enduro competition lies somewhere between
motocross and trials, being essentially an off-
road race against the clock for street-legal
machines with lights. No points are lost for
putting a foot down in sections; instead, riders
must make sure to arrive at a series of
checkpoints within strict time limits. The most
prestigious event is the International Six Day

Enduro, a punishing marathon fought out by
teams from all over the world.

The other main form of off-road competition
is desert racing, of which the best-known event
is the legendary Paris-Dakar Rally. Bikes are
generally huge, twin-cylinder four-strokes with
long-travel suspension, extra fuel in rear
pannier tanks and sophisticated computerized
navigation equipment. The Paris-Dakar crosses
the Sahara Desert and covers thousands of
miles in three weeks – barely one rider in three
makes it all the way. Other leading desert races
include the Pharaohs in Egypt, and the Baja in
Mexico.

Several manufacturers produce desert-
replica roadbikes, such as Yamaha's Super
Ténéré and Honda's Africa Twin, which are
particularly popular in Continental Europe.

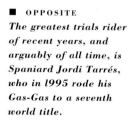

■ OPPOSITE
*The greatest trials rider
of recent years, and
arguably of all time, is
Spaniard Jordi Tarrés,
who in 1995 rode his
Gas-Gas to a seventh
world title.*

■ RIGHT *Top desert
racer Stéphane
Peterhansel stands high
on the footpegs as he
blasts his works Yamaha
through the Sahara
Desert in the 1994
Paris-Dakar Rally.*

SPEEDWAY, LONG TRACK AND ICE RACING

Speedway bikes have little in common with other motorcycles, being purpose-built for short, four-lap races on quarter-mile (400 metre) dirt ovals. Their engines are 500cc, single-cylinder four-strokes that run on methanol and have just one gear. Their chassis have minimal front suspension and none at the rear, no front brake, and a right footrest set low to take the rider's weight as the bike power-slides through the left-hand bends.

The sport became popular in Australia in the 1920s and took off in Europe after the first British meeting was staged in Essex in 1928. Speedway is essentially a team sport, with meetings consisting of heats between four riders from two rival teams. But the year's biggest event has traditionally been the individual World Final. Sweden's Ove Fundin and New Zealander Barry Briggs each won five

■ LEFT *Bruce Penhall, charismatic American former champion, leads England's Chris Morton in the World Team Final in 1980. The individual world title was also decided at a single meeting until 1995, when a series of points-scoring rounds was introduced to determine the champion.*

times in the 1950s and 1960s. Ivan Mauger, another New Zealander, won a record sixth title in 1979.

Several other types of racing share speedway's basic format of competing on a tight, anti-clockwise oval. The closest to speedway is long track, a German-dominated sport, also run on shale, whose longer straights

■ LEFT *Denmark's Tommy Knudsen shows typical speedway style as he remains perfectly in control while broadsiding out of a bend on his single-cylinder Weslake.*

and higher speeds demand engines with two gears. Ivan Mauger won three world titles in the 1970s but the most successful rider is Britain's Simon Wigg, who won his fifth in 1994. Grass-track and sand racing are related but less high-profile sports that require tyre-sliding skills on different surfaces.

The maddest form of bike sport is ice racing on bikes whose tyres bristle with scores of sharp steel spikes. These give excellent grip on the ice, allowing near-horizontal cornering angles, but they can turn a crash into an even nastier experience despite protective wheel-guards that extend part-way around the tyre. Ice racing has generally been dominated by Russians, but is also popular in parts of Eastern Europe and Scandinavia.

Japan has its own brand of speedway called autorace. Held solely to allow the large crowds to bet on the outcome, this takes place on concrete ovals. Eight riders contest each race, on 600cc single or twin-cylinder bikes, which are capable of 120mph (193kph). Prize money levels are high, and leading riders can earn as much as top Grand Prix stars. Nevertheless the temptation to fix results necessitates the imposition of strict rules to ensure that riders are kept away from the crowd before racing.

■ ABOVE *Three battling ice-racers demonstrate the radical cornering angles and aggressive, knee-down styles that are possible despite the slippery track.*

■ LEFT *Ice-race bikes do not slide in bends like speedway machines, but grip the track with long metal spikes fitted to their tyres, which can injure riders in a crash.*

■ BELOW *Speedway's short races and tight tracks combine to make the start particularly important; many races are won by the rider who gets away first.*

DIRT-TRACK AND HILL-CLIMBING

America's most spectacular bike sport takes place on one-mile (1.6-kilometre) ovals, where up to 16 riders thunder round on big Harleys with no front brakes. Through the turns they hold the bikes sideways under power from 100 horsepower V-twin engines, rear tyres throwing up dirt, and on the straights they slipstream or draft at speeds up to 130mph (209kph). The American Motorcycle Association (AMA) Grand National Championship also includes half-mile (800 metre) races, and quarter-mile (400 metre) short tracks, where 600cc single-cylinder bikes are used, and also steeple-chases, which combine elements of dirt-track and motocross.

Dirt-track began on horse tracks at country fairs across America before the First World War. Harley-Davidson's first official race entry was at

■ ABOVE *Jay Spring-steen (No.1) takes his XR750 wide through the "cushion" of loose dirt, while rivals use the firmer "groove" on the inside of the turn.*

the big 300-mile (482-kilometre) event at Dodge City, Kansas, on July 5 1914. The sport was America's most popular in the 1930s but it wasn't until 1946 that the AMA held a one-off championship race at the Springfield Mile, won by Norton-mounted Chet Dykgraff. Harley rider Joe Leonard was the winner in 1954, when the championship was first decided over a series of races, and the American marque has been the most successful ever since.

The most famous dirt-track bike is Harley-Davidson's XR750 V-twin, which was introduced in 1970 and has been taken to victory by dozens of riders, including multiple champion Scott Parker. Honda mounted a successful challenge with the RS750 V-twin, which took four consecutive titles after its introduction in 1984. But the Japanese firm pulled out after the AMA changed the rules to limit the RS's power.

A similar fate met the most outrageous dirt-track bike of all, the four-cylinder, two-stroke Yamaha TZ750 on which Kenny Roberts won the Indianapolis Mile in 1975. Bikes with more than two cylinders were banned at the end of that year and even Roberts didn't complain. The season-long battle for the champion's No.1

■ LEFT *European hill-climbing traditionally takes place on steep and twisty tarmac courses, often with spectacular backdrops such as this one in Devon, England.*

■ BELOW *Harley's in-line V-twin has been dirt-track's dominant engine for years partly due to its controllable power delivery.*

■ OPPOSITE *Scott Stump's left hand is tucked in to improve his XR750's aerodynamics as he enters a straight at the Sacramento Mile, one of the fastest dirt-track venues.*

plate included road races as well as dirt-tracks until separate series were set-up in 1986. Racing dirt-track from a young age has contributed to the road-racing success of many American riders including Roberts, Eddie Lawson and Wayne Rainey.

The other peculiarly American sport is that of hill-climbing – basically a test to see which

rider can go furthest and fastest up a dirt-covered slope that starts steep and gets steeper. Hill-climbing has a long tradition at events such as the famous Widowmaker, and produces long bikes with heavily-treaded rear tyres. An event called hill-climbing also takes place in Europe but this contest is based on timed sprints up a short, twisty tarmac course.

■ ABOVE *Ricky Graham, Bubba Shobert and others were successful on the RS750 before Honda quit after a rule-change made the V-twin less competitive.*

■ RIGHT *Kenny Roberts won the Indianapolis Mile on the TZ750 two-stroke, but still supported its ban.*

DRAG RACING

The quickest and most violent form of bike competition is drag racing – a straight duel of acceleration over a standing-start quarter-mile (0.4-kilometre). The fastest top fuel dragsters produce almost 1000bhp and reach over 220mph (354kph) in just 6.5 seconds – roughly the time a top sports car takes to reach 60mph (96kph). To keep the front wheel down and deliver maximum traction, drag bikes are built long and low, with massively wide rear tyres, and often using wheelie bars that extend far beyond the back of the machine.

Drag racing began in America, where most of the fastest times are still set, although the sport is popular in Europe and elsewhere too. In the early days, Indian and Harley V-twins raced against lighter Triumphs. Japanese motors took

over in the 1970s, when Californian Russ Collins built double and even triple-engined monsters using 750cc Honda power. Another star of the 1970s was Dutchman Henk Vink, known as the "Big Spender", who won many races on a 400bhp twin-engined Kawasaki. The extreme stresses that top fuel engines are exposed to make blow-ups frequent and big budgets essential.

Top fuel bikes have been limited to a single engine since the 1980s, but speeds have increased and in recent years riders have posted times below 6.5 seconds.

Harley-engined dragsters are also now faster than ever – and are often enlarged to over two litres, supercharged and fuelled by nitromethane. The Harley class has increased

■ ABOVE *Instant reactions are vital when the lights change.*

■ BELOW *Terry Vance takes his place on the start-line on one of the ultra-quick Suzukis with which he had much success in the 1980s.*

■ LEFT *Dutchman Henk Vink was Europe's best-known drag-racer of the 1970s, with his consistently spectacular performances on powerful Kawasakis.*

■ BELOW *Under its bodywork the Vance & Hines dragster's motor is based on a 16-valve Suzuki GSX four, but very few original components remain.*

■ BELOW *Twin-engined bikes such as the Weslake-powered machine of top British rider John Hobbs dominated drag racing in the 1970s, but are no longer permitted.*

in popularity to such an extent that some American racers are well-sponsored professionals.

Modern drag meets include numerous classes such as Funny Bike, for machines with roadster-based looks and power aids such as turbochargers or nitrous oxide, and Pro Stock, for highly tuned, near-standard-looking bikes that run on petrol. The cheapest and most basic class is one which allows riders to race on almost any motorcycle including standard or lightly modified roadsters.

RECORD BREAKING

The fastest motorcycles of all are the record-breakers: long, low and highly specialized machines built purely to reach phenomenal top speeds in wide open spaces. Aerodynamics are as vital as horsepower at very high speed, and the fastest machines run at places such as the Bonneville salt flats in Utah are streamliners, cigar-shaped projectiles in which the rider reclines with feet forward.

Bikes were much more simple when William Cook took his Peugeot-engined NLG to a recorded 75.9mph (122.14kph) at Brooklands in 1909, setting what is generally accepted as the first speed record. Indian's Jake de Rosier raised the figure to 88.9mph (143.06kph) at the same track two years later, only to be beaten by Matchless founder Charles Collier, who was recorded at 91.3mph (146.92kph) shortly afterwards. In 1920 Indian regained the

crown when Ernie Walker was timed at 104mph (167.36kph) at Daytona Beach. This is regarded as the first official world record, as by now contestants had to make two-way runs within a set time limit.

The 1930s were a great time for record-breaking in Europe, where Germany's Ernst Henne set several new marks on BMWs,

■ LEFT *In the 1930s Ernst Henne made use of Germany's autobahns to set a series of world records on streamliners powered by super-charged BMW twins.*

■ OPPOSITE *Bob Leppan at the 1966 London Motorcycle Show in Gyronaut X-1, the twin 650cc engined Triumph on which he set a record of 245.6mph (395.2kph).*

■ LEFT *Don Vesco poses on the Bonneville salt with Lightning Bolt, the twin-engined Kawasaki on which he set a record speed of 318.5mph (512.5kph) in 1978.*

culminating in 173.5mph (279.21kph) in 1937. Henne's great rival was Britain's Eric Fernihough, who earlier the same year had set a 169.7mph (273.09kph) record on his supercharged, JAP-engined Brough Superior. A year later Fernihough was killed when his bike got into a wobble at 180mph (290kph).

The 200mph (321kph) barrier was finally breached in 1956, when Wilhelm Herz

■ ABOVE *Bert Munro's streamlined Munro Special, based on a Model 596 Indian Scout built in 1920, set a class record of 183.5mph (295.3kph) at Bonneville in 1967.*

(427.26kph) on a 1480cc Harley. In 1978 Vesco set a record of 318.5mph (512.5kph) on his Lightning Bolt streamliner, powered by two turbocharged, four-cylinder Kawasaki Z1000 engines. Harley reclaimed the record in 1990 when Dave Campos, riding a twin-engined, 2400cc streamliner – sponsored by readers of the American magazine *Easyriders* – raised the record to 322mph (518.19kph).

■ RIGHT *Bert Le Vack on a Brough Superior SS100 Pendine V-twin, on which he set several speed records in the early 1930s.*

■ BELOW *NSU's 1956 Delphin III's size is emphasized in an aerial shot of the streamliner alongside a conventional racing machine.*

recorded 211.4mph (340.2kph) on a supercharged 500cc NSU. A year earlier Johnny Allen had taken a 650cc Triumph twin to 193.3mph (311kph) at Bonneville. The run was not recognized by the FIM, because no official observers were present, but Allen's exploits led to Triumph's most famous roadster being named the Bonneville.

In recent years the fight on the salt has been between Japan and Harley. American Don Vesco recorded 251.6mph (404.8kph) on a twin-engined, 700cc Yamaha two-stroke streamliner in 1970; a month later fellow road racer Cal Rayborn was timed at 265.5mph

A-Z OF MOTORCYCLES

The A-Z section that follows is a guide to the major manufacturers and the models they have produced since Gottlieb Daimler first fired-up Einspur back in 1885. No attempt has been made to cover all the makes: that would have been impossible. Motorcycling's history is littered with names of firms that built a few bikes and then went out of business, many of them before 1930. Names such as Abako, Abbotsford, ABC Scootamota, Abendsonne, Aberdale, Abe-Star.

The most important marques and their greatest hits, plus a few misses, are here, from AJS and Bimota to Yamaha and Zündapp. Between them they tell the story of an industry that has had many ups and downs, but which has produced many fine machines for the benefit of millions of riders worldwide. Some bikes have been cleverly engineered, others are simply beautiful to look at. The best have combined both style and performance, giving their riders the feeling of exhilaration and freedom that only a great motorcycle can provide.

AJS

■ AJS MODEL 30

Like most AJS roadsters, the 600cc Model 30 of the late 1950s suffered from a case of dual personality. Almost exactly the same bike, differing only in paint colour, badges and exhaust system, was also sold as the Matchless G11 – a result of the Wolverhampton-based AJS firm having been taken over by Matchless of London in 1931. The combined firm in turn became part of Associated Motor Cycles (AMC) in 1938, but the AJS and Matchless names were retained and used in an attempt to attract the continued support of each of the brand's enthusiasts.

AJS had originally been founded by Albert John Stevens in Wolverhampton

AJS MODEL 30 (1957)	
Engine	Aircooled 4-valve OHV pushrod parallel twin
Capacity	593cc (72 x 72.8mm)
Power	33bhp @ 6800rpm
Weight	180kg (396lb)
Top speed	95mph (152kph)

around the turn of the century, and won the Junior TT in 1914. But AJS's greatest racing feats came later, notably when Les Graham won the first ever 500cc world championship on the Porcupine twin in 1949.

The most popular AJS racebike was

the single-cylinder 350cc 7R, known as the "Boy Racer". Introduced in 1948, the 7R was hugely successful and was later enlarged to 500cc to make the Matchless G50.

Most of AJS's roadsters were less spectacular singles and parallel twins such as the Model 30, whose 600cc engine had almost square dimensions, and gave a smoother ride than most other models. Peak output was only 33bhp but the twin was capable of cruising fairly smoothly at 70mph (112kph). Handling was predictable and made for a relaxed, comfortable bike over distances. The Model 30 was also well-made, reliable and economical. Unfortunately such attributes were not

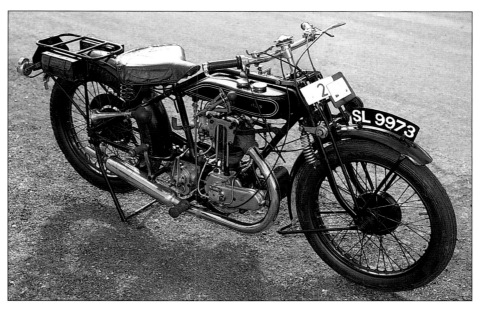

enough to keep AJS in business. Poor sales led to parent company AMC becoming part of Norton Villiers in 1967. Some AJS bikes were then built incorporating Norton parts, but they were not successful and the factory ceased production shortly afterwards.

OTHER MAKES

■ ABC
Best known of several ABCs in the 1920s was the 398cc flat-twin built by British aircraft firm Sopwith. Regarded as the predecessor of the first BMW, the engine's unreliability led to ABC's collapse.

■ ACE
American Bill Henderson set up ACE after selling his Henderson firm to the Schwinn cycle company in 1917, and produced bikes with a similar in-line four-cylinder layout. Best known was the XP-4, which set a record speed of 130mph (209kph) in 1923. Rights were later sold to Indian, who built a similar four.

■ ADLER
Germany's Adler built motorbikes for a short time from 1902, then concentrated on cars and bicycles before making a comeback in 1949. The firm's most popular model was the M250, a twin-cylinder two-stroke roadster released in

■ ABOVE *Four-cylinder ACE racers such as this were among the world's fastest bikes in 1923.*

1953. Adlers were ridden successfully in road races and enduros, but sales declined. Finally in 1958 the firm was taken over by the Grundig Corporation, who abandoned bikes to concentrate on producing typewriters.

■ AERMACCHI
The former aircraft factory at Varese in northern Italy built some fine 250 and 350cc single-cylinder four-strokes in the 1950s and 1960s, most notably racebikes such as the 100mph (160kph) Ala d'Oro 250 introduced in 1959. Aermacchi turned to two-strokes after being bought by AMF Harley-Davidson in the 1960s. Walter Villa rode Varese-built Harleys to four 250 and 350cc world titles between 1974 and 1976, but two years later the firm was declared bankrupt and sold to Cagiva.

■ ABOVE *A 350cc Aermacchi single from the mid-1960s in racing action.*

APRILIA

■ BELOW *Road-going RS250's massive twin-spar aluminium frame held a tuned Suzuki V-twin engine.*

■ APRILIA RS250

In recent years Aprilia has been one of the world's most dynamic and fastest growing motorcycle manufacturers, with an aggressive approach to design and performance typified by the RS250. Essentially a road-going replica of the two-stroke Grand Prix bike on which Italian idol Max Biaggi won the 1994 250cc world championship, the RS combined a high-revving two-stroke engine with a massive twin-beam aluminium frame, top-class cycle parts and stream-lined, racetrack-inspired styling.

Its engine was a subtly redesigned version of the V-twin powerplant from Suzuki's RGV250, and produced a maximum of 70bhp. With its aggressive

APRILIA RS250 (1995)	
Engine	Watercooled 90-degree V-twin two-stroke
Capacity	249cc (56 x 50.6mm)
Power	70bhp @ 11,900rpm
Weight	141kg (310lb)
Top speed	130mph (209kph)

riding position, peaky powerplant and ultra-light weight, the RS came closer than any other bike to providing Grand Prix style thrills on the road. Given enough frantic revving through the gears the Aprilia screamed towards a top speed of 130mph (208kph), and in the

■ LEFT *Its light weight and superb chassis made the RS250 almost unbeatable for fast cornering.*

■ BELOW *The title-winning 250cc Grand Prix racebike provided inspiration for the RS250 roadster.*

bends its superb suspension, powerful brakes and sticky tyres combined to make the RS250 almost unbeatable.

Aprilia certainly proved difficult to beat on the track in 1994, winning both the 250 and 125cc world titles with Biaggi and Japan's Kazuto Sakata. In all, it was quite a year for the small company from Noale, near Venice in northern Italy. Aprilia also began building the single-cylinder F650 for BMW, and announced that production of its own bikes had doubled in three years to 100,000 units. Yet it was only in 1973 that Ivano Beggio had taken control of the family bicycle firm and moved into the motorcycle business.

Beggio attributes much of Aprilia's subsequent success to an unusual policy of manufacturing virtually none of its components in-house. Instead, Aprilia relies on a network of suppliers for parts that are assembled at Noale. Also unusually, over a quarter of Aprilia's workforce of 500 is employed in racing or research and development. Racing has always been vital to Aprilia, providing important technical feedback as well as publicity.

Aprilia's roadbike production has traditionally been based on two-stroke sports and trail bikes of 125cc capacity, with names like Futura, Extrema and Pegaso. That went a step further in 1995 with the arrival of the RS250. At the same time Beggio was also planning an attack on the World Superbike Championship, and revealed a large-capacity four-stroke V-twin engine designed to power a range of sportsbikes and cruisers.

OTHER MAKES

■ **AJW**
British firm AJW built numerous parallel twins and singles dating back to the 1920s, and carried on after the Second World War with its best-known model, the 500cc, JAP-engined Grey Fox.

■ RIGHT *Aprilia's 1995-model Moto 6.5 roadster was created by brilliant French designer Philippe Starck.*

■ OPPOSITE *The RS250's colours matched those of the 400cc V-twin raced in 500cc Grands Prix by Loris Reggiani.*

■ ABOVE *In the 1930s AJW built 500cc singles, such as this one, using engines from Stevens and JAP.*

■ **AMAZONAS**
Notable for its size but not for its performance, the Brazilian-made Amazonas of the mid-1980s was powered by the flat-four VW car engine. Its astonishing vital statistics were an engine capacity of 1584cc, producing just 56bhp that needed to propel a massive 385kg (848lb).

■ LEFT *Ariel's 650cc Huntmaster parallel twin, introduced in 1954, was popular for both solo and sidecar use.*

🏍 ARIEL

■ ARIEL RED HUNTER

One of the oldest manufacturers of all, Ariel was known for its bicycles before they started to build motorcycles around the turn of the century. By the early 1930s, the firm from Selly Oak in the Midlands was one of Britain's most influential, and at that time employed Edward Turner, Val Page and Bert Hopwood – who would eventually

■ BELOW *A 1954 redesign failed to make the 500cc KH twin a success.*

ARIEL VH500 RED HUNTER (1937)	
Engine	Aircooled 2-valve OHV pushrod single
Capacity	497cc (81.8 x 85mm)
Power	26bhp @ 5600rpm
Weight	170kg (375lb)
Top speed	82mph (131kph)

become known as three of the British bike industry's greatest designers.

Ariel hit financial problems during the 1930s and the factory was closed for a time until Jack Sangster, son of founder Charles, bought the firm and restarted production of Page-designed single-cylinder four-strokes including the Red Hunter. These were handsome machines, built in 350 and 500cc sizes, that were produced from 1932 to the late 1950s, and were even successful in sidecar trials into the 1970s. Sammy Miller's successful GOV132 trials bike was based on a 1955 Red Hunter 500.

A late 1930s Red Hunter 500 was among the best bikes of its day, capable of well over 75mph (120kph) and reliable with it. Handling provided by

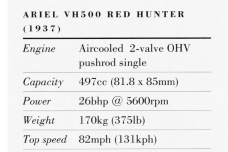

the combination of girder forks and rigid rear end was respectable too; rear suspension was not to be introduced until 1939. The Hunter was refined throughout the 1930s, gained telescopic forks when production recommenced after the Second World War and was kept going with an alloy cylinder head and new frame in the early 1950s.

After the firm's sale to BSA in 1944, Ariel built two main types of twin, firstly the softly-tuned 500cc KH, which was introduced in 1949 but sold poorly. More powerful and successful was the Huntmaster, which was powered by a slightly modified version of the 650cc twin-cylinder engine from BSA's A10. There was more to the Huntmaster than mere badge engineering, since most parts, including the frame, were its own.

The result was a pleasant bike, good for 100mph (160kph) that was particularly popular with sidecar enthusiasts in the late 1950s.

If Ariel's most famous bike is undoubtedly the Square Four, then the bravest must be the Leader, the innovative, fully enclosed 250cc two-stroke released in 1959. With an 18bhp, twin-cylinder engine based on that of the German Adler, a pressed steel frame, effective weather protection and optional panniers, the Leader was intended to be a proper motorcycle with the convenience of a scooter.

The Leader actually worked rather well, with a top speed of about 70mph (112kph) and excellent handling. But the public didn't take to it, partly because the new Mini car offered cheap

four-wheeled travel, and the bike had temperamental starting and poor brakes and finish. Ariel later stripped off the bodywork to produce the Arrow, tuning the engine to 20bhp to produce Super Sports and Golden Arrow versions. But although the Arrow sold quite well it wasn't enough to save Ariel, and the firm eventually ceased trading in 1967.

■ RIGHT *Leader was a sales flop.*

ARIEL

■ ARIEL SQUARE FOUR

One of the most famous roadsters of all, Ariel's Square Four was also one of the longest lived, remaining in production in various forms from 1931 to 1958. The Square Four, whose powerplant was effectively a pair of geared-together parallel twins, was designed by Edward Turner shortly after the future Triumph boss had joined Ariel in 1928. The Four's capacity of 500cc was soon afterwards increased to 600cc and then 997cc. In all three forms the "Squariel" was superbly smooth, but suffered from overheating problems with its rear cylinders. Although the biggest model was capable of more than 100mph (160kph), its performance was severely handicapped by its excessive weight.

After the Second World War the Square Four was comprehensively updated, first with a lighter aluminium engine and then, in 1954, with a new cylinder head and striking four-pipe exhaust system. By this time the Ariel had also gained telescopic front forks and plunger rear suspension. Despite this, the heavy Four was a soggy handler. Even in its final, more sophisticated guise the engine was prone to overheat. But the Square Four's smoothness, relaxed high-speed cruising ability, comfort and looks made the bike much loved by those who could afford one.

ARIEL SQUARE FOUR (1958)	
Engine	Aircooled 8-valve OHV pushrod square four
Capacity	997cc (65 x 75mm)
Power	45bhp @ 5500rpm
Weight	211kg (465lb)
Top speed	105mph (168kph)

■ BELOW *The looks of the later Square Fours, such as this 1958 model, were enhanced by a four-pipe exhaust system.*

■ BELOW *Square Fours such as this model from 1937 were supremely smooth and good for almost 100mph (160kph).*

■ RIGHT AND BELOW RIGHT *The 997cc Square Four from 1937 – with instruments set into fuel tank – produced 36bhp.*

OTHER MAKES

■ ARMSTRONG

The motorcycle arm of British car components giant Armstrong produced motocross, trials, road racing and military bikes in the 1980s, after taking over Barton Engineering and CCM. Most were powered by engines from Rotax of Austria. Armstrong's CF250 road-racer, introduced in 1983, featured a tandem-twin Rotax engine in an innovative twin-spar carbon fibre frame. Niall Mackenzie and Donnie McLeod dominated British racing, and scored some impressive results in Grands Prix. Armstrong also built a very successful single-cylinder, four-stroke military bike, rights to which were later sold to Harley-Davidson.

■ ATK

Utah-based ATK made its reputation building motocross bikes with both two-stroke and four-stroke engines, most of which were sold in the States. Following a

■ ABOVE *Future 500cc Grand Prix star Niall Mackenzie rose to prominence on Armstrong's rapid 250cc twin.*

change of ownership, the firm introduced a pair of purposeful street legal Dirt Sports machines in 1994.

■ BAKKER

Many superb specials and racebikes have emerged from Nico

Bakker's workshop in northern Holland, most with innovative chassis, and with engines ranging from Yamaha's TZ350 to BMW and Harley-Davidson four-strokes. His radical QCS (Quick Change System) sportsbike, most recently powered by Yamaha's FZR1000 engine, used an advanced non-telescopic front suspension system. Bakker has also done much chassis development work for manufacturers including BMW and Laverda.

■ BELOW *Bakker's Bomber used BMW's R1100 flat-twin engine.*

BENELLI

■ BENELLI 750 SEI

With its smart styling, Italian racing-red paintwork and the unique attraction of its six-cylinder engine – emphasized by an array of gleaming chromed exhaust pipes – the Benelli 750 Sei looked set to be a world beater when it was launched

■ LEFT *The Sei was supremely smooth and comfortable, but its straight-line performance was unexceptional.*

■ BELOW AND BOTTOM *The Sei's big aircooled engine and its six exhaust pipes dominate from every angle.*

BENELLI 750 SEI (1975)	
Engine	Aircooled 12-valve SOHC transverse six
Capacity	748cc (56 x 50.6mm)
Power	71bhp @ 8900rpm
Weight	220kg (485lb) dry
Top speed	118mph (189kph)

in 1975. Instead the Sei turned out to be softly tuned and no faster than Honda's CB750-four of six years earlier. Its modest performance led to the Benelli being overshadowed by more powerful superbikes, particularly its Italian rivals

from Ducati, Guzzi and Laverda.

Not that the Sei was a bad bike, indeed in most respects it was a very good one. The engine, although criticized for closely resembling one-and-a-half Honda CB500 units, was commendably narrow for a six. The

■ RIGHT
*Benelli's 250cc
four was raced
successfully by
Renzo Pasolini and
Kel Carruthers in
the 1960s.*

three dual-manifold Dell'Orto
carburettors allowed room for the rider's
knees, always a potential problem with a
six, and the engine made plenty of
smooth midrange power. But the
maximum output of 71bhp gave a top
speed of just 120mph (193kph), and
even the Sei's excellent handling,
roadholding and braking could not make
up for that in the eyes of riders looking
for an expensive Italian superbike.

The Sei's lack of blood and thunder
was surprising given Benelli's racing
pedigree. The firm was founded by six

Benelli brothers from Pesaro, and
produced its first bike in 1921. Tonino,
the youngest brother, was the first racer
to put Benelli on the map, notably on a
175cc four-stroke prepared by big
brother Giovanni in 1937. Tonino retired
shortly afterwards but Benelli's bikes
continued to win, culminating in Dario
Ambrosini's victory in the 250cc world
championship in 1950.

Ambrosini's death a year later shook
Benelli but the firm eventually returned
to racing and in 1960 built a four-
cylinder 250cc machine. Italian stars

Tarquinio Provini and Renzo Pasolini
won many races on it through the 1960s
but it was Australian Kel Carruthers who
did best of all, winning the 250cc world
championship in 1969.

Sadly, track success was not
matched in the showrooms and shortly
afterwards the Benelli family sold out to
Argentinian car baron Alejandro de
Tomaso. He aimed to relaunch Benelli
with the 750 Sei, but neither that nor the
slightly more powerful 900cc version
that followed it could recapture the
Pesaro firm's former glory.

OTHER MAKES

■ BARIGO

Founded by Patrick Barigault at La Roch-
elle on the west coast of France, Barigo is
a small firm with a background in the
peculiarly French supermoto, a combination of road racing and motocross. In 1992
Barigo produced the Supermotard roadster
– basically a street legal version of the
firm's competition machine – with a 600cc
Rotax single-cylinder engine, aluminium
twin-beam frame, long-travel suspension
and supermoto styling. Two years later
came the Onixa, which combined a similar
motor and frame with sportsbike parts and
striking, fully-faired bodywork.

■ LEFT
*Barigo's 600cc
Onixa sportster
looked peculiar
but was very
light and
handled well.*

BIMOTA

■ BIMOTA SB6

Seventeen years and a gulf in technology separated Bimota's 1994 model SB6 from its predecessor the SB2, yet the two bikes had much more in common than the fact that each was powered by a four-cylinder Suzuki motor. The GSX-R1100-engined SB6 featured a curvaceous full fairing, state-of-the-art frame design, a self-supporting seat unit, top-quality cycle parts — and was arguably the world's most desirable sportsbike. Exactly the same had been true of the GS750-powered SB2 back in 1977.

The gap between the two bikes' release ensured that their performance was very different. The SB6's 1074cc watercooled, 16-valve engine, tuned

BIMOTA SB6 (1994)	
Engine	Watercooled 16-valve DOHC transverse four
Capacity	1074cc (75.5 x 60mm)
Power	156bhp @ 10,000rpm
Weight	190kg (418lb)
Top speed	175mph (280kph)

with an exhaust system that curved up to twin silencers in the tailpiece, produced a claimed 156bhp and rocketed the Bimota to over 170mph (273kph). The impeccably rigid aluminium twin-spar Straight Connection Technology frame, massive 46mm (1.8in) diameter forks,

OTHER MAKES

■ BETA

Italian firm Beta built a rapid 175cc roadster in the late 1950s, but in recent years has concentrated on the off-road market, particularly trials bikes.

■ BFG

Powered by the 70bhp, 1300cc flat-four engine normally found in a Citroën GS car, the French-built BFG was intended

as a grand tourer. Strange styling and excess weight meant that sales were limited mainly to the French police, and BFG went bust in the mid-1980s.

■ BIANCHI

Best known for some impressive Grand Prix performances in the early 1960s, Bianchi built bicycles before becoming one of the first Italian motorcycle manufacturers in 1897. Bianchi won many races in the 1920s, built a spectacular supercharged four-cylinder 500cc racer in 1938, and sold motocross bikes as well as small-capacity roadsters before motorcycle production ended in 1967.

■ LEFT *In the early 1960s Bianchi produced both racing bikes, and roadsters such as this 300cc MT61.*

■ ABOVE *A strong aluminium frame, plus top-class suspension and tyres, gave the SB6 razor-sharp handling.*

sophisticated Öhlins shock, fat Michelin radial tyres and big Brembo brake discs gave superb cornering and stopping power. The SB2 came from a much earlier era of bike design, yet was considered even more exotic in its day.

Bimota was formed in Rimini, Italy in 1973 by Messrs Bianchi, Morri and Tamburini – the name of the company being derived from the first two letters of each name. The SB2 was the firm's first

purpose-built roadster, and held its 75bhp aircooled GS750 motor in a tubular steel frame. Suspension, brakes and tyres were the best available, and the seat-tank unit's fibreglass was lined with aluminium, meaning no rear subframe was needed. The Bimota's 130mph (209kph) top speed and heavy handling could not compare with the performance of its SB6 successor, but in 1977 the SB2 was the ultimate roadster.

■ RIGHT *With its sculpted bodywork and state-of-the-art chassis, Bimota's SB2 was a sensation in 1977.*

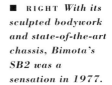

■ LEFT *The stylish and rapid SB6, powered by Suzuki's GSX-R1100 engine, was a great success for Bimota.*

BIMOTA

■ BIMOTA TESI 1D

When Bimota launched the Tesi in 1991, the radical sportster with its distinctive hub-centre front suspension arrangement was intended to lead the motorcycling world into a new era.

BIMOTA TESI 1D (1991)	
Engine	Watercooled 8-valve DOHC desmodromic 90-degree V-twin
Capacity	904cc (92 x 68mm)
Power	113bhp @ 8500rpm
Weight	188kg (414lb)
Top speed	153mph (245kph)

Named after the Italian word for thesis, the Tesi was the product of ten years' development by Bimota's chief engineer Pierluigi Marconi, who had begun his quest for an alternative to the traditional front forks while studying for his degree. The Tesi replaced conventional forks

with a twin-sided front swing-arm, working a single suspension unit. Handlebars were linked by a series of rods to the front wheel, which pivoted on a bearing inside its hub in order to steer the bike. Powered by the watercooled, V-twin engine from Ducati's 851 sportster, tuned

■ OPPOSITE
*With its forkless
front suspension
system correctly set
up, the Tesi was
very stable when
cornering.*

■ LEFT *Virginio
Ferrari's 1987
Formula One world
title was arguably
Bimota's greatest
racing success.*

■ ABOVE *This 1984 endurance racing
prototype was powered by a Honda VF750
V4 engine.*

■ ABOVE
*Engineer Federico
Martini's stylish,
Ducati-engined
DB1 gave Bimota
a vital sales boost
in 1986.*

■ OPPOSITE
*Beneath the Tesi's
bodywork, its
Ducati V-twin
engine was held by
u-shaped alloy
frame plates.*

■ RIGHT
*Bimota's desire to
broaden its market
led to the creation
of the distinctive
Mantra roadster
of 1995.*

by Bimota with a long-stroke crankshaft
that increased peak output to 113bhp,
the Tesi was fast and responsive.

But although the forkless front end
gave an advantage when braking into a
corner, the Tesi suffered some sus-
pension-related teething problems that
detracted from the theoretical handling
advantages to be gained by separating
steering and suspension actions. The
Tesi's price, inevitably, was high even by
Bimota's standards, and sales were poor.
Even the sleeker, limited-production
Tesi ES of 1993 could not convince the
motorcycling public that this was the
face of the future.

Bimota made its name in racing
by building the frames that were used by
Johnny Cecotto (Yamaha) and Walter
Villa (Harley) to win five 250 and 350cc
world championships. Jon Ekerold won
the 350cc title in 1980, again with a
combination of Bimota frame and
Yamaha TZ engine.

The factory's most important success
was Virginio Ferrari's 1987 World
Formula One championship win, on a
Yamaha FZ750-engined YB4. From that
bike Bimota developed a road-going
YB4 and a string of successful
FZR1000-powered models including the
YB8, Tuatara and Furano.

BMW

■ BMW R60/2

In recent years BMW has produced bikes with one, three and four cylinders, but the German firm's name is synonymous with flat-twins. The very first BMW motorcycle, the R32 of 1923, was powered by a boxer engine that produced 8bhp at 3300rpm and used shaft final drive. The R32 was rather expensive – but it was cleverly designed, nicely finished and sold well. Some things really don't change.

Among the most popular BMW twins during the 1950s and 1960s were the 600cc R60 and its successor the R60/2, which was launched in 1960. These models, and also the slightly slower 500cc R50 and R50/2 bikes of the same period, were hugely successful due to their relaxed, fuss-free nature, reliability and general ease of use. The R60/2 used a slightly tuned version of the 28bhp

BMW R60/2 (1960)	
Engine	Aircooled 4-valve pushrod flat-twin
Capacity	494cc (68 x 68mm)
Power	26bhp @ 5800rpm
Weight	195kg (430lb)
Top speed	87mph (139kph)

aircooled boxer motor from the R60, which gave superbly smooth running and a top speed of about 90mph (145kph). Although BMW had been among the first firms to use telescopic forks in the 1930s, the R60/2 was fitted with leading-link Earles forks which were particularly well suited to sidecar work. Heavy steering and soft suspension at both ends made the 60/2 ill-suited to sporty solo riding, but the

BMW had few equals for comfortable long-distance touring.

BMW has had little involvement in top level competition in recent years, but has a long and impressive history of racing and record-breaking. One of the most famous early stars was Ernst Henne, who set a number of speed records on streamlined, supercharged boxers in the 1930s. Schorsch Meier became the first foreign rider to win an Isle of Man TT when he took the 1939 Senior race on a supercharged 500cc flat-twin. Works BMW pilot Walter Zeller won many international races for BMW in the 1950s, finishing second in the 500cc world championship in 1956. And BMW flat-twins dominated sidecar racing for two decades, winning 19 out of 21 world championships between 1954 and 1974 with drivers including Max Deubel and Klaus Enders.

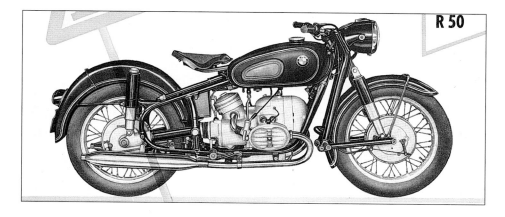

R 50

■ LEFT *The 494cc R50/2, seen here in 1955 with a single saddle, shared many parts with the 60/2.*

■ BELOW LEFT *Schorsch Meier's 1939 TT-winning supercharged twin had a top speed of over 125mph (201kph).*

■ BELOW *Fritz Scheidegger's world titles in 1965 and 1966 continued a long run of BMW sidecar success.*

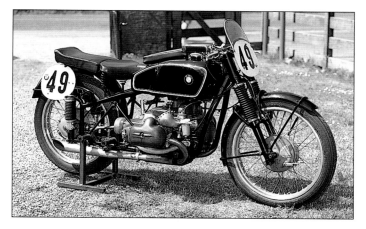

■ RIGHT
This 500cc, 12bhp R52 flat-twin dates from 1928, the first year BMW fitted lights as standard.

■ OPPOSITE
With its Earles forks, smooth 30bhp engine and all-round comfort, the R60/2 made a fine tourer.

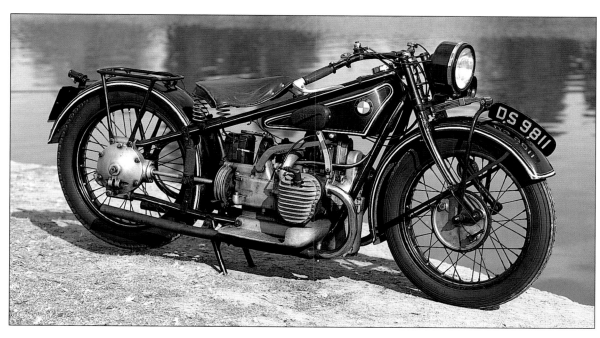

BMW

■ BMW R90S

BMW's traditional flat-twins were gradually refined over the years and reached new heights of performance and desirability with the R90S of 1974. The basis of the R90S was the familiar 898cc boxer lump from the R90/6, tuned slightly to give 67bhp at 7000rpm. To the normal specification the R90S added a neat bikini fairing, stylish smoked paintwork, twin front disc brakes and even the luxury of a clock in the dashboard.

The R90S couldn't match the sheer

■ **BELOW**
With its fairing and smoked orange paintwork the R90S had the looks to match its superb performance.

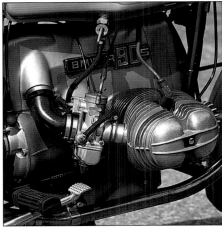

■ ABOVE *Increased compression ratio and 38mm Dell'Orto carburettors gave the R90S an output of 67bhp.*

■ OPPOSITE *The stylish and versatile F650 accounted for over 25 per cent of BMW's production in 1994.*

BMW R90S (1974)	
Engine	Aircooled 4-valve OHV pushrod flat-twin
Capacity	898cc (90 x 70.6mm)
Power	67bhp @ 7000rpm
Weight	215kg (474lb)
Top speed	125mph (201kph)

power of mid-1970s Japanese superbikes such as Kawasaki's four-cylinder Z1, or the handling finesse of Italian sportsters from Ducati and Moto Guzzi. But the German bike accelerated smoothly to a top speed of 125mph (201kph), handled very respectably, and was superbly comfortable, well-finished and reliable. In 1974 the R90S was more than twice as expensive as Honda's CB750 in most markets – but in many riders' opinion, BMW's majestic sports-tourer was simply the best production motorcycle in the world.

In the early 1980s the future looked bleak for the flat-twins, as BMW released its new range of watercooled K-series fours and triples. But demand for the traditional twins remained strong, several models were reprieved and updated, and BMW's management thought again. In 1993, came the new-generation boxer, the R1100RS, powered by a 1085cc fuel-injected, air/oilcooled, four-valves-per-cylinder, high-cam motor producing 90bhp.

The R1100RS's chassis was noteworthy, too, because it incorporated Telelever front suspension. Instead of telescopic forks, the system consisted of hollow fork legs, a horizontal arm pivoting on the engine, and a single suspension unit. Telelever worked well, giving good handling and a smooth ride, and the rest of the RS was equally impressive. With plenty of mid-range power, a 135mph (217kph) top speed, a protective fairing, generous fuel range and powerful, anti-lock brakes, the

R1100RS was a sports-tourer in the finest BMW boxer tradition.

BMW's tradition of building single-cylinder bikes dates back to the 250cc R39 of 1925, and singles were produced – effectively by mounting one cylinder of a twin vertically – until R27 production was halted in 1967. The F650 single, introduced in 1994, was an altogether different machine. The first chain-driven model in BMW's 70-year

history, the F650 also defied convention by being assembled in Italy, by Aprilia, and by using a watercooled, 652cc engine built by Rotax of Austria. The chassis was derived from that of Aprilia's Pegaso trail bike, and gave taut handling well suited to the BMW's 100mph (160kph) performance. The F650 worked well as a versatile and relatively inexpensive roadster, and its sales success surprised even BMW.

B M W

■ BMW K1

With its brightly-coloured, all-enveloping bodywork, the K1 was a startling bike by any manufacturer's standards when it was launched in 1989, let alone by the standards of traditionally conservative BMW. In conjunction with the huge front mudguard, the K1's fairing and large rear section combined to give a wind-cheating shape unmatched even by Japanese sportsbikes.

Behind the plastic was a tuned, 16-valve version of the watercooled,

BMW K1 (1989)	
Engine	Watercooled 16-valve DOHC longitudinal four
Capacity	987cc (67 x 70mm)
Power	100bhp @ 8000rpm
Weight	234kg (468lb) wet
Top speed	145mph (233kph)

987cc four-cylinder engine that had been introduced five years earlier in the K100. The K-series four aligned its

cylinders horizontally, in contrast to the transverse layout favoured by the Japanese. In K1 form the fuel-injected four produced 100bhp, sufficient to send the aerodynamically efficient BMW to a top speed of over 140mph (225kph). A strong steel frame, based on that of the K100, firm suspension (with the Paralever system to combat the effect of the drive-shaft) and powerful triple-disc braking gave good handling and stopping power. The K1 was too big and heavy to be a true sportsbike, but it did much to boost BMW's image.

■ BELOW *With its aggressive styling, the K1 was a radical departure for traditionally conservative BMW.*

■ **LEFT**
BMW's K-series engine held its cylinders horizontally, and in K1 form had 16 valves.

■ **BELOW**
The K1 was far less sporty than its looks suggested, but its handling was still exceptionally good.

OTHER MAKES

■ **BÖHMERLAND**

Notable for its vast length and for being designed to carry three people, the Böhmerland was produced in Czechoslovakia between 1923 and 1939. Designed and built by Albin Liebisch, the Böhmerland was powered by a 600cc, 16bhp single-cylinder engine. As well as the long wheelbase "Langtouren", with its rear pannier fuel tanks, there was a shorter Jubilee model, and a sportier bike called the Racer.

■ **BOSS HOSS**

Originally named Boss Hog until Harley-Davidson objected, and powered by America's ubiquitous Chevrolet V-eight engine – typically with a capacity approaching six litres and output of 300bhp – the Boss Hoss was arguably the biggest, heaviest and most powerful bike, but not the most sensible, in series production. Final drive was by chain and there was only one gear: fast forward. Claimed top speed was over 150mph (241kph) but the Hoss's handling, with 450kg (992lb) of weight and a square-section rear tyre, made for just as much excitement. Over 150 of these huge beasts had been produced by Tennessee-based Boss Hoss firm by the early 1990s.

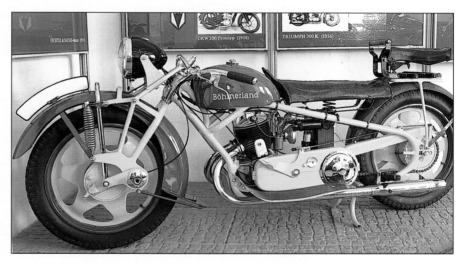

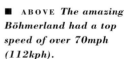

■ **ABOVE** *The amazing Böhmerland had a top speed of over 70mph (112kph).*

■ **ABOVE AND RIGHT**
Its awesome Chevy V-eight powerplant made the Boss Hoss very fast – in a straight line!

BRITTEN

■ BRITTEN V-1000

Impressive displays in international twin-cylinder races in recent seasons confirmed the Britten V-twin's status as one of the world's most exotic and brilliantly engineered motorbikes. Designed and almost totally hand-built by New Zealander John Britten and his small team, the Britten was powered by a watercooled, fuel-injected 60-degree V-twin motor. After the original V-1000 had made its mark at Daytona in 1991, its engine was enlarged to 1108cc, producing a phenomenal 171bhp. To allow the bike to compete in Superbike racing, Britten then developed a new V-1000 with a 985cc, short-stroke engine.

The rigid power unit acted as the V-1000's frame, supporting girder forks and the huge rear swing-arm, both of which were formed from lightweight Kevlar and carbon fibre. Front and rear

suspension systems were multi-adjustable and used Öhlins shocks. The rear unit was situated in front of the engine for optimum cooling. The Britten

BRITTEN V-1000 (1995)	
Engine	Watercooled dohc 8-valve 60-degree V-twin
Capacity	985cc (99 x 64mm)
Power	155bhp @ 12,400rpm
Weight	145kg (320lb) wet
Top speed	185mph (296kph)

featured an advanced, computerized engine-management system that recorded and could adjust the engine's performance as it ran. To top it all, the V-1000 was beautifully styled; its narrow width and sensuous curves contributed to recorded speeds of more than 180mph (289kph) at Daytona.

As well as the bikes raced successfully by Britten's own riders including Paul Lewis and Andrew

Stroud, small numbers of production racebikes were sold for sizeable sums of money. The V-1000's elaborate construction made the prospect of a road-going version appear remote.

In 1995, when the racebike was again successful at Daytona, John Britten's collaboration with the Indian marque's new Australian owner, Maurits Hayim-Langridge, looked likely to result in elements of the V-1000 being incorporated in Indian streetbikes due for release within a few years. When Britten tragically died of cancer only six months later, at the age of 45, the motorcycle world lost one of its greatest engineering talents.

■ ABOVE *Its engine-management system allowed the Britten, ridden here by Jim Moodie, to be fine-tuned to suit the conditions.*

■ OPPOSITE *The sculpted V-1000 was one of the most beautiful bikes ever built, as well as one of the fastest.*

OTHER MAKES

■ BRIDGESTONE
Motorcycle production was never any more than a sideline for the Bridgestone rubber company, which remains a major tyre manufacturer to this day. But in the 1950s and 1960s Bridgestone built a range of bikes, from mopeds to twin-cylinder two-stroke sportsters, the best of which was the 350GTR. Powered by a disc-valve, parallel-twin engine that produced a claimed 40bhp, the GTR was a quick and stylish motorcycle that was capable of over 90mph (145kph).

The six-speed Bridgestone was a sophisticated machine when it was launched on the American market in 1966. Its rubber-mounted motor was reasonably smooth, and its blend of steel twin-downtube frame, gaitered forks and twin shocks gave good handling with a plush ride. But the high price limited export sales and at the end of that year Bridgestone, who had declined to take on important tyre customers Honda, Kawasaki, Suzuki and Yamaha by selling bikes on the home market, quit motorcycle manufacture altogether.

■ LEFT AND INSET *The disc-valve 350GTR was fast and refined, but Bridgestone abandoned it to concentrate on tyre production.*

BROUGH SUPERIOR

■ BELOW AND BOTTOM *The final, 1939-model Superior SS100 was arguably the world's finest motorcycle.*

■ BROUGH SUPERIOR SS100

George Brough combined his own frames with bought-in engines and other parts to produce bikes which were innovative, exclusive, expensive and, above all, fast. Never one to sell his products short, he named his first machine the Superior to the displeasure of his motorcycle engineer father, William Brough, who built flat-twins and who commented that he supposed his was now to be known as the Inferior.

But superior George's bikes were — as they proved with a string of race wins and speed records in the 1920s and 1930s — ridden by Brough himself and other legendary figures such as Eric Fernihough, Freddie Dixon and Bert Le Vack. The machines built by the small

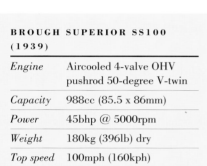

**BROUGH SUPERIOR SS100
(1939)**

Engine	Aircooled 4-valve OHV pushrod 50-degree V-twin
Capacity	988cc (85.5 x 86mm)
Power	45bhp @ 5000rpm
Weight	180kg (396lb) dry
Top speed	100mph (160kph)

■ LEFT *By 1939,
the SS100 was
powered by a 50-
degree Matchless
V-twin engine,
fitted with a four
speed gearbox.*

■ BELOW *Earlier SS100s, such as this
1926 example, used powerplants from JAP
of Tottenham, north London.*

■ BOTTOM *Had not the Second World
War intervened, Brough's flat-four Dream
might have proved an outstanding machine.*

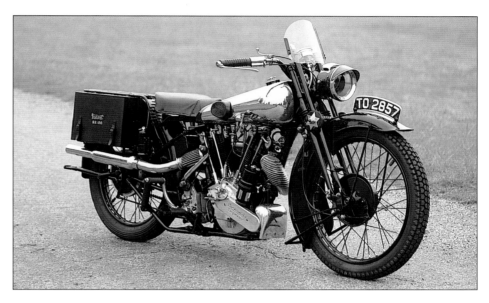

team from Nottingham were regarded by
many as the best in the world. When *The
Motor Cycle* summed up a test by saying
a Superior was the Rolls Royce of motorcycles, Brough seized on the line for his
advertising — and Rolls didn't object.

The SS100, produced between 1925
and 1940, was Brough's most famous
model. It was powered initially by a
980cc V-twin from JA Prestwich (JAP),
the big engine-making firm from north
London, and came with a signed guaran-
tee from Brough that the bike had been
timed at over 100mph (160kph) for a
quarter of a mile (0.4 kilometres).
Brochures also boasted of the hands-off
stability at speeds of 95mph (152kph).

Fewer than 400 SS100s were built,
most using the JAP engine but the last
100 or so models powered by a
Matchless V-twin. The bike's
specification was constantly changed,
with the result that no two SS100s were
identical. Optional rear suspension was

introduced in 1928, foot gearchange in
1935 and a four-speed Norton gearbox a
year later. Brough's numerous
innovations included flyscreens, twin
headlamps, crashbars and panniers.

TE Shaw, alias Lawrence of Arabia,
owned a series of Superiors (the last of
which cost him his life in a crash), each
of which he fitted with a special
stainless steel petrol tank.

The Brough Superior that might have
topped even the SS100 was the Dream, an
exotic 990cc flat-four roadster that George
Brough revealed in late 1938. Its engine
featured twin crankshafts, linked by
gears, and a firing arrangement that made
it supremely smooth. Development of the
promising Dream was halted when the
Second World War broke out, and Brough
Superior production was never restarted.

BSA

■ BSA GOLD STAR DBD34

For most of its life the Birmingham Small Arms Company was Britain's biggest motorcycle manufacturer, and in the years after the Second World War it was the largest in the world, producing over 75,000 bikes in some years during the 1950s. At that time BSA was an industrial giant, involved in producing guns, taxi-cabs and metal plate, and had also taken over Ariel and Sunbeam.

The firm's origins in armaments manufacture stretched back to 1863. Bicycle production followed in the 1880s and the Small Heath factory built its first motorcycle, powered by a Minerva engine, in 1905. BSA's reputation grew, notably with a series of reliable and successful V-twins in the 1920s.

BSA's best-loved early model was the S27, universally known as the Sloper

■ BELOW AND
BOTTOM *Lean,
functional and
stylish, the DBD34
did the most to
make the Gold Star
badge famous.*

BSA GOLD STAR DBD34 (1956)	
Engine	Aircooled 2-valve OHV pushrod single
Capacity	499cc (85 x 88mm)
Power	42bhp @ 7000rpm
Weight	159kg (350lb)
Top speed	110mph (177kph)

■ BELOW *This 1930s Champion spark plug advertisement featured the Sloper in an unflattering manner.*

■ LEFT
Over 125,000 of BSA's 500cc M20 singles were supplied to allied forces during the Second World War.

■ BELOW LEFT
This off-road Gold Star competed successfully in the International Six Days Trial in 1954.

■ BOTTOM
Slopers such as this model from the early 1930s were refined, quiet and good for 65mph (104kph).

due to its angled-forward single cylinder. Introduced with a 500cc engine in 1927, and later available in 350 to 595cc versions, the Sloper was stylish, sophisticated and notably quiet. It quickly became popular and was frequently updated through its ten years in production.

The Second World War was a particularly busy time for the BSA factory which, despite suffering heavy bomb damage that claimed 53 workers' lives, produced huge numbers of both guns and bikes.

The most famous BSA was the legendary Gold Star single, which was hugely successful as a roadster and as a competition bike in road racing, motocross and trials in the 1950s. The "Goldie" had its origins in 1937, when racer Walter Handley earned a Brooklands Gold Star award for lapping the banked track at over 100mph (160kph) on BSA's 500cc Empire Star. The next year's model was named Gold Star in recognition, and after a break for

the War it was relaunched, initially as a 350. Several tuning options were available, with power outputs ranging from 18bhp for the trials version, to over 30bhp for the track racer. Each bike was supplied with a factory certificate testifying to the machine's power.

Numerous revisions kept the Gold Star in top position throughout the 1950s. The archetypal model was the 500cc

DBD34 introduced in 1956, with its clip-on handlebars, polished tank and finned engine. An open-mouthed Amal carburettor and swept-back exhaust combined to give 110mph (177kph) top speed. The Gold Star dominated the Isle of Man Clubmans TT in that year and was successful in many unofficial burn-ups, remaining prized as a café racer after production ended in 1963.

BSA

■ BSA 650cc A10

BSA built two main versions of the trademark British parallel twin: the 500cc A7, which was introduced in 1946 and updated five years later, and the 650cc A10 that appeared in 1950. Both the A7 and A10 were sold in many forms in the 1950s, earning a reputation more for oil-tightness, economy and reliability than for looks or performance. In 1962 they were replaced by the 500cc A50 and the 650cc A65, which featured updates including a unit-construction engine and gearbox.

The original A10 was the Golden Flash, whose flexible, 35bhp single-camshaft engine gave a top speed approaching 100mph (160kph). In 1954 the Flash was updated with swing-arm rear suspension, instead of the old plunger design. Other A10s including

■ **BELOW** *The 646cc A10 of the mid-1950s was a handsome machine, and a big-selling success for BSA.*

BSA 650cc A10 GOLDEN FLASH (1958)	
Engine	Aircooled 4-valve OHV pushrod parallel twin
Capacity	646cc (70 x 84mm)
Power	34bhp @ 5750rpm
Weight	195kg (430lb)
Top speed	96mph (154kph)

the Super Flash and Road Rocket provided a little more power and speed, and in 1958 BSA produced the A10S Super Rocket, with a 43bhp engine and top speed of 105mph (168kph).

The best and rarest of the bunch was the Rocket Gold Star introduced in 1962. This consisted of a slightly tuned Super Rocket engine in a frame based on that of the Gold Star single. Forks, brakes and wheels also came from the

■ OPPOSITE PAGE, TOP *This A65L Lightning twin provided good performance by mid-1960s' standards.*

■ LEFT *John Cooper rode BSA's 750cc triple to some famous victories.*

■ ABOVE *BSA's smaller twin was the 500cc A7, like this 1956-model Shooting Star.*

Gold Star, and the twin featured a close-ratio gearbox, rearset footrests and a siamesed exhaust system. The result was the fastest and best handling A10. In recent years the Rocket Gold Star's higher value has led to fakes being built by fitting the more common Super Rocket with special parts.

BSA's last great roadster was the 750cc Rocket Three triple, which appeared at the same time as the Triumph Trident in 1969. The two models shared a 58bhp engine that owed more to Triumph than BSA, although the Rocket Three unit was angled at 15 degrees in a different twin-downtube frame. Like the Trident, the Rocket Three was a fast, competent bike, but by 1971 BSA was in financial trouble, recording a massive loss. The once mighty firm was swallowed up by the new Norton Villiers Triumph company, and the last batch of triples – wearing the well-known Triumph badges – left BSA's famous Small Heath factory in 1973.

■ BELOW *The ultimate BSA parallel twin is a genuine Rocket Gold Star such as this immaculate 1963 model.*

BUELL

■ BUELL RS1200

Harley-Davidson's reluctance to build a sportsbike in recent years has led many smaller firms and individuals to produce machines powered by the American firm's V-twin engine. Among those is Erik Buell, a former road-racer and Harley engineer, who designed and built an innovative, fully-faired bike called the RR1000, which was successful in twin-cylinder racing in the 1980s. The RR was followed in 1989 by the RS1200, a roadster whose half-fairing had the advantage of leaving the all important 1200cc Sportster V-twin unit in view.

The key to the Buell was its tubular steel frame, which held the engine via an ingenious rubber-mounting system.

BUELL RS1200 (1989)	
Engine	Aircooled 4-valve OHV pushrod 45-degree V-twin
Capacity	1200cc (88.8 x 96.8mm)
Power	70bhp @ 5000rpm
Weight	205kg (450lb) dry
Top speed	122mph (196kph)

Italian Marzocchi forks were matched with a rear shock set horizontally beneath the engine. The RS1200 roared to over 120mph (193kph) and handled well, but its high price kept sales low. Erik Buell's big break came in 1993, when Harley-Davidson – looking for a

■ RIGHT *The RS1200 was one Harley-engined bike that encouraged hard riding on twisty roads.*

■ BELOW *Buell's S2 Thunderbolt was developed and sold in collaboration with Harley-Davidson itself.*

way to diversify into the sportsbike market without spending a fortune on research and development or alienating its current riders – bought a 49 per cent stake in the firm, which was relaunched as the Buell Motorcycle Company.

In 1994, having moved into a newer and larger factory near Milwaukee, the new Buell firm launched its first bike: the S2 Thunderbolt. This too was powered by Harley's Sportster engine, and used a modified version of the RS frame. Reworked styling, new cycle parts and a free-breathing exhaust system made this the fastest and best Buell yet. Equally importantly, higher production levels allowed a lower price, and Buell now had input from Harley in development, finance and marketing. With plans for increased exports and a range of models including a roadster based on Harley's watercooled VR1000 race engine, the Buell Motorcycle Company looked set for an exciting future.

OTHER MAKES

■ BULTACO

Francisco Bulto founded Bultaco near Barcelona in 1958 after splitting from Montesa, which he had co-founded, due to that firm's reluctance to go racing. The new firm built a series of rapid small-

■ LEFT
Angel Nieto won two 50cc world titles for Bultaco.

■ FAR LEFT
Bultaco's trials stars have included world champion Yjrio Vesterinen.

capacity two-stroke racers through the 1960s, and had many high finishes in Grands Prix. Roadsters included the rapid 250cc Metralla, which had a claimed top speed of more than 100mph (160kph). Bultaco also specialized in off-road bikes. Sammy Miller's win on a Sherpa in the 1965 Scottish Six Days Trial heralded the two-stroke's takeover in trials. After the trials world championship was started in 1975, Bultaco won five years in a row. In road racing, Angel Nieto and Ricardo Tormo won a total of four 50cc world titles in the years up to 1981. But by then a series of strikes had crippled Bultaco, and production ended shortly afterwards.

■ CABTON

One of several Japanese firms that built bikes heavily based on British singles and parallel twins in the 1950s, Cabton failed to survive the more competitive decade of the 1960s.

CAGIVA

■ CAGIVA C593

The last years were the best ones for Cagiva's 500cc Grand Prix challenge, as the Italian team that had dared take on the mighty Japanese factories in racing's toughest class finally won races in 1992 and 1993 – and saw John Kocinski briefly lead the 1994 500cc world championship on the bright red V-four. Then Cagiva quit Grands Prix, amid reports of financial problems for the group that owned Ducati, MV Agusta, Morini and Husqvarna as well as the Cagiva brand name.

Racing has always been the first love of Cagiva's owners, the Castiglioni brothers Claudio and Gianfranco, but the firm has produced some impressive roadsters since it was set up on the site of the former Aermacchi Harley-Davidson factory at Varese in 1978. Cagiva's rapid growth was based on 125cc two-strokes,

■ ABOVE *John Kocinski won the US Grand Prix in 1993, and briefly led the championship in 1994.*

CAGIVA C593 (1993)	
Engine	Watercooled 80-degree V-four crankcase reed-valve two-stroke
Capacity	498cc (56 x 50.6mm)
Power	178bhp @ 12,500rpm
Weight	132kg (290lb)
Top speed	191mph (306kph)

most notable of which has been the race-replica Mito – a fine-handling 100mph (160kph) machine that has been regularly updated to provide cutting-edge style and performance.

Larger capacity Cagivas have included the 900 and 750cc Elefant trail bikes, derivatives of which have been successful in desert racing. The firm's withdrawal from Grands Prix in 1995 allowed more resources to be put into development of an exciting new range of 750 and 900cc four-cylinder machines destined for the street and World Superbike racetracks.

OTHER MAKES

CASAL

When Casal began production of its small-capacity two-strokes in the mid-1960s it relied on Zündapp engines. The Portuguese firm has since developed its own powerplants, and continues to build mainly 50cc bikes for the home market.

CCM

After building big-single motocross bikes based on BSA's B50 in the 1970s, British

specialist CCM was taken over by the Armstrong car components firm. Founder Alan Clews bought the company back in the mid-1980s and produced Rotax-engined motocross and trials bikes.

COTTON

Most of Cotton's production in the 1950s and 1960s consisted of modest roadsters with Villiers two-stroke engines. The firm had some racing history, though, and its "coTTon" badge was inspired by Stanley Woods' Isle of Man win in 1923.

CYCLONE

Famous for its exotic 1000cc, overhead-camshaft V-twins, Cyclone began to

build bikes in 1913 and won many races with them. But the American firm's roadsters were not profitable. Bigger firms, including Harley-Davidson and Indian, introduced eight-valve racers of their own, and Cyclone production lasted only for a few years.

CZ

Czech firm CZ began building bikes in the 1930s, and won several motocross world titles with its single-cylinder two-strokes in the 1960s. After the Second World War CZ was nationalized and produced utility roadsters in collaboration with Jawa, before Cagiva took control of the company in 1992.

■ ABOVE *The 1994 version of Cagiva's 125cc Mito featured a 30bhp two-stroke engine, aluminium beam frame and styling inspired by Ducati's 916.*

■ OPPOSITE *Cagiva's V4 has generally been the most stylish, if not the fastest, of the factory 500s.*

■ RIGHT *Cagiva's Elefant 900 was a sophisticated trail bike powered by a Ducati V-twin engine.*

DOUGLAS

■ **DOUGLAS DRAGONFLY**
The flat-twin engine was Douglas's trademark, and the firm from Bristol concentrated on that layout from 1906 – when the Douglas family began building bikes previously known as Fairys – until its demise in the late 1950s. Early

DOUGLAS DRAGONFLY (1955)	
Engine	Aircooled 4-valve OHV pushrod flat-twin
Capacity	348cc (60.8 x 60mm)
Power	17bhp @ 6000rpm
Weight	166kg (365lb)
Top speed	75mph (120kph)

models had boxer engines in line with the bike, including the banked sidecar outfit that versatile racing star Freddie Dixon used to win the 1923 sidecar TT. Roadsters such as the K32 were among the most sophisticated of the 1930s.

Later boxers such as the 350cc T35 of 1947 mounted the cylinders across the frame in BMW style, but although performance was good Douglas gained a reputation for dubious quality of both workmanship and materials. The last and best model was the 350cc Dragonfly, which was launched in 1955 and featured a headlamp nacelle that blended into the fuel tank. Aided by stout Earles forks and well-damped twin

rear shock units, the handling was excellent. But although the Dragonfly cruised smoothly and comfortably at 60mph (96kph), its low-rev performance and 75mph (120kph) top speed were moderate, and sales were not enough to keep Douglas in business.

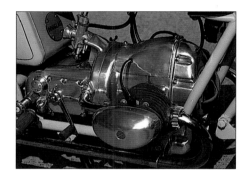

■ ABOVE *The Dragonfly's 348cc flat-twin engine was not highly successful, lacking real smoothness at low revs.*

■ LEFT *Flowing styling and a Reynolds-Earles pivoted front fork gave the Dragonfly a distinctive look.*

■ RIGHT *Early Douglas twins, such as this 2.75bhp model from 1914, had cylinders in line with the bike.*

■ FAR RIGHT *Douglas introduced the disc brake on this 6bhp racebike in 1922.*

OTHER MAKES

■ DAIMLER

German engineer Gottlieb Daimler is credited with building the world's first motorcycle, the wooden-framed Einspur that was first ridden by his son Paul in 1885. Daimler had no great interest in motorcycles, and shortly afterwards abandoned the project to concentrate on automobile development.

■ DERBI

Barcelona firm Derbi's name showed its roots, DERivados de BIcicletus meaning "derivative of bicycles" – which is what they had built until the 250cc Super was released in 1950. Early motorcycles included a 350cc twin but in the 1960s Derbi concentrated on small-capacity bikes such as the racy 49cc and 74cc Grand Sports. The firm's successful challenge in Grand Prix racing's smaller classes culminated in Angel Nieto winning five 50cc and 125cc world titles between 1969 and 1972, when Derbi pulled out to concentrate on road bikes and motocross. Over a decade later the firm returned to Grands Prix to win a string of titles with another legendary Spanish rider, Jorge "Aspar" Martinez.

■ DKW

Founded by Danish-born Joerge Rasmussen, two-stroke specialist DKW began building bikes in 1920 and by 1928 had become the world's largest manufacturer with a production of over 100,000 machines. In 1932 DKW merged with Audi, Horsch and Wanderer to form Auto Union, giving the four-circle logo still

■ ABOVE *Daimler's 265cc Einspur had a top speed of about 8mph (12kph).*

■ ABOVE *Spanish stars and Derbi teammates Jorge Martinex and Alex Criville were closely matched at Jerez in 1988.*

■ ABOVE *The SB500 Luxus became the 300,000th DKW bike to be built when it rolled off the German firm's line in 1935.*

used by Audi. Numerous racing successes included Ewald Kluge's 1938 Junior TT win on a supercharged 250cc split-single. After the Second World War the Zschoppau factory was taken over by MZ, and DKW moved to Ingoldstadt in West Germany. In 1957 the firm joined the Victoria and Express companies in the Zweirad Union, but in 1966 this was bought by two-stroke engine manufacturer Fichtel & Sachs, who dropped the DKW name.

■ DMW

Wolverhampton-based DMW was founded during the Second World War to make suspension systems for rigid framed bikes, and progressed to building complete machines in 1947. Most were Villiers-engined two-strokes, notably the 250cc twin-cylinder Dolomite. Roadster production ended in 1966, although DMW continued to build trials bikes on a limited basis.

■ DNEPR

For many years Ukrainian firm Dnepr has built shaft-driven flat-twins based on BMW designs from the 1940s. The Dnepr 11 was a 649cc twin, producing 36bhp. Designed for use with a sidecar, it had a reverse gear and a top speed of about 75mph (120kph). The broadly similar military-style Dnepr 16 outfit featured drive to both rear wheels.

■ DOT

DOT's Lancashire factory built Villiers-engined trials and motocross two-strokes in the 1950s and 1960s. The firm's best decade was the 1920s, when DOT riders competed in the TT and its roadster range included a 1000cc JAP-powered V-twin.

DUCATI

■ DUCATI 250 DESMO

In 1926 the Ducati brothers, Adriano and Marcello, founded a company in Bologna to produce electrical components. Badly damaged in the Second World War, the factory was taken over by the government in exchange for their investment. Ducati looked for new opportunities, and in 1946 began producing the Cucciolo, a 50cc four-stroke engine that clipped onto a bicycle frame and sold in huge numbers. In 1954 the firm appointed a new chief designer, Fabio Taglioni, who would be responsible for many great bikes, and

DUCATI 250 DESMO (1975)	
Engine	Aircooled 2-valve SOHC desmodromic single
Capacity	249cc (74 x 57.8mm)
Power	30bhp @ 8000rpm
Weight	132kg (290lb) wet
Top speed	95mph (152kph)

for adopting the desmodromic system of valve operation – that is valves closed by a cam, rather than springs – that has become the company's trademark.

■ ABOVE
Taglioni's classical single, featured bevel shaft, single overhead cam and desmo valvegear.

■ LEFT *The 250 Desmo single's uncompromising approach was emphasized by its simple and elegant styling.*

■ ABOVE LEFT *Ducati's first engine was the 50cc Cucciolo, or "little pup", which clipped to a bicycle.*

■ ABOVE RIGHT *The 450cc desmo engine was also used to power a successful Street Scrambler model.*

■ ABOVE *The 100cc Grand Sport, Taglioni's first design for Ducati, set the tone for many future models.*

■ RIGHT *Fine handling was always one of the light, firmly suspended Ducati singles' assets.*

By 1955 Taglioni had produced the 100cc Grand Sport, known as the Marianna, whose single-cylinder engine, with overhead camshaft driven by bevel shaft, would provide Ducati's basic format for the next 20 years. The single was very successful in events like the Giro d'Italia, and in 1958 a 125cc desmo racebike won several Grands Prix and finished second in the world championship. Ducati's range grew with singles like the 175cc Sport of 1957, and the 1964 model 250cc Mach 1 – fast, light, stylish and successful on road and track.

The fastest and best singles of all were the Desmo roadsters, produced in 250, 350 and 450cc versions from the early 1970s. With sleek, simple styling by Leo Tartarini, they were sportsters with clip-on bars, rearset pegs and single seats. Both larger models were capable of over 100mph (160kph), and even the smallest Desmo came close, with reasonable smoothness and fine handling to match. Ducati also built a Street Scrambler version of the single, which sold well and was a predecessor of modern trail bikes.

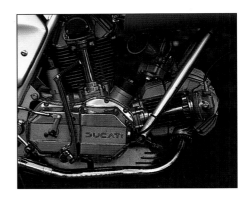

■ OPPOSITE *Top-class suspension and a rigid frame gave the 900SS excellent handling at speed.*

DUCATI

■ DUCATI 900SS

Lean, loud and built purely for speed, Ducati's 900SS was the most single-minded and arguably the finest of the great Italian sportsters of the 1970s. The 900SS combined a potent V-twin engine with a taut chassis, top-class cycle parts and a racy riding position to provide performance that few rivals could approach. Its gaping, filterless 40mm (1.5in) Dell'Orto carburettors, free-breathing Conti pipes and lack of such niceties as electric start or pillion seat, left no doubt about its aggressive nature.

Ducati had released its first V-twin, the 750GT, in 1971 and followed it shortly afterwards with the tuned 750 Sport, an unfaired roadster with bright yellow paintwork. Paul Smart's victory in the 1972 Imola 200 inspired the Bologna firm to build a street-legal replica called the 750SS with desmodromic valve operation like the racer's. In 1975 the engine was enlarged to 864cc to produce the 900SS, whose maximum of 79bhp and generous mid-range torque gave great acceleration and a top speed of over 130mph (209kph).

The 900SS carried virtually no components that were not strictly necessary,

DUCATI 900SS (1975)	
Engine	Aircooled 4-valve SOHC desmodromic 90-degree V-twin
Capacity	864cc (86 x 74.4mm)
Power	79bhp @ 7000rpm
Weight	188kg (414lb)
Top speed	132mph (211kph)

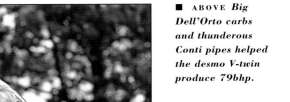

■ ABOVE *Big Dell'Orto carbs and thunderous Conti pipes helped the desmo V-twin produce 79bhp.*

■ LEFT *The original 900SS was the most singleminded of all 1970s superbikes – a pure-bred racer on the road.*

and the bike's light weight, strong tubular steel frame and firm Marzocchi suspension parts gave unshakeable high-speed handling. A useful cockpit fairing, Brembo brakes and elegant styling added to the charm of a bike that could be raced successfully in production events with few modifications.

Ducati's success in the 1970s owed much to two racing victories, both by Englishmen but in very different circumstances. Paul Smart's unexpected win at the prestigious Imola 200 in April 1972 was a landmark. Smart finished just ahead of team-mate Bruno Spaggiari, beating several factory entries including MV Agusta's Giacomo Agostini, for a result that did much to establish the Ducati name worldwide.

Six years later came another famous day, when Mike Hailwood returned from retirement to win the Isle of Man Formula One TT. Hailwood's emotional victory on the red and green Sports Motorcycles V-twin, at an average speed of 108.51mph (174.6 kph), led to Ducati producing a limited edition

Hailwood Replica of the 900SS in 1979. Like the standard 900, it remained in production until 1984, steadily losing its performance edge due to tightening emissions laws and Ducati's growing financial problems, which led to the state-owned firm being taken over by Cagiva in 1985.

■ TOP *Paul Smart's legendary victory at the Imola 200 in 1972 gave the reputation of Ducati's V-twins a big boost.*

■ ABOVE *Ducati celebrated Mike the Bike's 1978 TT win with a successful Hailwood Replica V-twin.*

■ BELOW *The 750 Sport of the early 1970s featured a 56bhp V-twin engine.*

DUCATI

■ **LEFT** *Superb handling combined with style and power to make the 916 an instant classic.*

■ DUCATI 916

Rarely has a new motorcycle generated as much excitement as Ducati's 916 did on its launch in 1994. The bike's styling was feline and gorgeous, from the sleek scarlet nose of its twin-headlamp fairing, via a single-sided swing-arm, to the tailpiece from which emerged twin high-level silencers. Its fuel-injected V-twin engine was magnificent, churning out mid-range torque and a peak of 114bhp. And its chassis was sublime, combining state-of-the-art suspension technology with the strength and simplicity of Ducati's traditional tubular steel frame.

The 916, designed by a team headed by former Bimota co-founder Massimo Tamburini, was the ultimate development of the watercooled, eight-valve desmodromic V-twin series that had begun with Massimo Bordi's 851 Strada in 1988. The 851 had brought Ducati, revitalized under Cagiva's control, roaring into the 1990s, combining the V-twin's traditional torque and charm with a new-found refinement. Over the next few years the Bologna firm's flagship was reshaped, its chassis was revised and its engine was enlarged to 888cc, giving additional speed and poise.

The 916 raised the stakes again, with a top speed of 160mph (257kph), even more mid-range acceleration and the addictive feel that only a V-twin can provide. Its uprated chassis gave light steering with impeccable stability, plus

DUCATI 916 (1994)	
Engine	Watercooled 8-valve DOHC desmodromic 90-degree V-twin
Capacity	916cc (94 x 66mm)
Power	114bhp @ 9000rpm
Weight	195kg (429lb)
Top speed	160mph (257kph)

■ **BELOW** *The 916 was beautiful, from its sharp nose to its high-level silencers.*

■ BELOW *In 1990 French ace Raymond Roche began Ducati's world Superbike domination.*

■ RIGHT *The sophisticated eight-valve 851 (left) was joined by the simpler, four-valve 900SS in 1989.*

huge amounts of cornering clearance and grip. Parent company Cagiva's financial problems resulted in delayed production, increasing the demand for what had already been the most eagerly awaited new bike for years. Everyone who finally got to ride the 916 knew that this was a very special motorcycle.

Much of Ducati's sales success in the 1990s was due to domination of the World Superbike Championship, in which the Italian firm benefited from rules allowing twin-cylinder bikes a capacity and weight advantage over fours. Frenchman Raymond Roche won the title in 1990, and American Doug Polen followed with successive championships on the factory V-twins. After coming second to Kawasaki's Scott Russell in 1993, Britain's Carl Fogarty gained revenge with victory on his works 916 the following season.

Ducati also developed a fine line of less high-tech V-twins, after reviving the 900SS name for a new SOHC, two-valves-per-cylinder desmo sportster in 1989. That red and white model suffered from mediocre carburation and suspension, but two years later it was uprated and reshaped to produce a thrillingly raw superbike. In the following years the 900SS line was broadened to include the single-seat Superlight and the stylish, unfaired M900 Monster, plus lookalike Super Sport models in 750 and 600cc sizes.

■ ABOVE AND INSET LEFT *The M900 Monster's brutal styling and wheelie-happy performance made it a big hit.*

ENFIELD

■ ENFIELD BULLET 500

The single-cylinder Bullet was one of the most popular models of Britain's old Royal Enfield firm, which manufactured the simple, light bike between 1949 and 1962, initially in 350cc and later in 500cc form. The Bullet was widely exported, and was used by the Indian armed forces. In 1958 production was started in Madras, using machinery from the old Royal Enfield factory. The 350cc bike sold well in India, and by the mid-1980s it was also being exported to

much-improved front brake. By modern standards the Enfield was inevitably crude, with modest acceleration, a realistic cruising speed of 65mph (104kph), considerable vibration and harsh handling. It was also cheap, economical, reliable and provided an unmistakable classic feel that some riders enjoyed.

countries including Britain.

The 500cc model followed a few years later and was also successful, despite its basic layout having remained unchanged since the mid-1950s. The pushrod-operated engine produced 22bhp, and was held in a simple tubular steel frame. For domestic use many of the details had changed little, too, but export bikes incorporated numerous refinements including a

ENFIELD BULLET 500 (1990)	
Engine	Aircooled 2-valve OHV pushrod single
Capacity	499cc (84 x 90mm)
Power	22bhp @ 5400rpm
Weight	169kg (270lb)
Top speed	80mph (128kph)

■ BELOW *The 500cc Bullet was built in 1990 but looks almost identical to its predecessor of the 1950s.*

■ RIGHT *Bullet handling is inevitably crude but can be uprated by specialists such as Fritz Egli.*

■ OPPOSITE MIDDLE *Even when tuned the pushrod Bullet engine lacks power, but it is economical and fairly reliable.*

OTHER MAKES

■ ECOMOBILE

Looking like a large, wingless glider, the Ecomobile produced by Swiss engineer Arnold Wagner was one of the most unusual machines on two wheels. The first versions, produced in 1982, held a BMW flat-twin engine in the Kevlar/fibreglass monocoque body. In 1988 the design was uprated using the four-cylinder K100 engine, giving the streamlined Ecomobile a top speed of over 150mph (241kph).

■ EGLI

Swiss engineer Fritz Egli has built chassis, invariably featuring his trademark large-diameter steel spine frame, for a huge variety of engines since starting with the Vincent V-twin on which he became Swiss racing champion in the late 1960s. In the 1970s he turned to four-cylinder Hondas and Kawasakis, and his bikes were highly successful in endurance racing. In recent years he has produced his first Harley-Davidson special. And as the Swiss and Austrian importer of Enfield Bullets, he tuned the Indian-made single's engine and

■ ABOVE *Egli's 1983 Harley special, nicknamed Lucifer's Hammer, was fast, loud and powerful.*

uprated its chassis to produce the considerably improved Swiss Finish Bullet.

■ ELF

The string of racebikes backed by French petrochemicals giant Elf were some of the most innovative of recent years, all using non-telescopic suspension of various designs. Radical early models such as the Honda-powered Elf E endurance racer of 1981 pioneered features including carbon fibre disc brakes. In 1985 Elf moved into Grands Prix with backing from Honda, using a more conventional forkless chassis. Despite a works V-four engine, British rider Ron Haslam could never make the Elf 3 truly competitive, and Elf pulled out after the 1988 season. Honda's involvement yielded benefits including development of the single-sided swing-arm found on many recent roadsters.

■ EMC

Austrian-born two-stroke tuning wizard Dr Joe Ehrlich came to England in the 1930s and set up his Ehrlich Motor Co in London after the War. His Model S and Model T 350s used unusual split-single engines, and were unsuccessful. In the early 1960s

■ LEFT *The amazing 170mph (273kph) Turbo Ecomobile combined superbike speed and cornering ability with sports car comfort.*

■ ABOVE *Ron Haslam lifts the Elf 3's forkless front wheel at the 1988 French Grand Prix.*

Ehrlich built a 125cc racer on which Mike Hailwood scored good results. After a successful move to F3 car racing Ehrlich returned to bikes in the early 1980s, when his 250cc Rotax-engined racers were highly competitive in Grands Prix and the TT. After another absence, the veteran Dr Joe – now in his 80s – returned with yet another EMC racebike in 1995.

EXCELSIOR

■ EXCELSIOR MANXMAN

Excelsior became Britain's first motor-cycle manufacturer when it began selling bikes in 1896 under the firm's original name of Bayliss, Thomas and Co. In

1910 the company's name was changed to Excelsior, following the demise of a German manufacturer of the same name. Excelsior specialized in small-capacity bikes and produced racers, notably the 250cc Mechanical Marvel – which won the Lightweight TT in 1933.

That result increased interest in Excelsior and led to the firm producing a replica racer, but a loss of nerve by the

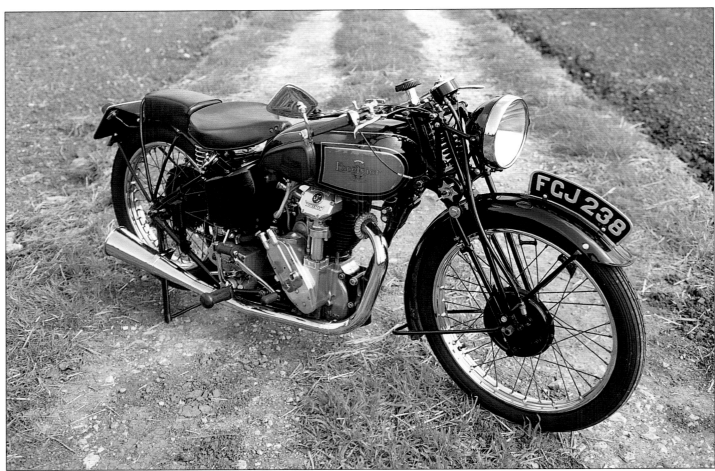

EXCELSIOR MANXMAN 250 (1936)

Engine	Aircooled 2-valve SOHC single
Capacity	246cc (63 x 79mm)
Power	25bhp approx
Weight	132kg (290lb) dry
Top speed	80mph (128kph)

OTHER MAKES

■ EXCELSIOR

The American motorcycles of this name were built in Chicago by the Schwinn bicycle company, and ranged from small two-strokes to the big four-stroke V-twins for which Excelsior was famous. The firm built its first machine in 1907. By 1931,

when Excelsior fell victim to the Depression, the factory had taken over production of the four-cylinder Henderson, becoming America's third largest marque behind Indian and Harley-Davidson. Excelsior's best known model was the Super X, a 750cc (45ci) V-twin introduced in the mid-1920s.

engineers – who thought club racers would be unable to maintain such a complicated engine – prompted a simpler motor with a single overhead camshaft. The Manxman was released in 1935 in

250cc form, and was later produced in 350 and 500cc capacities too. Its good performance and impressive strength made the single popular with road riders and club racers.

After the Second World War, Excelsior concentrated on Villiers-engined two-stroke roadsters such as the 250cc Viking and Talisman, but sales fell and production came to an end in 1962.

■ OPPOSITE TOP
A Manxman at speed on the TT circuit from which its name is derived.

■ OPPOSITE MIDDLE *The Excelsior's SOHC engine, seen here in 350cc form, was simple and reliable.*

■ OPPOSITE BELOW *As well as being a competitive racer, the Manxman was a popular roadster in the late 1930s.*

■ RIGHT
Excelsior's 250cc four-valve Mechanical Marvel was ridden to TT victory by Sid Gleave in 1933.

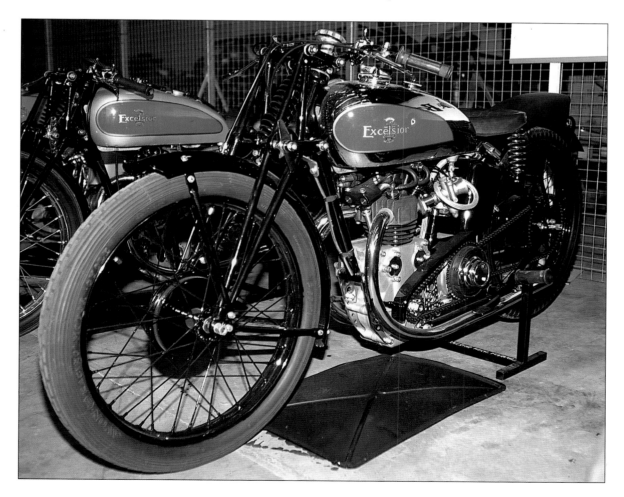

F N

■ FN FOUR

The world's first mass-produced four-cylinder motorcycle was the Belgian-built FN, which was a revelation when it was introduced in 1904. The company had been founded near Liège in 1899 to manufacture arms and ammunition, and began making single-cylinder bikes in 1902. But it is the four-cylinder bike, designed by Paul Kelecom, for which FN is remembered. The 362cc in-line engine was notable for its high tension magneto ignition and fully-enclosed shaft final drive; the chassis incorporated one of the earliest forms of telescopic forks.

Initial doubts led *France Automobile* magazine to regard it as more of a curiosity than a practical motorcycle,

FN FOUR (1911)	
Engine	Aircooled 8-valve inlet-over-exhaust in-line four
Capacity	491cc
Power	4bhp
Weight	75kg (165lb) dry
Top speed	40mph (64kph)

despite its remarkable engine. But the FN was far more than that, and would be gradually updated over two decades of production. Engine capacity grew to 412cc and then to 491cc in 1911, by which time the FN Four produced about 4hp, had gained a clutch and two-speed gearbox, and was capable of 40mph. An

updated 748cc four was introduced just before the First World War during which the occupied factory produced bikes for the German army. The FN did not recapture its popularity after the War, although a 1923 redesign – when chain final drive replaced the shaft – kept the model going for three more years.

OTHER MAKES

■ FANTIC

After starting production in the 1960s, Fantic gained a reputation for small-capacity two-strokes, particularly the range of Caballero trail bikes. The Italian firm has built many bikes for motocross and particularly trials, where it has been a leading contender for many years.

■ FATH

German racer-engineer Helmut Fath's greatest achievement came not in 1960, when he won the world sidecar championship for the first time, but eight years later, when he returned from serious injury to regain the title on a machine he had designed and built himself. The URS, named after Fath's village of Ursenbach, was a 500cc DOHC transverse four that revved to 15,000rpm and produced a reported 80bhp. The URS was also raced as a solo using chassis from Seeley and Metisse, most successfully in 1969 by veteran German Karl Hoppe. After selling his team to Friedel Münch, Fath built a powerful 500cc flat-four two-stroke engine that was raced in both solo and sidecar classes in the 1970s.

■ FRANCIS-BARNETT

Never the most glamorous of manufacturers, Francis-Barnett specialized in producing economical roadsters from its start in 1919 until its demise in 1966. The firm's most famous model was the 250 Cruiser of the 1930s, which combined its single-cylinder Villiers two-stroke engine with pressed-steel leg-shields, large mudguards and partial engine covers. In 1947, the Coventry firm was taken over by Associated Motor Cycles, after which it continued to build small-capacity roadsters, as well as trials and scrambles bikes, profitably for several years. But the rise of Italian scooters hit sales, and Francis-Barnett's attempt to design and build its own engines was unsuccessful. "Fanny-B" returned to Villiers engines for its single and twin-cylinder models, also called Cruisers, in the 1960s.

■ RIGHT *This single-cylinder Francis-Barnett Falcon provided reasonable small-capacity performance in 1959.*

■ LEFT *Helmut Fath won the 1968 sidecar world title with his own four-cylinder URS.*

■ ABOVE *Fantic is known for trials bikes such as this 125cc, seen tackling the Scottish Six Days Trial in 1991.*

■ ABOVE *The bodywork of this 1936-model Francis-Barnett Cruiser gave its rider useful protection.*

GILERA

■ GILERA SATURNO

Gilera was one of motorcycling's big names in the 1950s, racing with great success and building some fine road-sters. The firm was founded by a youth-ful Giuseppe Gilera in 1909, and represented Italy in the International Six Days Trial in the 1930s. Gilera's most famous roadsters were four-stroke singles, notably the 500cc Saturno that was much loved for its blend of clean, handsome styling and lively performance.

The Saturno was designed and briefly raced just before Italy entered the Second World War but was first produced in 1946, in Sport, Touring and Competition versions. Early models had girder forks and Gilera's own brand of rear suspension – horizontal springs in tubes, with friction dampers. Telescopic forks and vertical shocks were intro-duced in the early 1950s. The bike quickly became popular thanks to its

■ ABOVE *In recent years, the once-proud Gilera name has only been used for Piaggio-built scooters.*

GILERA SATURNO (1951)	
Engine	Aircooled 2-valve OHV pushrod single
Capacity	499cc (84 x 90mm)
Power	22bhp @ 5000rpm (Sport version)
Weight	170kg (374lb) dry
Top speed	85mph (136kph)

■ LEFT *The Saturno racer's look and performance changed little throughout most of the 1950s.*

■ LEFT *The
CX125, a two-
stroke sportster
introduced in
1991, featured
single-sided
suspension at front
and rear.*

excellent road-going performance and some impressive racing results, notably Carlo Bandirola's win at the new Sanremo circuit in 1947, which led to the Saturno racer being known as the Sanremo.

Saturnos were not competitive at Grand Prix level but continued to be raced successfully in Italy several years after production had ended in the late 1950s. But by then Giuseppe Gilera had lost enthusiasm following the early death, of a heart attack, of his son Feruccio in 1956.

In 1969 the company was sold to small-bike specialist and Vespa scooter producer Piaggio, who developed a range of new models in the late 1980s. These included a new Saturno, a stylish 500cc four-stroke single with half-fairing, disc brakes and single-shock rear suspension, which was produced mainly for export to Japan. Later models included the Nordwest 600 single and

the CX125, an innovative two-stroke sportster with forkless front suspension. Sales, however, were moderate, and Gilera's 250cc Grand Prix comeback in 1992 was sadly an expensive failure

that the company could ill-afford. In 1993 Piaggio announced the closure of the factory at Arcore, near Milan, although the Gilera name continued to be used for scooters.

OTHER MAKES

■ GARELLI
When Garelli began production in 1913 it was with an unusual 350cc twin-pistoned two-stroke single, which won many races. Recent production has concentrated on

■ LEFT *Angel
Nieto cornering his
125cc works Garelli.*

■ FAR LEFT
*Spain's trials
superstar Jordi
Tarrés takes a rare
"dab" to steady his
factory Gas-Gas.*

small-capacity two-strokes and mopeds. Garelli's most successful racing years were the 1980s, when the Italian firm's monocoque-framed 125cc parallel twins, acquired from Minarelli, won seven consecutive world titles at the hands of Fausto Gresini, Luca Cadalora and Angel Nieto.

■ GAS-GAS
Spanish specialist firm Gas-Gas has made a huge impact in trials over recent years, scoring numerous wins through their riders, including the great Jordi Tarrés who clinched his seventh world championship in 1995.

■ LEFT *Piero Remor's 500cc powerplant set the pattern for modern transverse four-cylinder engines.*

■ BELOW *Unlike the "dustbin" fairings often used, this 1956 Gilera's fly-screen leaves the engine visible.*

GILERA

■ GILERA 500cc FOUR

Gilera's 500cc four-cylinder racer made even more of an impact than its impressive haul of six world champion-ships between 1950 and 1957 suggests. Its transverse four-engine layout provided the inspiration not only for MV Agusta, whose similar machines domi-nated the 500cc world championship after Gilera's withdrawal, but later also for the Japanese factories on both road and track.

The original 500 four was designed as early as 1923 by Carlo Gianini and Piero Remor, two young engineers from Rome. Initially aircooled and with a gear-driven single overhead camshaft, by 1934 the four was called the Rondine, featured twin cams and a

supercharger, and was producing an impressive 86bhp. Gilera bought the project, and the four was soon winning races and setting a world speed record of 170.15mph (273.8kph).

After the War supercharging was banned, halving the four's power output. Piero Remor, one of the original designers, produced a new aircooled, twin-cam powerplant, then in 1949 left for MV, who soon adopted a similar layout. Nevertheless Gilera's Umberto Masetti won two championships and Geoff Duke added three more between 1953 and 1955. After Libero Liberati's win in 1957 the Arcore firm joined rivals Guzzi and Mondial in pulling out of Grand Prix racing completely.

GILERA 500cc-FOUR (1956)

Engine	Aircooled 8-valve DOHC transverse four
Capacity	499cc (52 x 58.8mm)
Power	70bhp @ 11,000rpm
Weight	150kg (330lb) dry
Top speed	145mph (233kph)

■ RIGHT *John Hartle howls his Gilera through Quarter Bridge on the way to second place in the 1963 Senior TT.*

OTHER MAKES

GNOME & RHÔNE

Between the Wars the Paris-based factory moved from aircraft engine production to build a variety of bikes with single-cylinder and flat-twin engines of up to 750cc. After 1945 Gnome & Rhône built small-capacity two-strokes, but didn't survive the 1950s.

GREEVES

Best known for its trials and motocross bikes, Essex firm Greeves also built road-sters and the Silverstone road-racer in the 1950s and 1960s. Most of the roadsters were 250 and 350cc two-strokes, with engines bought from British Anzani or Villiers, and given names such as Fleet-master, Sportsman and Sports Twin. Off-road successes included many wins for the

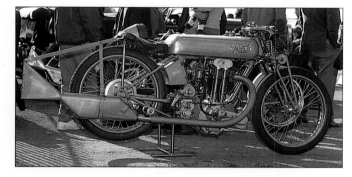

■ LEFT *The exhaust of this Grindlay-Peerless racer from the 1920s is fitted with a huge "Brooklands can" to reduce noise.*

Greeves Hawkstone scrambler, and the European 250cc championships won by Dave Bickers in 1960 and 1961. Bill Wilkinson's Scottish Six Days Trial victory on a 250cc Greeves Anglian in 1969, ahead of Sammy Miller's Bultaco, brought to an end British bikes' domination of the trials world.

GRINDLAY-PEERLESS

Bill Lacey gave Grindlay-Peerless its greatest success when he covered over 100 miles (160km) in an hour to set a world record in 1928. Roadsters ranged from big 1000cc V-twins to 150cc two-strokes, but although the bikes were regarded as stylish, production ended in 1934.

■ LEFT *This 250cc Sports Twin two-stroke from 1963 was typical of Greeves' roadster production.*

■ LEFT *Bill Wilkinson won the 1969 Scottish Six Days Trial on a 250cc, Villiers-engined works Greeves Anglian.*

HARLEY-DAVIDSON

■ HARLEY-DAVIDSON MODEL 9E

William S Harley and Arthur Davidson were former school friends who, while working for a Milwaukee engineering firm, dreamt of producing a motorbike. In 1902 they built a 400cc (25ci) single-cylinder engine, and a year later, after being joined by Davidson's elder brothers Walter and William A, they fitted it into a bicycle frame to complete the prototype Harley-Davidson motorcycle. The motor proved reliable but underpowered, so was enlarged. The frame was too weak so it was replaced with a more substantial structure built along similar lines.

HARLEY-DAVIDSON MODEL 9E (1913)	
Engine	Aircooled 2-valve inlet-over-exhaust single V-twin
Capacity	1000cc (61ci)
Power	10bhp
Weight	150kg (330lb) dry
Top speed	60mph (96kph)

Two more bikes were produced in 1903, and another three the following year. By 1907 the Harley-Davidson's growing reputation for reliability had helped push annual production above

150. In that year Harley-Davidson raised money for expansion by becoming a corporation, with shares divided among 17 employees. The firm had by now moved across Milwaukee from its first base, a small shed in the Davidsons' yard, to bigger premises in what would become Juneau Avenue, the firm's current address.

Very early models had no lights or suspension but within a few years Harley had fitted leading-link forks, a carbide gas headlamp and magneto ignition. The Model 5 of 1909 produced about 4bhp from its 494cc (30ci) inlet-over-exhaust engine, and was good for 45mph (72kph). It had bicycle pedals to

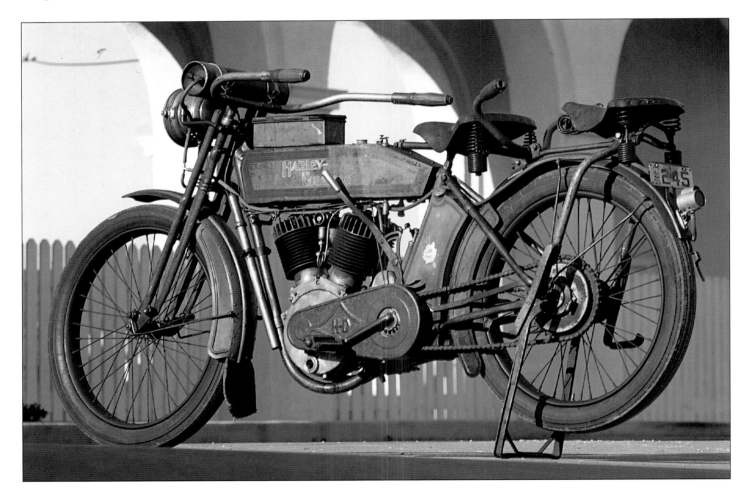

■ RIGHT *Harley made a late start in racing, but tuned and lightened V-twins such as this were successful after 1914.*

start the engine and set the bike in motion, after which the leather drive belt was tightened using a hand lever.

Harley's first V-twin, the Model 5D, was built in 1909, but was not an immediate success. It produced about 7bhp, almost twice as much as the

■ FAR LEFT *This official photograph from 1910 shows founders William, Walter and Arthur Davidson and William Harley.*

■ LEFT *The Harley legend began in this tiny shed at the rear of the Davidsons' home in Milwaukee.*

■ BELOW *Harley launched a new 5bhp single in 1913, and a year later introduced a kickstart and rear drum brake.*

single, but was hard to start and suffered from a slipping drive belt. Two years later the 45-degree V-twin was reintroduced with revised valvegear and a new frame; soon afterwards it was fitted with chain drive and a full floating seat. The improvements made a big difference and the V-twin grew rapidly in popularity. By 1913, the Model 9E's 1000cc (61ci) powerplant was producing about 10bhp, giving a top speed of 60mph (96kph).

Harley-Davidson had initially been reluctant to get involved in racing, preferring reliability runs, but in 1914 finally entered a factory team. The Milwaukee firm's so-called "Wrecking Crew", riding powerful eight-valve V-twins, were very competitive against rivals Indian, Merkel and Excelsior both before and after the First World War. This period was one of great fluctuation for Harley-Davidson. Production rose to over 22,000 bikes and 16,000 sidecars in 1919, before halving two years later due mainly to the rise of the Model T Ford, which put most of the American motorcycle firms out of business.

HARLEY-DAVIDSON

■ OPPOSITE *A neat pair of V-twins on show at Harley riders' unofficial meeting place at Daytona Beach, Florida.*

■ HARLEY-DAVIDSON WL45

Harley is best known for large-capacity V-twins, but the smaller 45ci (750cc) Forty Five also played a vital part in the company's history. The first 45ci model, a basic machine with a total-loss oil system, was produced in 1928. Nine

years later, it was restyled and updated to create the W series. Simple and strong, if not particularly fast even in its day, the Forty Five kept Harley going through the Depression of the 1930s. As the WLA model it also proved an ideal military machine, with around 80,000 being used in the Second World War.

After the War many ex-army 45s were converted for civilian use, which did much to popularize Harleys worldwide, and the Milwaukee factory recommenced building the W in various forms, including the WR racer. The WL name denoted a sportier version of the basic W, with slightly raised compression increasing power to 25bhp. The three-speed gearbox was operated by a hand lever, with a foot clutch. In 1949 Harley introduced its Girdraulic damping system on the WL's springer front forks,

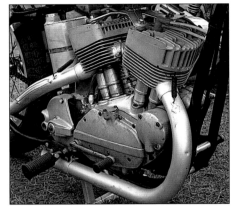

■ ABOVE *The K-series V-twin, introduced in 1952, featured unit construction and a four-speed gearbox.*

HARLEY WL45 (1949)	
Engine	Aircooled sidevalve 45-degree V-twin
Capacity	742cc (70 x 97mm)
Power	25bhp @ 4000rpm
Weight	240kg (528lb) wet
Top speed	75mph (120kph)

■ BELOW *The look of this "hard-tail" 1949 WL45 is reflected in the styling of many modern Harleys.*

in place of the simple friction damper used previously. The bike had a sprung saddle and no rear suspension.

Nevertheless the ride was fairly comfortable, handling was adequate and the WL was capable of cruising steadily and reliably at 60mph (96kph). It remained in production until 1952, when it was replaced by the Model K,

featuring a unit-construction engine and four-speed gearbox, with foot change. The three-wheeled Servicar, powered by the faithful 45ci engine, was built until 1974.

In 1936, with America still suffering the effects of the Depression, Harley bravely introduced the Model 61E. The new bike's 61ci (1000cc) V-twin engine

was a major advance due to its over-head-valve design and recirculating oil system. The 61E was also neatly styled, and became a big success. Known as the Knucklehead after the shape of the engine's rocker covers, it gave Harley the technical edge over great rivals Indian and became the illustrious ancestor of all modern Harleys.

■ RIGHT *The shape of this 1946 Knucklehead's rocker covers clearly shows where it got its name from.*

■ ABOVE *Harley's wartime WLA and WLC, built for Canadian forces, proved to be rugged and reliable.*

■ ABOVE *The three-wheeled Servicar, produced for commercial use in 1931, was a long-running success.*

HARLEY-DAVIDSON

■ HARLEY-DAVIDSON XLCH SPORTSTER

At its peak in the early 1960s, the XLCH Sportster lived up to its name by being one of the quickest bikes on the road. It roared to a top speed of over 100mph (160kph), turned standing quarters in around 14 seconds and, in a straight line at least, was a match for lighter British 650cc twins. That was then. In recent decades the name has remained while the Sportster models, smallest machines in a range of cruisers, have become about as far from a sports motorcycle as possible.

The Sportster was launched in 1957, with an overhead valve V-twin motor

HARLEY-DAVIDSON XLCH SPORTSTER (1962)	
Engine	Aircooled 4-valve OHV pushrod 45-degree V-twin
Capacity	883cc (76.2 x 96.8mm)
Power	55bhp @ 5000rpm
Weight	220kg (485lb)
Top speed	110mph (177kph)

■ LEFT *The original XLCH's 883cc engine-capacity is also used for the smaller of the two current Sportster models.*

■ BELOW *Lean, loud, powerful and respectably light, the Sportster fully lived up to its name back in 1959.*

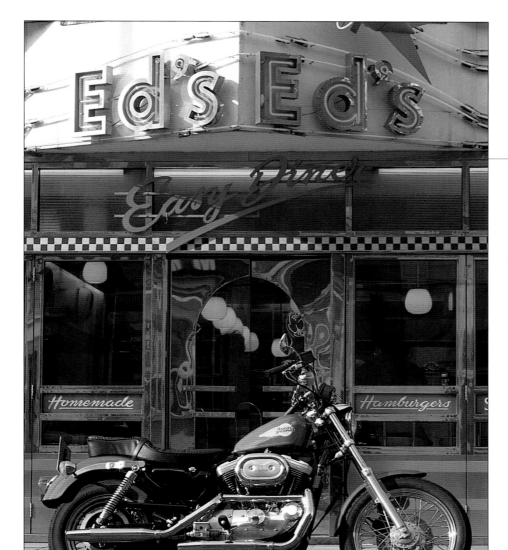

■ LEFT *By 1991, the Sportster's capacity had grown to 1200cc but its performance had barely changed at all.*

■ BELOW *Harley attempted to build a true sportsbike with the XLCR Café Racer of 1977, but it was not a great success.*

for mediocre suspension and brakes by plenty of others, the current XLHs are the best yet, combining age-old charm with five-speed gearboxes, belt final drive systems and reliability unheard of from Milwaukee in 1957. Its name may not ring true any more, but the Sportster looks set to stick around for many more years to come.

In contrast, one of Harley's most distinctive but least successful, and shortest-lived, models of all was the lean black XLCR Café Racer that was introduced in 1977. Consisting of the 1000cc Sportster engine in a new frame developed from that of the XR750 racebike, the Café Racer incorporated racy features such as a bikini fairing, twin front discs, matt-black siamesed exhausts and single seat. The look was attractive and by Harley standards the performance was good, but the XLCR appealed neither to traditional riders nor to the café racer crowd. Few were sold and the model was quickly dropped; ironically it has become quite highly sought-after in recent years.

whose 54ci (883cc) capacity was the same as its KH predecessor, but used a larger bore and shorter stroke to allow higher revs. The original XL model had a big gas tank and fenders, but a year later Harley produced the XLCH, complete with tuned engine, small headlamp, tiny gas tank, lower bars and loud pipes: the classical Sportster style had arrived.

The Sportster's look and performance have varied remarkably little over the years. Capacity has increased via 1000cc to 1200cc, joined in 1986 by the Evolution-engined 883cc model that has served as a popular entry-level Harley. Although frequently derided by riders of big-twin Harleys, and criticized

HARLEY-DAVIDSON

■ HARLEY-DAVIDSON ELECTRA GLIDE

For many people the Electra Glide is the quintessential Harley-Davidson: big, simple, traditional, ostentatious; a bike built by Americans, for Americans, for travelling across the vast country of its birth. More than just a comfortable, slow-revving V-twin tourer, the Electra Glide has become a rumbling, rolling symbol of two-wheeled freedom — albeit one hampered over the years by dubious reliability, handling and braking.

The Electra Glide was launched in 1965, when Harley added an electric starter to the 74ci (1200cc) V-twin that had been steadily developed since

1947. The legendary name followed a pattern; the 1949 model Hydra-Glide featured hydraulic front suspension and the Duo-Glide of 1958 had added rear

suspension. With high handlebars, big gas tank and fenders, footboards, a single saddle, and fat white-wall tyres on wire-spoked wheels, the Electra

■ LEFT *Harley introduced fuel-injection with the range-topping Ultra Classic Electra Glide in 1995.*

■ BELOW *This 1978 Glide shows classic features, including big fenders, fat tyres and lots of chrome.*

■ LEFT *The Hydra-Glide was introduced in 1949, taking its name from its new hydraulic front forks.*

to benefit from the hugely improved alloy Evolution engine introduced by a revitalized Harley in 1984 – from which point it has been success all the way. In 1995, the range-topping Ultra Classic Electra Glide debuted the fuel-injection system designed to take Harley's faithful aircooled, pushrod V-twin towards the 21st century.

The Electra Glide may have been the most famous Harley, but the Softail model introduced in 1984 was perhaps the most significant. As well as the new Evolution engine, the Softail featured clean, traditional looks and rear suspension cleverly hidden under the engine to give the illusion of a solid or "hard-tail" rear end.

The Softail marked Harley's entry into the nostalgia market that has served the company so well ever since. Its most vivid interpretation came in 1993 with the Heritage Softail Nostalgia – complete with two-tone paint, white-wall tyres and cowhide patches on both the seat and the saddlebags.

HARLEY-DAVIDSON ELECTRA GLIDE (1965)

Engine	Aircooled 4-valve OHV pushrod 45-degree V-twin
Capacity	1198cc (87.1 x 100.6mm)
Power	60bhp @ 4000rpm
Weight	350kg (770lb)
Top speed	95mph (152kph)

■ ABOVE *Styling chief Willie G Davidson, grandson of William A, has played a big part in Harley's recent success.*

■ BELOW *The Heritage Softail Nostalgia sums up Harley's approach to design.*

Glide looked elegant. Despite plenty of engine vibration and poor suspension and braking – problems exaggerated by its massive 350kg of weight – the bike was well received.

Just a year later, in 1966, Harley changed the engine from the Panhead to the Shovelhead – named after the shape of their cylinder head covers – which added a modicum of reliability. Other changes over the years included adding a fairing and hard luggage, enlarging the V-twin lump to 80ci (1340cc) in 1978, and rubber-mounting the powerplant to combat vibration. All helped make the Glide ride better and in more comfort.

The biggest shake-up in Harley-Davidson history came in 1981 when the management, led by Vaughn Beals, raised the money to buy Harley from parent company AMF, under whose control in the 1970s Harley had seen a deterioration in quality and sales. The Electra Glide was one of the first models

HARLEY-DAVIDSON

■ HARLEY-DAVIDSON XR750

One bike has dominated American dirt-track racing since the early 1970s: Harley's XR750, the thundering V-twin that has captured countless victories

HARLEY-DAVIDSON XR750 (1978)	
Engine	Aircooled 4-valve pushrod OHV 45-degree V-twin
Capacity	750cc (79 x 76mm)
Power	95bhp @ 8000rpm
Weight	145kg (319lb) wet
Top speed	130mph (209kph)

while retaining almost the same look and layout. The XR was introduced in 1970, when race-team manager Dick O'Brien put a modified Sportster engine into the chassis of Harley's outdated KR racer. The result was initially underpowered, unreliable and unsuccessful; the original XR's best performances were arguably made by car-jumping stunt rider Evel Knievel. But in 1972 the XR's iron-barrelled engine was replaced by a new aluminium V-twin, and Mark Brelsford won the first of its many titles.

The Harley has not always been on top since then. Yamaha's Kenny Roberts won in 1973 and 1974, and in the mid-1980s Honda won four titles with the

RS750, which was based on a CX500 V-twin engine turned through 90 degrees. But the XR750 has generally ruled the roost, with championships for riders including Jay Springsteen, who won three in a row from 1976-8, and Randy

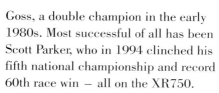

■ LEFT *Rodney Ferris crouches low and revs his Harley XR750 towards 130mph (209kph) at the Sacramento Mile.*

■ FAR LEFT TOP *Scott Parker and his factory XR have been successful in recent seasons.*

■ FAR LEFT BOTTOM *Italian star Walter Villa won four 250 and 350cc world titles in the mid-1970s.*

■ BELOW *Harley revealed a new generation of V-twin technology in the alloy-framed V1000 racebike.*

Goss, a double champion in the early 1980s. Most successful of all has been Scott Parker, who in 1994 clinched his fifth national championship and record 60th race win – all on the XR750.

Since 1980, Harley has not built complete XRs, instead selling engines which are then built into bikes using parts from firms such as frame specialist Champion. A modern XR750 produces over 100bhp, and reaches over 130mph (209kph). In over 30 years the lean and purposeful XR look has barely changed, despite the appearance of upside-down forks, cast wheels, rear brakes – early XRs had none at all – and huge silencers. Many road machines have copied its style, including Harley's own 1983 model XR1000, and Sportster-based XR specials from firms such as Storz Performance and Los Angeles dealer Bartels.

The XR750 has never made as good a road racer as it has a dirt-track bike, but the Harley has had its moments over the years. Some of its best performances came from Cal Rayborn at the Anglo-American match race series in 1972. The Californian won three races and set

two lap records on his fully-faired XR, finishing joint top rider with British Triumph ace Ray Pickrell, and proving once and for all that Americans could ride road-race bikes with the best.

Harley recently produced a very different competition machine in the VR1000, a road-racer whose fuel-injected, watercooled, DOHC eight-valve, 60-degree V-twin engine heralded

a new era for the American firm. With its modern twin-beam aluminium frame, the VR had little apart from its V-twin layout and its colour scheme in common with previous Harleys. The VR was first raced at Daytona in 1994, ridden by Miguel Duhamel, and remained down on power compared to rival Superbikes a year later. But Harley showed no signs of giving up the fight.

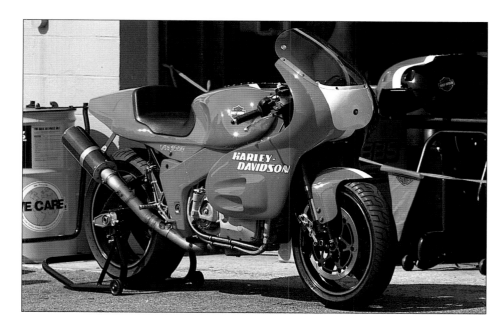

■ BELOW *By 1920s' standards, Henderson's in-line four-cylinder engine was supremely smooth and powerful.*

■ BOTTOM *The KJ model, known as the "Streamline", was a fast, refined and inevitably expensive machine.*

HENDERSON

■ HENDERSON KJ

Arguably the finest and most sophisticated machines in the years up to 1930, American-built Hendersons featured four-cylinder engines mounted in-line with the bike. The firm began production in 1911, using the engine layout and long wheelbase format that would become its trademark. Six years later, founder Bill Henderson sold the firm to Schwinn, makers of bicycles and Excelsior motorbikes, and left to found Ace. The Henderson firm continued development, and its 1301cc K model of 1920 produced 28bhp to give an impressive top speed of 80mph (128kph). Among its several advanced features were electric lighting and a fully-enclosed chain.

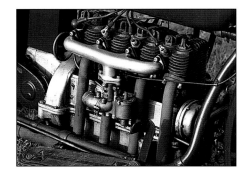

HENDERSON KJ (1929)	
Engine	Aircooled 8-valve inlet-over-exhaust in-line four
Capacity	1301cc
Power	40bhp
Weight	225kg (495lb) approx.
Top speed	100mph (160kph)

In 1929, Henderson reached new heights of luxury with the Model KJ, known as the "Streamline", which featured improved cooling to a stronger, 40bhp engine of the familiar in-line four-cylinder layout. The Streamline was fast – capable of a genuine 100mph (160kph) – and typically advanced,

with leading-link forks and such details as an illuminated speedometer set into the fuel tank. But it failed to sell during America's Depression, and Schwinn halted production in 1931. By then Indian had bought the rights to produce Ace machines, and continued to build its own four into the 1940s.

OTHER MAKES

■ HARRIS

Brothers Steve and Lester Harris set up their chassis firm in Hertford in the 1970s, and made their name with a series of fine-handling café racers, known as the Magnums. These featured Harris-made tubular steel frames, with a range of top-quality cycle parts. Engines were normally Japanese fours, ranging from the Kawasaki Z1000-engined Magnum 1 of the late 1970s to the recent Magnum 4, powered by Suzuki's GSX-R motor.

Throughout the 1980s Harris produced numerous chassis for racing, and developed aluminium beam frames for road and track. In recent years the firm has been heavily involved in 500cc Grands Prix and, along with French company ROC, has worked in conjunction with Yamaha to produce bikes powered by the Japanese factory's V-four engines.

■ HERCULES

After building bicycles for several years, Germany's Hercules produced its first motorbike in 1904. After the Second World War, Hercules concentrated on small-capacity two-strokes with engines from Sachs. The firm rapidly built up a large range of bikes in the 1950s, notably its first twin-cylinder model, the 318. This was billed as a luxury tourer, and had a 247cc engine that produced 12 bhp. Sachs took control of the firm in 1969. The Hercules name survived, notably with the W2000 of the mid-1970s – the world's first commercially built Wankel rotary-engined motorbike. Its 294cc – or 882cc, depending how it was measured – motor produced a claimed 27bhp at 6500rpm and gave a top speed of almost 90mph (145kph). But the rotary, which was marketed as a DKW in Britain, did not sell well, and recent production has been limited to two-stroke motorcycles of below 100cc.

■ RIGHT *The Hercules/DKW W2000 rotary had lively performance but was not a sales success.*

■ FAR RIGHT *Post-war Hercules production concentrated on two-strokes such as this enduro machine.*

■ ABOVE *The Harris Magnum 4 held a four-cylinder Suzuki GSX-R engine in a frame of traditional steel tubes.*

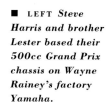

■ LEFT *Steve Harris and brother Lester based their 500cc Grand Prix chassis on Wayne Rainey's factory Yamaha.*

HESKETH

■ HESKETH V1000

When it was launched in 1981, the Hesketh V1000 was billed by its creator as being the finest machine in the world, a two-wheeled Aston Martin which would prove that the British could still build motorcycles. Lord Alexander Hesketh had money, he had run a high-profile Formula One car-racing team, and on paper his handsome V1000 was very promising. Its aircooled, 992cc, 90-degree V-twin engine, designed by four-stroke specialist Weslake, used twin cams and four valves per cylinder to produce an impressive 86bhp. The Hesketh's frame was a neat structure of nickel-plated steel tubing, and it held top quality motorcycle parts including Marzocchi suspension and Brembo disc brakes from Italy.

■ LEFT *When cruising on an open road, the Hesketh felt impressively fast, smooth and relaxed.*

■ BELOW *The V1000's neat bodywork, nickel-plated frame and V-twin engine made an attractive combination.*

■ RIGHT *Numerous problems with its engine and gearbox were the main reason for the V1000's failure.*

■ BELOW *The fully-faired Vampire tourer was as unsuccessful as the V1000.*

HESKETH V1000 (1982)

Engine	Aircooled 8-valve DOHC 90-degree V-twin
Capacity	992cc (95 x 70mm)
Power	86bhp @ 6500rpm
Weight	230kg (506lb) dry
Top speed	120mph (193kph)

Despite an excessive weight of 230kg (506lb), the bike handled and braked very well. It was also reasonably fast and smooth, too, with a top speed of 120mph (192kph) and a pleasantly relaxed cruising feel at 90mph (145kph). But the Hesketh was plagued by problems from the start. In particular, the V-twin engine was noisy, unreliable, leaked oil and suffered from a horribly imprecise and noisy transmission. Production was delayed, faults were slow to be corrected, losses mounted, and Hesketh Motorcycles went bust in May 1982. The following year Lord Hesketh set up a new firm to build a fully-faired Vampire tourer, but most of the faults remained and few were produced.

OTHER MAKES

■ HILDERBRAND & WOLFMÜLLER

The world's first motorcycle to achieve series production was the 1488cc four-stroke built by brothers Heinrich and Wilhelm Hilderbrand, and Alois Wolfmüller. Starting in 1894, the Munich-based partnership produced about 1000 examples of the watercooled parallel twin, which developed 2.5bhp and had a top speed of 25mph (40kph). Normal braking was by a steel spoon that pressed on the front tyre, supplemented if necessary by a large rear bar that could be released to dig into the road. Motorcycling's rapid development at that time meant the twin soon became outdated, and production ended in 1897.

■ HOLDEN

Colonel Sir Henry Capel Holden was one of the great characters of motorcycling's pioneering years. He designed the world's first four-cylinder motorbike, a 1054cc watercooled, flat-four that was built in Coventry between 1899 and 1902. The four-stroke engine produced 3bhp, giving the bicycle-style Holden a top speed of about 25mph (40kph). Colonel Holden went on to design Brooklands, the world's first purpose-built race circuit, in 1906.

■ ABOVE *Hilderbrand & Wolfmüller's 1488cc twin, the world's first production bike, revved to just 240rpm.*

■ ABOVE *As well as designing the world's first four, Holden produced this stem-powered bike in 1898.*

■ BELOW LEFT *For a 305cc parallel twin, the CB77's smoothness and 95mph (152kph) top speed were impressive.*

■ BOTTOM *Honda's CB77 and the similar 247cc CB72 were fast, well-made and reliable machines.*

HONDA

■ HONDA CB77

The world's largest motorcycle manufacturer was founded in October 1946, when Soichiro Honda set up the Honda Technical Research Institute in a small wooden shed in Hamamatsu. Aiming to provide cheap transport for a population hit by defeat in the Second World War, Honda first bolted army-surplus engines to bicycles. A year later he built his own 50cc two-stroke engine, and in 1949 Honda and his 20 employees produced their first complete bike: the 98cc two-stroke Model D, or "Dream". Sales were good, progress was rapid and by 1953 Honda had developed the more sophisticated Model J Benly, whose

90cc four-stroke single-cylinder engine design owed much to Germany's NSU.

The first Hondas to make an impact in export markets were the 250cc CB72 and 305cc CB77 of the early 1960s. Sportier versions of the four-stroke

HONDA CB77 (1963)	
Engine	Aircooled 4-valve SOHC parallel twin
Capacity	305cc (60 x 54mm)
Power	28.5bhp @ 9000rpm
Weight	159kg (350lb) dry
Top speed	95mph (152kph)

■ LEFT *Soichiro Honda built and raced cars before starting his bike firm in 1946.*

■ BELOW LEFT *Honda's first complete bike was the 98cc Model D of 1949.*

■ BELOW *Clever advertising made the C100 a success.*

■ BELOW *Much of Honda's success in the 1960s was due to simple, reliable roadsters like this 125cc Benly.*

■ BOTTOM *Although it was neither fast nor successful, the CB450 heralded Honda's big-bike challenge.*

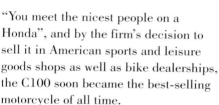

parallel twin C72 and C77 models, the Hondas differed from British twins by using a 180-degree crankshaft, with the pistons rising and falling alternately. Honda's conventional pressed-steel frame, as used on the popular 125cc CB92, was replaced by a tubular steel structure, holding telescopic forks, twin shocks and powerful front and rear drum brakes. With a top speed of 95mph (152kph) and good handling, the CB77– known as the Super Hawk in the States – was a match for many larger British bikes. It was also reliable and oil-tight, and did much for Honda's growing reputation – as did Mike Hailwood's 250cc world championship win in 1961.

Of all Honda's bikes over the years, the most important was arguably the humble C100 Super Cub that was launched in 1958. Combining scooter-style full enclosure with large wheels and an engine placed in the conventional motorbike position instead of under the seat, the Super Cub offered convenience, economy, reliability, cleanliness and even a certain style. Boosted by the famous advertising line,

"You meet the nicest people on a Honda", and by the firm's decision to sell it in American sports and leisure goods shops as well as bike dealerships, the C100 soon became the best-selling motorcycle of all time.

The bike that proved Honda was becoming a major force in motorcycling was the CB450 of 1965. Until the CB's arrival, the Japanese firm had been content to build small-capacity bikes. But with its DOHC, parallel twin engine

displacing 445cc and producing 43bhp, the bike, publicized as the "Black Bomber" or "Black Hawk", was a clear challenge to the long-dominant British twins. In fact, the CB450 turned out to be smooth, comfortable and softly tuned, with a top speed of around 100mph (160kph). Despite respectable handling it couldn't keep up with the British opposition, and was not a great success, but the CB450 signalled the start of Honda's attack on the big bike market.

HONDA

■ HONDA CB750

Modern day motorcycling arrived with
Honda's CB750, which offered a new
level of performance and sophistication
when it was released in 1969. The
CB750 was the first mass-produced
four-cylinder bike, a fact emphasized by
its impressive array of chromed
tailpipes, and it incorporated an electric
starter, disc front brake and five-speed
gearbox, all at a competitive price. The
CB750 dominated the early 1970s,
became known as the first superbike
and had a great influence on machines
that followed.

The CB750's major attraction was its
736cc, four-cylinder engine, which was

■ LEFT *The
CB750's chassis
was less impressive
than its engine, but
the Honda handled
reasonably well.*

■ OPPOSITE
*With its four-
cylinder engine
and front disc
brake, the CB750
was in a class of its
own in 1969.*

■ BELOW *As well
as being powerful,
the 736cc four was
smooth, reliable,
oil-tight and came
fitted with an
electric starter.*

HONDA CB750 (1969)

Engine	Aircooled 8-valve SOHC transverse four
Capacity	736cc (61 x 63mm)
Power	67bhp @ 8000rpm
Weight	218kg (480lb) dry
Top speed	125mph (201kph)

smooth, reliable and produced an impressive 67bhp. Although the four-pot motor was an SOHC, two-valves-per-cylinder design, its development could be traced to Honda's racing exploits with high-revving twin-camshaft fours in the 1960s. The CB750 was a big and rather heavy bike with high handlebars, intended as an all-rounder. But it still whistled to a top speed of about 125mph (201kph), handled reasonably well and sold in huge numbers worldwide.

In the 1970s, Honda did relatively little to uprate the CB750, which meant that it lost ground to newer rivals including Kawasaki's 900cc Z1, which arrived in 1973. The Honda actually lost some performance, as its engine was detuned to reduce emissions. When it was given a facelift to produce the CB750F in 1976, the new bike's flat handlebars, racier styling, vivid yellow paintwork and four-into-one exhaust system were let down by a top speed of below 120mph (193kph). The DOHC, 16-valve CB750K of 1979 had an unreliable engine and poor handling, all of which seemed a far cry from the

■ BOTTOM *Handsome, agile and capable of 100mph (160kph), the CB400 was dubbed the "poor boy's superbike".*

■ BELOW *Ten years after the first four, the 16-valve CB750K was unreliable and handled very poorly.*

■ MIDDLE *Dick Mann's 1970 Daytona-winning CB750 is seen here ridden by racer/journalist Alan Cathcart.*

brilliance of the original CB750.

Although the CB750's engine formed the basis for many specials and racebikes throughout the 1970s, the Honda made less of an impact on the track than in the showrooms. One racing highlight was veteran American star Dick Mann's victory at Daytona in 1970, which did much to boost the four's image. Some of the most successful straight-four racers were the RCB endurance bikes of the mid-1970s, which dominated long distance events in the hands of riders such as French duo Christian Léon and Jean-Claude Chemarin.

The CB750's success inspired Honda to produce several smaller fours in the 1970s, starting with the CB500 that arrived in 1971, and which was in some respects an even better bike. Its 498cc, 50bhp engine gave a top speed of just over 100mph (160kph), and the CB500's reduced size and weight gave improved handling and manoeuvrability. Honda produced another winner in 1975

with the CB400. Designed mainly for the European market with flat handlebars, sporty styling and a neat four-into-one exhaust system, the CB400 was much loved for its blend of lively performance and taut handling.

HONDA

■ BELOW *The GL1000's flat-four engine was smooth, powerful and refined.*

■ BELOW MIDDLE *The Gold Wing name means flying with a first-class ticket.*

■ BOTTOM *Even the original, unfaired GL1000 was a big, fat and heavy bike.*

■ HONDA GL1000 GOLD WING

Few bikes provoke such extreme reaction as Honda's Gold Wing. Much more than simply a motorcycle, the large and luxurious Wing has inspired, over two decades of production, a cult following that no other single model can match. Throughout most of that time it has offered unmatched levels of two-wheeled comfort and civility. Yet to many motorcyclists the Wing – always most popular in America, and built in Ohio since 1980 – is merely overweight, overpriced and overrated.

The original, unfaired GL1000 Gold Wing was the world's biggest and heaviest bike when it was introduced in 1975. Most notable for its unique, watercooled flat-four engine, the GL also

HONDA GL1000 GOLD WING (1975)	
Engine	Watercooled 8-valve SOHC transverse flat-four
Capacity	999cc (72 x 61.4mm)
Power	80bhp @ 7000rpm
Weight	260kg (571lb) dry
Top speed	122mph (196kph)

featured shaft drive, twin front disc brakes and an under-seat fuel tank. The Wing produced 80bhp, had a top speed of 120mph (193kph), and accelerated hard despite 260kg (571lb) of weight. Its smoothness and comfort rapidly won a large following, especially among middle-aged Americans.

■ LEFT *Its handling was inevitably ponderous, but the GL1000 was unbeatable for relaxed long-distance cruising.*

■ BELOW *Gold Wing riders have traditionally been older and more presentable than the average motorcyclist.*

Many riders fitted accessories to their Gold Wings, prompting Honda to introduce a fully-dressed model in 1980. Called the Interstate in America and the De Luxe in Europe, it combined an enlarged 1100cc engine with a fairing, hard luggage and crash-bars. The bike was a hit, as was the Aspencade – named after a big American rally – that was launched two years later with a sound system, passenger backrest and on-board compressor for the air suspension. Two-wheeled luxury touring

had finally come of age.

For many owners the Gold Wing provides an entry to club runs, rallies and other social events. The two main American Wing owners' clubs each have branches all over the States. Thousands of riders gather together at the annual Wing Ding, for entertainment, custom contests, technical seminars and accessory stands. Similar meetings are called Trefferns in Europe, where there are Gold Wing owners' groups in 15 different countries.

The size and sophistication of the Gold Wing reached new levels in 1988 with the introduction of the GL1500, powered by an all-new flat-six engine. Fully-enclosed, complete with big fairing, built-in luggage, cruise control and an electronic reverse gear to help when parking, the GL1500 was the heaviest and most complex Gold Wing yet. More to the point, it was also the fastest, smoothest and most responsive. For such a huge bike, it also handled and braked remarkably well.

■ ABOVE *Back in 1984, the Aspencade's lavish control console looked like something out of an aeroplane.*

■ RIGHT *For comfortable two-wheeled travel in your old age, nothing could beat the six-cylinder GL1500.*

HONDA

■ HONDA CBX1000

The stunning six-cylinder CBX1000 was released in 1978 to demonstrate Honda's ability to build powerful, race-developed motorbikes. At its heart was an aircooled, 1047cc motor containing twin camshafts and 24 valves. A descendant of Honda's multi-cylinder racers of the 1960s, the engine produced 105bhp to send the CBX accelerating smoothly to a top speed of 135mph (217kph), with a spine-tingling note from its exhaust. The huge powerplant, with six shiny exhaust downpipes jutting from its bank of angled-forward cylinders, was left uncovered by frame tubes for maximum visual effect.

Designed as an out-and-out sports-bike by former Grand Prix engineer Shoichiro Irimajiri, the CBX featured sleek, restrained styling and used its engine as a stressed member of the steel frame. Firm suspension helped give

■ **ABOVE** *The CBX1000's steel frame was designed to leave the huge six-cylinder engine on show.*

■ **BELOW** *Despite its high bars, the CBX was a sportsbike by 1978 standards, complete with lean, aggressive styling.*

good handling despite the bike's considerable weight, and no rival superbike could match the Honda's blend of speed, smoothness and six-cylinder soul. Unfortunately that was not enough to make the CBX successful, particularly in the important American market. In 1981 the bike was detuned slightly and fitted with a fairing and single-shock, air-assisted suspension. The CBX-B was a competent sports-tourer, and sold well. But it had none of the raw appeal of the original six.

Arguably Honda's most singleminded roadster of the early 1980s was the CB1100R, an exotic 1062cc straight-four produced in small numbers mainly

■ BELOW *In Ron Haslam's hands, the superb CB1100R made an almost invincible production racer.*

■ BOTTOM *The CX500 Turbo was a magnificent technical achievement, but not an outstanding motorcycle.*

■ BELOW *For such a big, heavy motorcycle, the firmly suspended CBX1000 handled exceptionally well.*

HONDA CBX1000 (1978)	
Engine	Aircooled 24-valve DOHC transverse six
Capacity	1047cc (64.5 x 53.4mm)
Power	105bhp @ 9000rpm
Weight	263kg (580lb) dry
Top speed	135mph (217kph)

to win prestigious long-distance production races such as the Castrol Six-Hour in Australia. A development of the CB900, the 1100R combined a tuned, 115bhp engine – the most powerful four-cylinder unit in motorcycling – with an uprated chassis and a racy fairing. Not only was the CB1100R almost unbeatable on the track, but it also made a superb road-going Superbike too.

Among Honda's many innovative bikes of the 1980s was the CX500 Turbo, which was launched in 1981. Less of a practical motorcycle than a corporate statement of engineering expertise, the Turbo used the world's smallest turbocharger to boost the output of the CX500 V-twin – one of the least suitable engine layouts for forced induction – from 50 to 82bhp. The CX chassis was comprehensively redesigned

and given a large fairing. Although heavy, the result was a fast, stable and comfortable sports tourer. But the CX Turbo's performance did not justify its complexity and high price and few riders were tempted to buy one. After first enlarging the engine to produce the CX650 Turbo – and seeing the other three Japanese firms follow with turbo-bikes of their own – Honda abandoned the turbocharging experiment.

HONDA

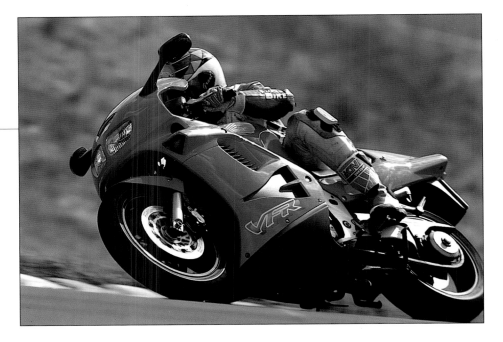

■ **HONDA VFR750F**

In the early 1980s Honda produced a series of roadsters powered by four-stroke V-four engines, and the water-cooled, 90-degree layout – which is well-suited to bike use due to its narrow width, smoothness and low centre of gravity – looked set to challenge the transverse four's domination. The VF750F of 1983, in particular, was a fast and fine-handling machine. A year later, Honda's range included five different VF models, from 400 to

HONDA VFR750F (1994)	
Engine	Watercooled 16-valve DOHC 90-degree V4
Capacity	748cc (70 x 48.6mm)
Power	100bhp @ 9500rpm
Weight	209kg (460lb) dry
Top speed	150mph (240kph)

1000cc. But the VF750 developed mechanical problems that proved hugely expensive and embarrassing to Honda, and the V-four revolution faded.

In the circumstances the VF's successor, the VFR750F, became one of the most important bikes Honda has ever produced when it was launched in 1986. Happily for Honda, it was also one of the best. Its V-four motor produced an improved 105bhp, was smooth and flexible and supremely

■ **BELOW** *The 1994-model VFR, like its predecessors, was arguably the best all-round motorcycle money could buy.*

■ OPPOSITE *The VFR750 has always handled well, despite being less sporty than most of its 750cc rivals.*

■ BELOW *For both performance and race-replica style, the magnificent RC30 was in a class of its own in 1988.*

■ BELOW *Handsome, swift and agile, the VF750 was a fine bike in 1983 – until its engine self-destructed.*

■ BOTTOM *The exotic NR750 had oval pistons and great looks, but it was far too heavy and expensive.*

reliable. The VFR's chassis, based around an all-new aluminium frame, gave good handling. And the Honda's efficient bodywork and high-quality finish contributed to a uniquely well-balanced bike.

The VFR was gradually refined over the next decade, becoming sportier without losing the sophistication and all-round ability that made it unique. Its biggest change came in 1990 with the VFR750FL model, which featured sleeker styling, a stronger, race-derived twin-spar frame and a single-sided swing-arm. Four years later came another revision, with new bodywork and numerous detail changes, but the essential character and appeal of the VFR remained intact.

Honda redefined the limits of sportsbike design with the release of the VFR750R – better known by its code-name RC30 – in 1988. Essentially a road-going copy of the factory RVF racebike that had dominated Formula One and endurance competition in the mid-1980s, the hand-built RC30 was powered by a tuned, 112bhp version of the standard VFR750 engine. The RC30's twin-headlamp fairing, compact layout, light weight and huge twin-beam aluminium frame – rumoured to have been cast in the same dies as the RVF's – made for a super-fast, fine-handling

bike that was virtually unbeatable on both road and track.

The most exotic V-four of all was the oval-pistoned NR750, descendant of the NR500 with which Honda had taken on the two-strokes in 1979, when returning to Grand Prix racing. In 1992, over ten years after abandoning that attempt,

came the gorgeously styled and hugely expensive NR roadster, whose 32-valve motor produced a class-leading 125bhp at 14,000rpm. Its chassis was superb, too, but despite much use of lightweight materials the NR weighed an excessive 222kg (489lb) and was no faster than 750s costing a fraction of the price.

HONDA

■ HONDA CBR600F

The world's most popular bike of recent years has been Honda's CBR600F, which has sold in huge numbers due largely to its ability to provide high performance at a reasonable price. Never intended as a state-of-the-art Superbike, the Honda has nevertheless maintained an excellent balance between power, handling and

HONDA CBR600F (1995)	
Engine	Watercooled 16-valve DOHC transverse four
Capacity	599cc (65 x 45.2mm)
Power	100bhp @ 12,000rpm
Weight	185kg (407lb) dry
Top speed	155mph (248kph)

practicality. The CBR's success – over 100,000 were produced in the eight years following its introduction in 1987 – has vindicated Honda's decision to move away from the V-four engine layout, back to the transverse four-cylinder format popularized by the CB750.

The original CBR600F, launched alongside a bigger CBR1000F model with similar fully-enclosed bodywork, was built to compete directly with

Kawasaki's GPZ600 four. Neither Honda model contained much innovative engineering. But the performance of the 600F, in particular – a top speed of 135mph (217kph) from its smooth, 85bhp engine, allied to excellent handling, reasonable comfort and impressive reliability – rapidly

■ **BELOW** *The 1995-model CBR600F maintained the traditional balance between high performance and reasonable price.*

■ RIGHT *Full bodywork has kept both engine and frame hidden since the CBR600F was introduced in 1987.*

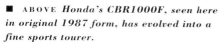
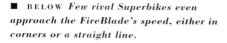

■ ABOVE *Honda's CBR1000F, seen here in original 1987 form, has evolved into a fine sports tourer.*

■ BELOW *Few rival Superbikes even approach the FireBlade's speed, either in corners or a straight line.*

established the Honda as the leader in motorcycling's most popular class.

In contrast to the way in which the CB750 was allowed to become decreasingly competitive throughout the 1970s, the CBR600F has repeatedly been refined to keep it at, or near, the head of the pack. An important revision came in 1991, with the introduction of a new 100bhp engine and bodywork restyled to good effect. In 1995 a revised induction system and numerous chassis modifications combined to give improved mid-range performance, top speed of over 150mph (240kph) and even sharper handling.

Like its 600cc sibling, the four-cylinder CBR1000F was designed to provide high performance at an acceptable price – and over the years it has proven to be a very capable sports tourer. The motorcycle's watercooled, 998cc engine has consistently produced over 130bhp with impressive mid-range torque, and its steel-framed chassis, although quite heavy, has given solid handling allied to long-distance comfort. Honda's CBR900RR heralded a new

level of Superbike performance when it was launched in 1992. The CBR, known as the "FireBlade" in most markets, relied on a conventional format of 893cc, 16-valve, straight-four engine and twin-beam aluminium frame. It gained its edge by housing a 123bhp motor – good for a top speed of 165mph (265kph) –

in a motorcycle which, at just 185kg (407lb), weighed less than most 600cc middleweights. The smooth, high-revving motor, racy steering geometry and taut suspension gave a blend of straight-line and cornering speed that no mass-produced machine could match and the FireBlade was another success.

HONDA

■ HONDA RC166 SIX

Soichiro Honda had raced cars with some success before turning to motorcycle production, and knew competition could bring both prestige and technical knowledge. Honda entered some Japanese meetings in the mid-1950s, and in 1959 made a first visit to the Isle of Man TT. The early 125cc racebikes were based on German NSU twins but proved uncompetitive against the dominant MV Agustas, but Honda learned fast. In 1961, aided by MV's retirement from the smaller classes, Honda's Tom Phillis and Mike Hailwood won the 125 and 250cc world championships.

In the next season Honda was even more successful. Swiss star Luigi Taveri won the first of his three 125cc titles, and Jim Redman of Rhodesia took both 250 and 350cc championships. Redman

HONDA RC166 (1967)	
Engine	Aircooled 24-valve DOHC transverse six
Capacity	247cc (39 x 34.5mm)
Power	60bhp @ 18,000rpm
Weight	120kg (264lb) dry
Top speed	153mph (245kph)

went on to win a total of six titles on Honda's fours. But it was the six-cylinder machine, raced to 250 and 350cc championships by Mike Hailwood in both 1966 and 1967 that was Honda's finest four-stroke racebike.

The six was designed to resist Yamaha's increasingly strong two-stroke challenge by allowing very high revs. In 250cc form its compact engine, containing 24 tiny valves, emitted an

unforgettable exhaust howl and produced 60bhp at a heady 18,000rpm. The six was debuted prematurely by Redman in late 1964, and improved for both reliability and handling during the following season. In 1966 Hailwood won ten out of 12 Grands Prix on the 250cc RC166, and also took the 350 title on a bored-out 297cc version. Hailwood retained both championships on the six before Honda quit Grand Prix racing in 1968.

Despite success in the smaller classes, Honda could not win the 500cc championship in the 1960s. Mike Hailwood came agonizingly close on a four-cylinder 500 whose handling and reliability did not match its power. In 1966 a breakdown in the final round at Monza cost Hailwood the title, which Giacomo Agostini won for MV Agusta by six points. In the next season's

■ LEFT *Even Freddie Spencer could not make the NR500 competitive against the 500cc Grand Prix two-strokes.*

■ BELOW *Swiss star Luigi Taveri, here in action on a 250, won three 125cc titles for Honda in the 1960s.*

■ ABOVE *Mike Hailwood, riding this 250cc six, won the Junior TT on his way to the world title in 1967.*

■ BELOW *The oval-pistoned, monocoque-framed NR500 proved uncompetitive when it was first raced in 1979.*

penultimate race, Hailwood broke the lap record and led by half a lap — before his Honda stuck in top gear. Mike won the final race but Ago took the title — not on points or even race wins, which were equal, but on his greater number of second places.

When Honda returned to Grands Prix to take on the two-strokes in 1979, company policy dictated using a four-stroke. Thus was born the NR500: a watercooled V-four whose oval pistons — in fact shaped like running tracks, with two plugs, two conrods and eight valves

to each cylinder — were intended to give the next best thing to a V-eight now that engines had been limited to four cylinders. The radical bike also used a monocoque aluminium frame and 16-inch wheels. Its engine revved to 20,000rpm, but Honda had attempted too much and the NR was slow and unreliable. Simplifying the chassis and redesigning the engine brought improvements by 1981, but Honda abandoned the NR that year without having come close to a Grand Prix win let alone the championship.

■ ABOVE *Honda's four Japanese riders all managed respectable placings at the firm's first Isle of Man TT in 1959.*

HONDA

■ HONDA NSR500

After giving up with the four-stroke NR500, Honda finally won a first 500cc world championship with a two-stroke that was almost as unconventional. Freddie Spencer beat the four-cylinder Suzukis and Yamahas in 1983 with the NS500 – a reed-valve triple whose 125bhp output was 10bhp down on the opposition's, but which had an advantage in manoeuvrability. Fast Freddie's second championship, though, was won in 1985 on the bike that would be Honda's weapon for the next decade: the NSR500 V-four.

Since then, the NSR has generally been the most powerful of the factory 500s, partly due to its unique single-crankshaft design which reduces friction but increases width. After unsuccessful experiments with the fuel tank under the engine in 1984, the NSR has used a conventional chassis layout, with an aluminium twin-beam frame. In Honda tradition, the V-four's handling has often failed to match its horsepower – notably in 1989, when Eddie Lawson tamed a wayward NSR to win the title.

HONDA NSR500 (1994)	
Engine	Watercooled 112-degree V-four crankcase reed-valve two-stroke
Capacity	499cc (54 x 54.5mm)
Power	187bhp @ 12,000rpm
Weight	130kg (286lb) dry
Top speed	197mph (315kph)

■ OPPOSITE BOTTOM *The NSR500's basic layout has changed little since 1986.*

■ RIGHT *By 1994, Doohan's NSR had the handling to match its traditional horsepower advantage.*

■ BELOW *Eddie Lawson tamed the NSR and won the title in 1989.*

Recent years have seen the gradual evolution of the NSR, the biggest change coming in 1992 with the introduction of the "big bang" engine. Timing its four cylinders to fire in quick succession made the awesome 185bhp NSR easier to ride, a trick quickly copied by rival teams. Japanese ace Shinichi Itoh was

the first Grand Prix rider to be timed at 200mph (320kph), on an NSR500 at Germany's Hockenheim in 1993. In the following season Australian Mick Doohan overcame the effects of a serious leg injury, sustained two years earlier, to dominate the championship on the NSR.

Honda found more success after

effectively cutting the 500cc V-four motor in half to produce the NSR250 V-twin. Championship wins included Sito Pons' double in 1988 and 1989, and Luca Cadalora's in 1991 and 1992. Perhaps the finest achievement was by Freddie Spencer, who won both 500 and 250cc titles on NSRs in 1985.

OTHER MAKES

■ HOREX

A leading German make for many years, Horex was founded in 1923 and built many sophisticated road and race bikes in the following years. The firm's most successful model was the Regina, a 350cc OHV single, produced from the late 1940s. The 400cc Imperator, a stylish and technically advanced SOHC parallel twin introduced in 1951, featured telescopic or leading-link forks, twin-shock rear suspension and an enclosed drive chain.

Horex hit problems in the mid-1950s, partly due to the disastrous 250cc Rebell scooter, and the factory closed in 1958. In the 1970s, Friedel Münch and fellow enthusiast Fritz Roth attempted to revive the name with a 1400cc turbocharged

■ FAR LEFT *Former racer Sammy Miller on Husqvarna's 1930's V-twin in a TT classic parade.*

four, based on Münch's Mammut, and a series of small-capacity two-strokes. More recently the Horex name was used on a Honda 650cc single-cylinder engined sportster called the Osca, which was built and sold in Japan.

■ HRD

Howard Raymond Davies was a racer and former First World War air ace who in 1924 set up a firm to build bikes under his own name. The following year Davies won the Senior TT on an HRD, and Freddie Dixon scored a Junior win two years later. But roadster sales were disappointing, and the firm went into liquidation shortly afterwards. The HRD

name was later bought by Philip Vincent, to add credibility to his own machines.

■ HUSQVARNA

Best known in recent years for motocross and enduro bikes, Swedish firm Husqvarna was an armaments firm that diversified into motorcycle production in 1903. In the 1930s the firm built innovative 350 and 500cc V-twins that were raced successfully by riders including Stanley Woods. Husqvarna continued to build successful off-road competition machines after roadster production was ended in the early 1960s. In 1986 the firm became part of the Cagiva Group, and Husqvarna production was moved to Italy.

■ ABOVE *French rider Vuillemin corners his twin-cylinder Horex in a classic event.*

■ ABOVE *Husqvarna rider Jan Carlsson in the 1983 International Six Days Enduro.*

INDIAN

INDIAN POWERPLUS

Indian was founded in 1901 by George Hendee and Oscar Hedstrom, two former bicycle racers, who teamed up to produce a 1.75bhp single in Hendee's home town of Springfield. The bike was successful, and sales increased dramatically during the next decade. In 1904, the so-called diamond framed Indian single, whose engine was built by the Aurora firm in Illinois, was made available in the deep red colour that would become Indian's trademark. By now production was up to over 500 bikes annually, and would rise to a best-ever 32,000 in 1913.

In 1907, Indian built its first V-twin, and in following years made a strong showing in racing and record-breaking. One of the firm's most famous riders was Erwin "Cannonball" Baker, who set many long-distance records. In 1914, he rode an Indian across America, from San Diego to New York, in a record 11 days,

■ ABOVE *The power and refinement of Indian's new side-valve engine earned it the name Powerplus.*

INDIAN POWERPLUS (1918)	
Engine	Aircooled 4-valve 42-degree V-twin
Capacity	998cc (79.4 x 100.8mm)
Power	18bhp
Weight	186kg (410lb) wet
Top speed	60mph (96kph)

12 hours and ten minutes. Baker's mount in subsequent years was the Powerplus, a side-valve V-twin that was introduced in 1916. Its 61ci (1000cc), 42-degree V-twin engine was more powerful and quieter than previous designs, giving a top speed of 60mph (96kph). The Powerplus was highly successful, both as a roadster and as the basis for racing bikes. It remained in production with few changes until 1924.

■ BELOW *The 1918-model Powerplus had only minor differences from the machine introduced two years earlier.*

■ LEFT *In 1904 Indian's single offered a 30mph (48kph) top speed, excellent build quality and optional red finish.*

■ BELOW *This 1913-model Indian V-twin has the earlier F-head (or inlet-over-exhaust) valve layout.*

Competition success played a big part in Indian's rapid growth, and spurred technical innovation. One of the American firm's best early results came in the Isle of Man TT in 1911, when Indian riders Godfrey, Franklin and Moorehouse finished first, second and third. Indian star Jake De Rosier set several speed records both in America and at Brooklands in England, and won an estimated 900 races, on dirt-tracks and boards. He left Indian for Excelsior and died in 1913, aged 33, of injuries sustained in a board-race crash with Charles "Fearless" Balke, who later became Indian's top rider. Work at the Indian factory was stopped while De Rosier's funeral procession passed.

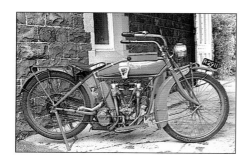

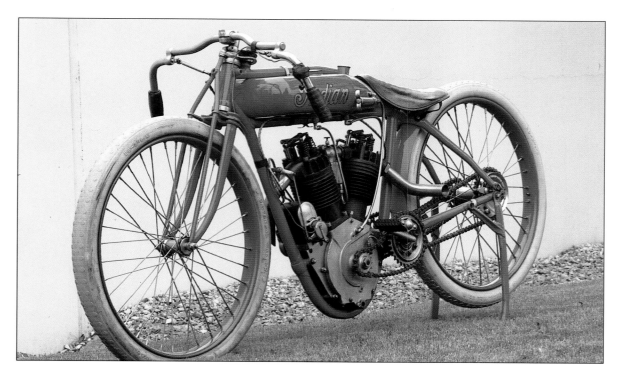

■ RIGHT *Indian's powerful eight-valve racers were very successful on the American tracks in 1916.*

INDIAN

■ INDIAN CHIEF

The Scout and Chief V-twins, introduced
in the early 1920s when Indian could
claim to be the world's largest motorcycle manufacturer, became the Springfield firm's most successful models.
Designed by Charles B Franklin, the
middleweight Scout and larger Chief
shared a 42-degree V-twin engine

INDIAN CHIEF (1947)	
Engine	Aircooled 4-valve sidevalve 42-degree V-twin
Capacity	1200cc (82.5 x 113mm)
Power	40bhp @ 4000rpm
Weight	245kg (539lb) dry
Top speed	85mph (136kph)

■ ABOVE *The 1200cc Big Chief was
introduced in 1923, and immediately
outsold Indian's smaller Scout model.*

■ RIGHT *Almost all Indian V-twin engines,
including this 74ci (1200cc) unit, had a
42-degree cylinder angle.*

■ BELOW *This 1947-model Chief, with
headdress mascot on its skirted front
fender, epitomizes the Indian look.*

■ ABOVE FAR
RIGHT *Scouts were
raced successfully
for many years,
and still compete
in classic events.*

■ RIGHT *The
500cc (30.5ci)
Scout Pony, seen
here in 1939 form,
was aimed at the
entry-level rider.*

■ BELOW RIGHT
*The Model 741
Military Scout
served with
distinction in the
Second World War.*

layout. Both models gained a reputation
for strength and reliability, which led to
the old Indian saying: "You can't wear
out an Indian Scout, or its brother the
Indian Chief. They're built like rocks to
take hard knocks; it's the Harleys that
cause the grief."

The first 1922 model Chief had a
1000cc (61ci) engine based on that of
the Powerplus; a year later the engine
was enlarged to 1200cc (73ci). Numerous improvements were made over the
years, including adoption of a front
brake in 1928. After Indian had been
bought by E Paul DuPont in 1930, the
new owner's paint industry connections
resulted in no fewer than 24 colour
options being offered in 1934. Models of
that era featured Indian's famous headdress logo on the gas tank. Indian's huge
Springfield factory was known as the
Wigwam, and native American imagery
was much used in advertising.

In 1940 all models were fitted with
the large skirted fenders that became an

Indian trademark, and the Chief gained
a new sprung frame that was superior to
rival Harley's unsprung rear end. The
1940s Chiefs were handsome and
comfortable machines, capable of
85mph (136kph) in standard form and
over 100mph (160kph) when tuned,
although their increased weight

hampered acceleration. In 1950, the
V-twin engine was enlarged to 1300cc
(80ci) and telescopic forks were adopted.
But Indian's financial problems meant
that few bikes were built, and production
of the Chief ended in 1953.

The Scout, initially with a 596cc
(37ci) engine that was bored-out to
745cc (45ci) in 1927, rivalled the Chief
as Indian's most important model. The
most famous version was the 101 Scout
of 1928, which featured improved
handling from a new, lower frame. In
1932, cost-cutting led to the Scout using
the heavier Chief frame, which was less
successful. Many Scouts were used in
the Second World War, but the model
was dropped when civilian production
restarted in 1946. In 1948, Indian built
just 50 units of the Daytona Sports
Scout, one of which took Floyd Emde to
victory in that year's Daytona 200-mile
(322-kilometre) race. Smaller, 500cc
(30.5ci) Scouts were also built between
1932 and 1941, known as the Scout
Pony, Junior Scout and Thirty-Fifty.

INDIAN

■ INDIAN FOUR

The Indian Four is one of the most
famous American motorcycles, though it
was by no means one of the most
successful. Indian bought the Ace firm,
makers of a 1265cc in-line four, in
1927, and the first Indian Four was
simply an Ace with smaller wheels and
Indian badges. In subsequent years
Indian improved the design with a front
brake, new forks and a new frame,
before introducing the Model 436 Four
in 1936. Known as the "upside down"
Four because its valvegear was reversed
to put intake valves at the side of the
engine and exhausts above, the Model
436 was unreliable and short-lived.

Indian returned to the original engine
layout and added other improvements in
1938. An early 1940s Four produced
40bhp, was very smooth and had a top
speed of 90mph (144kph). But the price
was high, rear cylinder overheating
remained a problem, and the Four
tied up money that Indian might
have better spent on developing
an overhead-valve V-twin rival to
Harley's 61E. Production of the
Four eventually ended in 1943.

INDIAN FOUR (1942)	
Engine	Aircooled 8-valve sidevalve longitudinal four
Capacity	1265cc (69.9 x 82.5mm)
Power	40bhp @ 5000rpm
Weight	255kg (561lb) dry
Top speed	90mph (144kph)

■ OPPOSITE *Factory windshield was a
popular accessory for both the Four and
Chief in the 1940s.*

■ BELOW LEFT *The in-line four motor was
handsome and smooth, but had a tendency
to overheat.*

■ BELOW *This well-used Four, built in
1941, has been updated with later forks
and foot gearchange.*

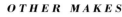

Indian's decision to build middleweight vertical twins in the late 1940s also contributed to its demise. The verticals were unreliable and unpopular, and production at Springfield ceased in 1953. Indian continued in business by importing British machines, notably the Royal Enfields which were sold as Indians. The firms split in 1960, after which Indian sold Matchless bikes for a few years before ceasing trading.

The Indian name was also used to sell small Italian-made bikes in the late 1960s and 1970s. More recently, two rival American firms claimed rights to the name and announced plans to build modern V-twins. Those came to nothing, but in 1994 the Indian name was acquired by Australian entrepreneur Maurits Hayim-Langridge. He appointed New Zealander engineer John Britten as a consultant, and announced development of a range of V-twin roadsters to be produced in America by 1998.

■ JAMES

Starting out as a bicycle firm in the last century, Birmingham-based James built four-stroke singles and large-capacity V-twins in the 1930s. In the 1960s, production was based on two-strokes, notably the 250cc Commodore single and its twin-cylinder successor the Superswift. The firm also built a number of trials bikes, and ran a factory team for many years. James became part of AMC in 1963, and ceased production when the group collapsed three years later.

■ ABOVE *The Superswift, introduced in 1962 and powered by a 250cc Villiers two-stroke engine, was one of the last and best James roadsters.*

■ JAWA

Jawa was founded in Czechoslovakia in 1929 and built numerous road and race bikes before the Second World War. Production continued after 1945, in conjunction with CZ, most notably with simple two-stroke roadsters. Jawa also built many highly successful speedway bikes, after taking over the Eso factory in 1962.

■ ABOVE *This 350cc two-stroke from the mid-1960s is a typical Jawa – competent, cheap and strangely styled.*

■ KAHENA

Powered by a 1600cc, flat-four VW car engine producing 50bhp, the Brazilian Kahena was a huge, fully-faired tourer built for the growing South American market of the early 1990s.

KAWASAKI

■ BELOW *The H1's fierce power-band and flex-prone frame made fast cornering an exciting business.*

■ **KAWASAKI 500cc H1**

The motorcycle division forms a relatively small part of Kawasaki Heavy Industries, a vast firm that produces trains, boats and planes. Kawasaki's involvement with bikes began in the 1950s, when the aircraft division was looking for civilian work, and was stepped up when the industrial giant wanted to increase awareness of its name. In 1960 Kawasaki built its first complete bike, a 125cc two-stroke, and took over Meguro, Japan's oldest motorcycle manufacturer, which had been making copies of British bikes including the BSA A7 parallel twin.

Kawasaki moved into the big bike market in 1966 with the W1, a 650cc

■ LEFT *High bars and sleek styling give this American-market H1-B a deceptively docile look.*

■ OPPOSITE LEFT *The H1's two-stroke triple engine was compact, powerful and very thirsty.*

■ OPPOSITE MIDDLE *The production of triples formed just a tiny part of Kawasaki Heavy Industries' work.*

■ OPPOSITE RIGHT *Kawasaki's first big bikes were 650cc parallel twins such as this W1 SS, produced in 1968.*

■ RIGHT *The fearsome 748cc H2 triple had similar looks to the H1, plus even more power, noise and speed.*

twin, which again owed much to BSA. It sold well in Japan, but flopped against the quicker British bikes on the American market. Kawasaki's response came with lighter, smaller-capacity two-strokes, the 250cc A1 Samurai and similar 350cc A7 Avenger, which were exported more successfully. In 1969 Kawasaki released the 500cc H1, the first of the triples that would earn the firm a well-deserved reputation for outrageous high performance.

With a peak output of 60bhp at 7500rpm from its aircooled, two-stroke engine, and a weight of just 174kg (383lb), the H1 – also known as the Mach III – had an unmatched power-to-weight ratio. It looked good, scorched to

KAWASAKI 500cc H1 (1969)	
Engine	Aircooled two-stroke transverse triple
Capacity	499cc (60 x 58.8mm)
Power	60bhp @ 7500rpm
Weight	174kg (383lb)
Top speed	120mph (192km/h)

a top speed of 120mph (192kph), and had handling that made life just a little exciting. The combination of an insubstantial frame, rearwards weight distribution and an abrupt power step at 6000rpm were responsible for introducing the words "wheelie" and "tankslapper" to motorcyclists' vocabularies. Poor fuel economy completed the triple's antisocial image, but owners could live with that.

Kawasaki also built two smaller triples, the 250cc S1 and 350cc S2, and in 1972 enlarged the three-cylinder engine to 748cc to produce the H2, or Mach IV. Its 74bhp motor gave blistering acceleration and a top speed of 125mph (201kph). Handling was slightly better than the H1's, but the H2 was a wild ride and remained so until emissions regulations finally killed off the big two-strokes in the mid-1970s.

KAWASAKI

■ KAWASAKI Z1

Kawasaki's Z1 was released in 1973 and dominated superbiking for much of the decade with its combination of powerful, unburstable motor, handsome looks and competitive price. The Z1's four-cylinder, 903cc engine featured twin camshafts, unlike Honda's SOHC CB750-four, and produced a maximum of 82bhp to give the Kawasaki a top speed of 130mph (208kph). Its straight-line performance outclassed that of the

Honda, whose launch in late 1968 had caused Kawasaki's engineers to delay and revise their four-cylinder project, code-named "New York Steak", which had originally been designed as a 750.

The Z1's chassis did not come close to matching the brilliance of its engine, but the Kawasaki handled reasonably well and was quite comfortable despite high handlebars. Its styling was superb, with a rounded tank, rear ducktail and four shiny silencers. Best of all, the Z1 was far cheaper than rival European

KAWASAKI Z1 (1973)	
Engine	Aircooled 8-valve DOHC transverse four
Capacity	903cc (66 x 66mm)
Power	82bhp @ 8500rpm
Weight	230kg (506lb) dry
Top speed	130mph (208kph)

■ ABOVE *The twin-cam Z1 motor was superbly strong and powerful.*

■ BELOW *Strong styling matched the Z1's awesome performance.*

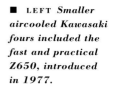

■ LEFT *Smaller aircooled Kawasaki fours included the fast and practical Z650, introduced in 1977.*

■ LEFT *Although it was prone to wobbles at high speeds, the Z1 went round slower corners quite well.*

■ BELOW *The Z1-R, with a tuned motor and uprated handling, faced fierce competition in 1978.*

superbikes. It became massively popular, acquired the nickname the "King" and earned Kawasaki a lasting reputation for horsepower and reliability.

Improvements in subsequent years included the addition of a second front disc brake in 1976, when the bike was renamed the Z900. A year later its engine was enlarged to 1015cc to produce the Z1000. In 1978 Kawasaki produced the Z1-R café racer, which featured a tuned, 90bhp engine, strengthened frame and angular styling incorporating a handlebar fairing. It was the best big "Zed" yet but faced renewed opposition from Suzuki's GS1000 and Honda's CBX1000.

The Z1's speed and reliability made it a natural for many forms of racing. In standard form the Kawasaki won Australia's prestigious Castrol Six-Hour race in 1973. In Europe the four-cylinder motor was used to power many endurance racers, notably the factory-

backed bikes on which Frenchmen Georges Godier and Alain Genoud won several 24-hour events in the 1970s.

In the late 1970s and early 1980s Kawasaki also built several smaller fours whose layout followed the Z1's pattern. Among the best was the Z650, released in 1977, which provided

typically smooth, reliable 110mph (177kph) performance with manoeuvrability and a competitive price. But although Kawasaki had billed the bike as being the 650 that would outperform any 750, they had not reckoned on Suzuki's faster GS750, which was launched at the same time.

■ ABOVE *French ace Jean-Claude Chemarin led Kawasaki's endurance team to success in the early 1980s.*

■ ABOVE *New Zealander Graeme Crosby won races and fans on a high-barred Moriwaki Kawasaki.*

KAWASAKI

■ KAWASAKI Z1300

The huge six-cylinder Kawasaki Z1300 was in some ways the ultimate late 1970s Superbike, the inevitable end product of the Japanese manufacturers' race towards bigger, heavier and more complex machines. Its watercooled, 1286cc engine produced a highest-yet 120bhp, and the slab-sided Z1300 weighed over 300kg (661lb) with fuel. Yet, ironically, its large radiator meant the Kawasaki had little of the visual impact of Honda's six-cylinder CBX1000, and the Z1300's performance was less startling than its specification suggested.

Despite all its weight, the Z1300 handled reasonably well, thanks to a

■ RIGHT *With an output of 100bhp, Kawasaki's six was motorcycling's most powerful engine in 1979.*

■ BELOW *The Z1300's styling and sheer bulk made the six-cylinder engine look almost ordinary.*

■ LEFT *Cornering was never going to be the Z1300's strength, but for such a big bike it handled well.*

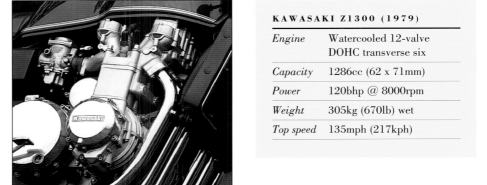

KAWASAKI Z1300 (1979)	
Engine	Watercooled 12-valve DOHC transverse six
Capacity	1286cc (62 x 71mm)
Power	120bhp @ 8000rpm
Weight	305kg (670lb) wet
Top speed	135mph (217kph)

strong frame and good suspension, and remained stable all the way to its impressive 135mph (217kph) top speed. But the Kawasaki's exposed, upright riding position limited its high-speed cruising ability, and the six-cylinder motor had a rather busy feel. Despite its unmatched power and bulk the Z1300 offered nothing that several smaller, simpler and cheaper bikes could not provide. The expensive six marked the end of Japan's apparent belief that bigger was better.

One of the outstanding bikes of the 1980s was Kawasaki's GPZ900R, the firm's first watercooled four, which was released in 1984. The GPZ's 908cc,

16-valve engine produced 113bhp at 9500rpm, and was impressively strong in best four-cylinder Kawasaki tradition. It pulled the GPZ smoothly to a top speed of over 150mph (241kph), aided by the excellent aerodynamics of the sharply styled full fairing.

A compact, light chassis provided handling to match, making the "Ninja", as the bike was known in America, hard to beat both on the road and in production racing. Better still, the GPZ matched its speed with genuine long-distance comfort. It immediately became popular and was still being sold almost ten years later having outlasted its supposed successor, the GPZ1000RX.

KAWASAKI

■ KAWASAKI ZZ-R1100

In the ultra-competitive motorcycle world of the 1990s, it was some achievement for Kawasaki to produce a Superbike whose awesome 145bhp powerplant and 175mph (280kph) top speed simply blew away all opposition. Not only did the ZZ-R1100 make just such an impact when it was launched in 1990, but the watercooled, 1052cc

■ OPPOSITE ABOVE *Handling was good, despite the 22-R1100's size and weight.*

■ OPPOSITE BELOW *The 1993-model ZZ-R1100 had a revised chassis, but its engine remained the star attraction.*

■ RIGHT *With a potent 600cc engine and twin-spar alloy frame, the 1995-model ZX-6R was a fast and agile sportster.*

KAWASAKI ZZ-R1100 (1990)

Engine	Watercooled 16-valve DOHC transverse four
Capacity	1052cc (76 x 58mm)
Power	145bhp @ 9500rpm
Weight	228kg (502lb) dry
Top speed	175mph (280kph)

■ ABOVE *Scott Russell won the 1993 World Superbike title and three Daytonas.*

■ ABOVE *High performance and bold styling made the original ZXR750 a big hit.*

Kawasaki was still the world's fastest production streetbike five years later.

Its straight-line performance came from a 16-valve engine developed from that of the 1988 model ZX-10. Big valves and lightened pistons increased power but the real boost came from the ZZ-R's ram-air system, based on Formula One car-race technology, which ducted cool air from a slot in the fairing nose to a pressurized airbox. The faster the Kawasaki went, the deeper it breathed – with thrilling result.

The ZZ-R was also a smooth and refined motorcycle that handled well thanks to a highly rigid aluminium frame and very good suspension. Heavy at 228kg (502lb), and with a fairly upright riding position, the Kawasaki made a practical and genuinely comfortable sports tourer, and on a straight road, it showed a clean pair of silencers to any other standard motorcycle.

Kawasaki's entrant in the 750cc sportsbike class in recent years has been the ZXR750. Conventional in layout – holding a watercooled, 16-valve engine in a twin-beam aluminium frame – the ZXR has consistently provided aggressive looks and 150mph (241kph) performance to match. It has also formed the basis of Kawasaki's World Superbike challenge, which reached a peak with Scott Russell's championship win in 1993.

Having popularized the 600cc class with the GPZ600 in 1985, Kawasaki spent the following years failing to match the sales success of Honda's CBR600F. The ZZ-R600, launched in 1990, provided big bike speed but lacked agility. The 1995 model ZX-6R – featuring ram-air induction and a new aluminium beam frame and sportier geometry – was outstanding, combining speed with superb handling.

K A W A S A K I

■ KAWASAKI KR750

Kawasaki's first international racing success came in the 125cc class, when Dave Simmonds won the world championship in 1969 on a factory-backed twin. The firm's fearsome two-stroke triple roadsters were naturals for racing, and a competition version of the 500cc H1, the H1R, took New Zealander Ginger Malloy to second

KAWASAKI KR750 (1975)	
Engine	Watercooled two-stroke transverse triple
Capacity	747cc (68 x 68mm)
Power	120bhp @ 9500rpm
Weight	140kg (308lb) dry
Top speed	180mph (288kph)

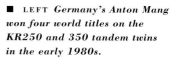

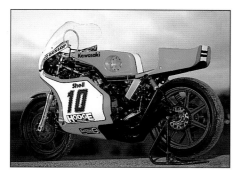

■ LEFT *Germany's Anton Mang won four world titles on the KR250 and 350 tandem twins in the early 1980s.*

■ LEFT *Even the fast and stylish Kork Ballington could not make the KR500 square-four a Grand Prix winner.*

place in the 500cc world championship in 1970. The later 750cc H2R triples became known as "Green Meanies" after their lime-green colours and dubious handling. American star Gary Nixon and Canadian Yvon Duhamel tamed the triple to take several big wins.

In 1975 Kawasaki replaced the roadster-based H2R with a purpose-built racer, the KR750. This was an all-new triple whose watercooled engine produced a considerably increased 120bhp, with a pronounced power step at 6000rpm that made the bike difficult to ride. Despite early reliability problems Mick Grant and Gregg Hansford were very successful on the KR in 1975, in Britain and Australia respectively. In that season Grant was timed at over 180mph (283kph) as he set a new Isle of Man TT lap record of 109.82mph (176.73kph). The following year privateer Gary Nixon led the F750 world championship on a KR, but controversially finished second after one of the rounds he had won was discounted.

Kawasaki's most successful racebikes were the KR250 and KR350, water-cooled two-stroke tandem twins that dominated Grand Prix racing between

1978 and 1982, winning no fewer than eight world championships and 73 Grands Prix. The KR was introduced in 250cc form in 1975, but initially proved unreliable. Its engine was then re-designed with a 360-degree crankshaft, where pistons rose together, instead of the original 180-degree layout. The new KRs were reliable and very fast, producing a maximum of 75bhp at 11,800rpm in 350cc form. They also handled well thanks to a chassis that included a rigid frame of chrome-moly-bdenum steel tubes, and Kawasaki's Uni-Trak rising-rate rear suspension.

South African Kork Ballington began the KR's domination, winning both 250 and 350cc titles in 1978 and 1979. Germany's Anton Mang added two further titles on each bike, including a double in 1981, and the KR350 retired as undefeated champion when the larger class was dropped after the 1982 season. By then Kawasaki had moved up to 500cc Grand Prix racing with the four-cylinder KR500, which featured an innovative aluminium monocoque chassis. Despite persevering for several seasons, however, even Ballington could not make it competitive.

OTHER MAKES

■ KOBAS

Talented engineer Antonio Cobas created many innovative racebikes in the late 1970s and early 1980s. The Spaniard's Rotax-engined 250cc racer of 1983 pioneered the use of a twin-beam aluminium frame with rising-rate rear suspension, adopted in recent years as the standard format for both racing and sports road machines.

■ KRAUSER

Some of the most exotic café racers of the 1980s were the Krausers that combined a tuned, flat-twin BMW engine with an intricate tubular steel spaceframe. Mike Krauser's German firm, best known for bike luggage, also built a BMW-powered road-going sidecar, the Domani, whose chassis was based on that of a Grand Prix racing "worm" outfit. Krauser's racing exploits have ranged from long-standing sidecar involvement to the championship-winning 80cc Grand Prix racers of the mid-1980s.

■ KREIDLER

German moped specialist Kreidler made its name with a string of 50cc world championships in the 1970s, in a team run by Dutch importer Henk Van Veen. But the firm hit financial problems and ceased production in the early 1980s.

■ KTM

Austrian firm KTM established a strong reputation, particularly in motocross and enduro racing, after beginning production in 1953. Early roadsters were mainly small-capacity two-strokes, powered by engines from fellow Austrian firm Rotax. KTM went bankrupt in 1991, victim of losses in its bicycle and radiator manufacturing operation, but recommenced motorcycle production shortly afterwards under new ownership. Recent production has concentrated on large-capacity four-stroke singles, notably enduro bikes and the Duke, a classy 620cc roadster launched in 1993.

■ LAMBRETTA

Scooter specialist Lambretta was established after the Second World War

■ LEFT *Thanks to excellent suspension and a rigid steel spaceframe, Krauser's BMW-powered MKM handled superbly.*

■ LEFT *KTM's Duke roadster showed signs of the firm's off-road traditions in its aggressive supermoto styling.*

■ LEFT *The Duke was far from practical, but its light weight and agile handling made it fun to ride.*

and stylish, fully-enclosed machines such as the LD150 were hugely popular in the 1950s and in the UK in the 1960s when they were a symbol of the Mods. Italian production was halted in the 1970s, but Lambrettas continued to be built under licence in Spain and India.

■ BELOW *Lanying gave this 745cc flat-twin unit an electric starter, but its output remained a modest 34bhp.*

■ BOTTOM *Apart from additions such as its fairing and pillion backrest, the CJ750 was essentially a 1950s' BMW.*

LANYING

■ LANYING CJ750F

China had become the world's largest motorcycle manufacturing nation by the mid-1990s, its annual output of well over three million units exceeding even that of Japan.

In 1994 the Lanying factory in Hunan province employed 13,000 workers and produced 10,000 bikes per month, the majority of them simple, small-capacity machines destined for use by China's vast population. Typical of the larger bikes was the Chang Jiang or CJ750F, a flat-twin four-stroke whose design – like that of Ural and Dnepr twins from the former Soviet Union – was based on BMWs from the 1950s.

Lanying had made some attempts to modernize the Chang Jiang by fitting an

LANYING CJ750F (1994)	
Engine	Aircooled 4-valve OHV pushrod flat-twin
Capacity	745cc (78 x 78mm)
Power	34bhp @ 5000rpm
Weight	230kg (506lb) dry
Top speed	70mph (112kph)

angular twin-headlamp fairing and an electric starter. But essentially the twin remained little changed. Its shaft-drive engine produced just 34bhp, good for only 70mph (112kph), its drum brakes were feeble and handling was limited. (In China most CJs were used with a sidecar, by police and medical services.)

By modern standards the Lanying was a crude device, and initial attempts to export it to Europe were unsuccessful. But the fast-growing Chinese motorcycle industry was increasingly setting its sights on lucrative export markets, and looked set to become an important force in the future.

LAVERDA

■ LAVERDA JOTA 1000

Motorcycles were just a sideline for a large agricultural machinery firm from north-eastern Italy when Francesco Laverda built his first bikes — tiny 75cc four-strokes — in the late 1940s. Small-capacity Laverdas were raced successfully in long-distance events such, as the Milano-Taranto and Giro d'Italia, in the 1950s, but the firm's later concentration on humble, economical bikes coincided with the rise of cheap cars, such as the Fiat 500, and nearly proved disastrous.

Laverda changed tack just in time in the late 1960s, releasing a 650cc four-stroke parallel twin that was quickly enlarged to produce the successful 750GT tourer and 750S sportster. Handsome, rugged and quick, especially the

■ ABOVE *The Jota's greatest asset was its powerful 981cc, three-cylinder engine.*

■ BELOW *Muscular looks and performance to match made the Jota one of the greatest superbikes of the 1970s.*

LAVERDA JOTA 1000 (1976)	
Engine	Aircooled 6-valve DOHC transverse triple
Capacity	981cc (75 x 74mm)
Power	90bhp @ 8000rpm
Weight	236kg (520lb) wet
Top speed	140mph (225kph)

later 750SF models, the twins earned Laverda a growing reputation for performance. Best and fastest of all was the exotic SFC, basically a road-going endurance racer with half-fairing, bright orange paint and tuned engine. Laverda also built an exotic V-six racebike, which was timed at 176mph (283kph) before retiring in its first and only ever

■ ABOVE *Enlarging the mighty three-cylinder powerplant's capacity to 1200cc gave even more mid-range grunt.*

■ ABOVE *The SFC1000 of 1985, the last of the aircooled triples, could not save Laverda from financial disaster.*

■ ABOVE *In 1994, under new management, Laverda began production of the parallel twin 650 sportster.*

■ ABOVE *Laverda's legendary 1000cc V-six racer proved fast but fragile in its only ever appearance in 1978.*

■ LEFT *The exotic, half-faired SFC750 parallel twin of the 1970s was basically an endurance racer built for the road.*

race, the Bol d'Or 24-Hours in 1978.

It was for three-cylinder sportsters, however, that the firm from Breganze became most famous. The first DOHC, 981cc triple, called the 3C, was powerful, good-looking and fairly successful when introduced in 1973. Three years later, at the request of the British Laverda importer, the factory tuned the motor with hot cams, high-compression pistons and free-breathing exhausts to produce the Jota. This was a big, raw 90bhp beast that bellowed to a top speed of 140mph (225kph) and needed a firm hand on the reins. The Jota was aggressive, demanding and expensive. In the mid-1970s it was the fastest thing on two wheels, as numerous production race victories confirmed.

The triple was modified in various ways in following years, without ever matching the success of the original Jota. The 1000cc sportster gained a fairing and a smoother-running, 120-degree crankshaft engine. A 1200cc version was also built, largely for the American market. Tightening emissions legislation prompted the quieter, less aggressive RGS and RGA triples of the 1980s. But although they performed well, prices were high, sales were disappointing and Laverda found itself in financial problems that led to receivership in 1987.

Several new Laverda operations rose only to fall again in the following years until finally, in 1994, production started once again at a new factory in nearby Zane, of the 650 – a model that had been developed several years earlier. This featured a 70bhp parallel twin engine, modern twin-beam aluminium frame and stylish full fairing, and was a fairly quick and agile sportster. Meanwhile Laverda's engineers were planning a new generation watercooled 1000cc triple to take the firm into the 21st century.

OTHER MAKES

■ LEVIS

Between 1911 and its demise in 1940, British firm Levis built many two- and four-stroke roadsters. Racing successes included victory in the 1922 Lightweight TT, and later wins in trials and motocross.

■ ABOVE *Levis produced this attractive 500cc four-stroke roadster in 1938.*

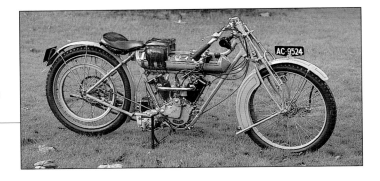

MATCHLESS

■ MATCHLESS G50

One of the great names of motorcycling's
early years, Matchless was founded by
the Collier family at Plumstead in south
London in 1899. Brothers Charlie and
Harry Collier were leading racers,
Charlie winning the single-cylinder

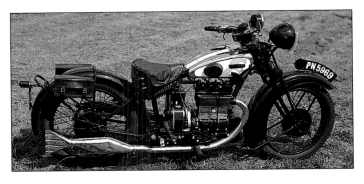

■ BELOW LEFT
*Good looks and
comfort were not
enough to make the
400cc Silver Arrow
V-twin of 1930 a
success.*

MATCHLESS G50 (1961)	
Engine	Aircooled 2-valve SOHC single
Capacity	496cc (90 x 78mm)
Power	51bhp @ 7200rpm
Weight	132kg (290lb) dry
Top speed	135mph (217kph)

■ BOTTOM *The
legendary G50
single lived up to
its "winged M"
badge, winning
races throughout
the 1960s.*

event at the first ever Isle of Man TT on
a Matchless in 1907, and Harry
following with a victory two years later.
Matchless took over the Wolverhampton-

based AJS firm in 1931, and many later
models of motorcycles were produced as
both AJS and Matchless machines, with
very few differences.

■ LEFT *Matchless also built bikes for off-road competition, such as this 500cc G80CS scrambler from 1958.*

■ RIGHT *Colin Seeley bought rights to G50 production and built the Seeley G50, still a force in classic racing.*

In 1930, Matchless released the Silver Arrow, a 400cc V-twin designed by Charlie Collier, but its performance was mediocre and sales poor. Younger brother Bert took over to produce the Silver Hawk, with a more powerful 600cc V-four engine, but despite 80mph (128kph) top speed it could not compete with Ariel's Square Four and was another failure. Matchless had more success with singles, such as the 350cc G3L that was produced in huge numbers for military use in the Second World War. This was one of the first bikes to use telescopic forks, and was later adapted for civilian use in models such as the G3LS of 1959.

The most famous Matchless was the G50 single-cylinder racer, basically a 500cc version of the 350cc AJS 7R. The G50 was first seriously produced in 1959, as a rival to Norton's Manx. Although slightly less powerful, with its 50bhp engine giving a top speed of about 135mph (217kph), the Matchless was lighter and had the edge on twisty circuits. AMC, which Matchless had become part of in 1938, suffered financial problems and went bust in 1966, after which rights to G50 production were bought by Colin Seeley, who continued engine development and built his own chassis to create the Seeley G50. The four-stroke single G50 held its own against the two-strokes until the 1970s, and in recent years has been competitive in classic racing.

OTHER MAKES

■ MAICO

Best known for its highly successful two-stroke motocross and enduro machines, German firm Maico began production in 1933 and built trials and road race bikes, notably the 125cc machines on which Borge Jansson won several Grands Prix in the early 1970s. Roadsters such as the twin-cylinder 350 and 400cc Taifun models were popular in the 1950s. In later years Maico concentrated on dirt bikes, before going bust in 1987.

■ MAGNI

Arturo Magni, team manager of the all-conquering MV Augusta race team, set up in business under his own name after MV's closure in the mid-1970s. Magni

■ ABOVE *In the 1960s, Maico built some rapid small-capacity road-racers.*

produced chassis kits for MV roadsters, and then complete bikes based around Honda's CB900 four. Later Magnis have used Moto Guzzi's V-twin engine, notably the retro-styled Sfida and the sleek, fully-faired Australia sportster.

■ MARUSHO

A leading Japanese manufacturer in the 1950s and early 1960s, Marusho was best known for its Lilac range of 125, 250 and 300cc V-twins. The firm produced a series of flat-twin roadsters before going out of business in the late 1960s.

■ LEFT *Magni's Guzzi-engined Australia sportster was fast and stylish.*

MONDIAL

■ BELOW *Mike Hailwood raced a pair of ex-works 250cc Mondials with great success in 1959 and 1960.*

■ MONDIAL 250cc RACER

Small Italian firm FB Mondial produced some fast and beautifully engineered racebikes in the 1950s, its finest moments coming when Tarquinio Provini and Cecil Sandford won the 125 and 250cc world championships in 1957. The company's origins dated back to 1929, when the four Boselli brothers founded FB to sell other firms' bikes. The first Mondials, built at FB's Bologna workshop, were DOHC, single-cylinder 125s. They were immediately successful, winning the world title for three years after its inception in 1949.

MONDIAL 250cc (1957)	
Engine	Aircooled 2-valve DOHC single
Capacity	249cc (75 x 56.4mm)
Power	29bhp @ 10,800rpm
Weight	125kg (275lb) dry
Top speed	135mph (216kph)

■ BELOW *Cecil Sandford won the TT and the 250cc world title in 1957 on this twin-cam Mondial single.*

Mondial also produced roadsters, starting with a 125cc four-stroke that was introduced in 1950, but the firm's main interest remained in racing. After

OTHER MAKES

■ MARS

The most memorable of several manufacturers called Mars was the German firm that produced a 959cc flat-twin roadster, the MA20, which featured an innovative pressed-steel frame in the 1920s. Mars built small-capacity two-strokes until ceasing production in the late 1950s.

■ MEGOLA

One of the strangest motorbikes of all time, the Munich-built Megola was powered by a radial five-cylinder engine situated inside its front wheel. Almost as unusual was the sheet-steel frame, which gave an armchair riding position. The 640cc side-valve motor produced 10bhp, and in sports form the single-speed Megola was timed at 90mph (144kph). Despite its unconventional design, some 2000 Megolas were built between 1922 and the firm's closure in 1925.

■ MEGURO

Founded in 1924, Meguro was one of the earliest Japanese motorcycle manufacturers. In the 1930s the firm's main bike was the 500cc Z97, a copy of the Velocette MSS. Meguro expanded to build twins in the 1950s, such as the 500cc K1, a copy of the BSA A7. But sales fell, and following a strike the firm was taken over by Kawasaki in 1960.

■ MIG

Chinese firm MIG has built an increasingly large number of bikes in recent years, many based on earlier Japanese designs. Most have been mopeds, scooters and commuter bikes, but

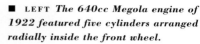

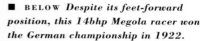

■ LEFT *The 640cc Megola engine of 1922 featured five cylinders arranged radially inside the front wheel.*

■ BELOW *Despite its feet-forward position, this 14bhp Megola racer won the German championship in 1922.*

■ ABOVE *MIG's QJ100 roadster is typical of the many small bikes built by Chinese firms in recent years.*

MIG did build a version of Honda's CB500-four of the 1970s.

■ MONTESA

Spain's first major bike manufacturer was founded in 1944 by Francisco Bulto, who

later left to form Bultaco, and Pedro Permanyer. Early bikes included successful two-stroke road racers and the Impala roadster. In recent years the Barcelona firm has been best known for trials, winning the world championship in 1980 and producing the long-running Cota model. Financial problems in the 1980s led to an association with Honda, whose engines have been used by Montesa in recent years.

■ MONTGOMERY

Founded in 1902, Montgomery built a wide variety of bikes using bought-in engines ranging from 150cc Villiers two-strokes to 1000cc JAPs. A typical mid-1930s bike was the Greyhound, a 500cc JAP-powered single capable of 75mph (120kph). It was well-made but expensive, and Montgomery did not resume production after the Second World War.

the triumphant 1957 season Mondial, who could not sell enough roadsters to finance the racing team, quit the sport. Two of the 250s were sold to Mike Hailwood, who won many races on them in Britain. In the 1960s Mondial made a partially successful return to racing using two-stroke engines. In 1992 the Mondial name resurfaced again, in the shape of a KTM-engined 560cc single-cylinder racebike produced by Pierluigi Boselli, son of the firm's former owner.

■ ABOVE *Mondial won a hat-trick of 125cc world titles with twin-cam singles similar to this 1949 machine.*

■ ABOVE *Former champion Cecil Sandford revived memories on a "dustbin-faired" 125cc at a Monza classic event.*

MOTO GUZZI

■ **MOTO GUZZI FALCONE**

Italy's largest motorcycle manufacturer for much of its long history, Guzzi dates back to the closing years of the First World War when three air corps friends, Carlo Guzzi, Giorgio Parodi and Giovanni Ravelli, planned a bike firm. After Ravelli was killed in a flying crash, the other two adopted the air corps' eagle symbol in his honour. In 1920 Carlo Guzzi designed the firm's first bike, a 500cc four-stroke with a

■ ABOVE *Founding partner Carlo Guzzi designed the road and race bikes that made Guzzi a leading marque in the 1920s.*

■ LEFT *Fergus Anderson riding his works Falcone on the way to victory in the 250cc Lightweight TT in 1952.*

single, horizontal cylinder. The Normale model was released two years later and, boosted by racing success, rapidly became popular.

Guzzi retained and updated the 500cc flat-single format for many years, leaving many of its more adventurous engine layouts for racing. Landmark singles included the GT luxury tourer of 1928, with its novel sprung frame, and the Sport 15 of 1931, finished in the bright red that became a favourite

MOTO GUZZI FALCONE (1950)	
Engine	Aircooled 2-valve OHV pushrod single
Capacity	498cc (88 x 82mm)
Power	23bhp @ 4500rpm
Weight	170kg (374lb) dry
Top speed	85mph (136kph)

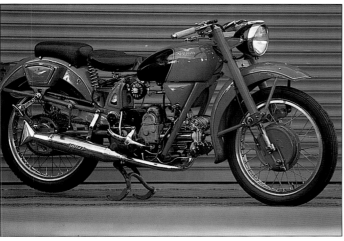

■ ABOVE *Guzzi's decision to quit racing in 1957 meant the exotic and super-fast V-eight never won a Grand Prix.*

■ LEFT *The quick and practical 250cc Airone, launched in 1939, was still popular when this bike was built in 1953.*

Sport and Touring forms. Further updates kept it in production until 1976.

Guzzi's horizontal singles were hugely successful in racing, winning three 250cc world titles between 1949 and 1952, and then being enlarged to 350cc to take five consecutive championships from 1953. The first two championships were won by Scottish ace Fergus Anderson, who then took over as Guzzi's competition manager.

The greatest machine of all was the legendary 500cc V-eight, which was designed by Giulio Carcano and first raced in 1956. The watercooled, quad-cam, 90-degree V-eight revved to 12,000rpm, produced 72bhp and was timed at a phenomenal 178mph (286kph) at the Belgian GP in 1957. Despite these feats, Guzzi unfortunately pulled out of Grand Prix racing at the end of that season, so the V-eight never really fulfilled its true potential.

Guzzi colour. The colour was also used for the famous series of production racers, which began in 1938 with the 28bhp, 100mph (160kph) Condor, and continued with the Dondolino, Gambalunga and the 250cc Albatros – all of which won at the highest level.

The best loved road-going single was the Falcone, which was introduced in 1950 showing clear links with the Normale of almost three decades earlier. Essentially a sports version of the previous year's Astore tourer, the Falcone featured flat handlebars and rearset footrests.

In standard trim its top speed was 85mph (136kph), but when tuned with Dondolino engine parts the Falcone was good for over 100mph (160kph) which, along with the lazy, low revving power delivery, helped to explain its popularity. From 1953 the Falcone was built in

OTHER MAKES

■ MORBIDELLI

Self-made businessman and fanatical motorcyclist Giancarlo Morbidelli used his huge woodwork machinery firm to finance production of some superb race-bikes. Morbidellis won three consecutive 125cc world titles in the mid-1970s, plus

the 250cc crown in 1977. Another 125cc title was added the following year, after the MBA firm had been created to produce replicas, and the two-stroke twins remained competitive for several more years. A four-cylinder 500cc racer proved less successful, and Giancarlo Morbidelli finally quit racing. In 1994, he returned to motorcycling with a prototype roadster – an exotic sports-tourer – powered by a purpose-built, 850cc watercooled V-eight engine.

■ LEFT *Morbidelli's V-eight prototype featured controversial styling by leading car-design studio Pininfarina.*

MOTO GUZZI

■ MOTO GUZZI
LE MANS 850

Guzzi's trademark transverse 90-degree V-twin engine design was first seen in an unusual 754cc three-wheeled mountain vehicle called the 3 x 3, built in small numbers for the Italian ministry of defence between 1960 and 1963. In 1964 Guzzi revised the engine for a military bike, and realized the machine had potential for civilian use too.

The V7 went into production in 1967, and two years later was followed by the V7 Special, whose 757cc engine produced 45bhp. With its shaft final drive, the Special was a practical machine whose smooth, 110mph (177kph) performance and stable

■ RIGHT *Fine handling combined with the Le Mans' power and smoothness to make a formidable Superbike.*

■ BELOW *The Le Mans Mk.1's tiny fly-screen added the finishing touch to the Guzzi's classically elegant profile.*

MOTO GUZZI 850 LE MANS MK.1 (1976)

Engine	Aircooled 4-valve OHV pushrod 90-degree transverse V-twin
Capacity	844cc (83 x 78mm)
Power	71bhp @ 7300rpm
Weight	215kg (473lb) dry
Top speed	130mph (209kph)

handling did much to establish Guzzi in the large-capacity market. In 1972 Guzzi released its first genuine high-performance V-twin, the V7 Sport. It featured a reworked 748cc motor and a lower frame that gave 125mph (201kph) performance with excellent handling.

Four years later came the most famous model of all – the 850 Le Mans. This lean sportster, with its neat headlamp fairing and striking, angular seat, was powered by a tuned version of the existing 844cc motor. High-compression pistons, big valves and unfiltered 36mm Dell'Orto carburettors helped raise peak output to 71bhp, which gave a top speed of 130mph (209kph). The shaft-drive motor's long-legged power delivery, coupled with good handling and excellent braking – using Guzzi's new system, which linked the front and rear discs – made the Le Mans one of the finest superbikes of the 1970s.

Times have often been difficult at Guzzi since the firm's great days in the early 1960s, when the big, modern factory at Mandello del Lario, on Lake

Lecco, employed over 1500 people, and boasted its own hydro-electric power stations and an advanced wind-tunnel. By the mid-1960s, factors including the changing bike market, the retirement of the firm's founders and a misguided move into moped production had left Guzzi in serious financial trouble. In 1966 the company went into receiver-ship, reopening a year later with a new owner. In 1973 Guzzi was bought by Alejandro De Tomaso, the Argentinian car baron, who maintained control for the next two decades without providing the investment that many enthusiasts had hoped for.

Guzzi's best-selling model for much of that time was the California, which was initially produced in 1971 as an American market version of the V7 Special, complete with higher bars, "buddy" seat and standard-fitment

screen and panniers. Over the years the California has seen several restyles and revisions, notably in its engine capacity which has grown to 850, 950 and finally 1100cc. In 1994 the California's aircooled, pushrod V-twin engine was fitted with optional fuel-injection, making an even more sophisticated and practical motorcycle tourer.

■ BELOW *Inspiration for the Daytona came from American "Dr John" Wittner's highly successful racing Guzzis.*

■ BOTTOM *The Daytona's sleek styling, updated V-twin engine and race-bred chassis made an impressive combination.*

M O T O   G U Z Z I

■ MOTO GUZZI DAYTONA 1000

Guzzi took a long time to produce a fitting successor to the original Le Mans, which was gradually developed through the 1980s while becoming decreasingly competitive. Finally, in 1992, came a new generation sportsbike, the Daytona 1000. Its design owed much to "Dr John" Wittner, an American dentist-turned-engineer who had achieved much success with Guzzi-powered racebikes in the late 1980s before coming to work at Mandello.

The roadster's chassis, consisting of a steel spine frame and single-shock rear suspension – incorporating a linkage to counteract the shaft drive's adverse

■ BELOW *Despite its shaft final drive and relatively narrow rear tyre, the Daytona went round corners exceptionally well.*

MOTO GUZZI DAYTONA 1000 (1992)

Engine	Aircooled 8-valve high-cam 90-degree transverse V-twin
Capacity	992cc (90 x 78mm)
Power	95bhp @ 8000rpm
Weight	205kg (451lb) dry
Top speed	150mph (241kph)

affect on handling – was developed from the one on Wittner's racebikes. It held a revised 992cc version of the aircooled V-twin, with fuel-injection, four valves per cylinder and a high camshaft design in place of the old engine's pushrod-operated layout. The handsome, 95bhp Daytona combined a 150mph (241kph) top speed with good handling plus Guzzi's traditional long-legged feel. Along with the cheaper, carburetted 1100 Sport that followed in 1994, the Daytona proved there was still sporting life in Guzzi's V-twin format.

■ **MOTO MARTIN**
Frenchman Georges Martin was one of the leading chassis specialists of the 1970s and early 1980s, producing stable-handling and beautifully styled café racers typically based on four-cylinder motors such as Kawasaki's Z1000 and Suzuki's GSX1100. Arguably the best of all was the Martin CBX1000, which was powered by a tuned version of Honda's six-cylinder engine.

■ ABOVE *The Martin CBX1000 was one of the fastest and most aggressively styled specials of the early 1980s.*

■ **MOTO MORINI**
Alfonso Morini began building bikes in partnership with Mario Mezzetti, under the MM name in the 1920s, and rode one himself to a class win in the 1927 Italian Grand Prix at Monza. After setting up under his own name after the War, Morini built roadsters and successful racers, most notably the superb DOHC 250 on which Tarquinio Provini was runner up in the 1963 world championship. The Bologna firm's best known roadster was the handsome and

■ ABOVE *Morini's pretty and fine-handling 3¹/₂ Sport was great fun on twisty roads, and despite the V-twin's modest power even made a useful racer.*

very quick 344cc 3¹/₂ Sport of the mid-1970s. Cagiva bought Morini in 1987, since when the name has been little used.

■ **MOTOSACOCHE**
Swiss brothers Henri and Armand Dufaux began by making a successful 215cc motorized bicycle in 1900, and by the 1920s had progressed to building 350 and 500cc four-stroke singles that gained many race wins and speed records. When sales fell in the 1930s, Motosacoche left bike production to concentrate on industrial engines.

■ **MOTOTRANS**
After being founded in 1957 to produce Ducati singles under licence, Spanish firm Mototrans became a manufacturer in its own right. Models included the Yak 410 trail bike plus some Zündapp-powered lightweights that were built in 1982, shortly before the factory was taken over and closed by Yamaha.

■ **MÜNCH**
The car-engined monster-bikes produced by German engineer Friedel Münch since 1966 have been some of the biggest and most expensive on two wheels. The first Münch Mammut models were powered by an aircooled, 1000cc four-cylinder NSU car engine, held in a huge chassis based on a twin-shock, tubular steel frame. By the early 1990s almost 500 had been built, later models with capacity of up to 1996cc and weight of over 350kg. The most recent Münch, the turbocharged Titan 2000, produced 150bhp and featured a hydraulic centre-stand.

■ ABOVE *The mighty Münch Mammut – or Mammoth – was one of the biggest, most powerful and most expensive superbikes of the 1970s.*

■ BELOW *MV's twin-cam four produced phenomenal performance both as a 500 and in 350cc form, as seen here.*

■ BOTTOM *John Surtees won MV's third 500cc world title on this Four in 1959.*

MV AGUSTA

■ MV AGUSTA 500cc FOUR

There is no greater name in motorcycle racing than MV Agusta, whose record of 17 consecutive world 500cc championships between 1958 and 1974 will probably never be equalled. In all, the small factory from Gallarate won 38 riders' world titles, 37 manufacturers' championships and over 3000 international races, as well as building the mighty four-cylinder roadsters that were arguably the fastest and most glamorous superbikes of the 1970s.

The Meccanica Verghera motorcycle firm was founded in the village of Verghera towards the end of the Second World War by Count Domenico Agusta, the eldest of four brothers whose late father, a Sicilian aristocrat, had been a noted aviation pioneer. Domenico turned to bikes, and in 1945 released a 98cc two-stroke that sold well and was also raced with instant success. Pure racers as well as other roadsters followed, and

MV AGUSTA 500cc FOUR (1956)	
Engine	Aircooled 8-valve DOHC transverse four
Capacity	498cc (53 x 56.4mm)
Power	70bhp @ 10,500rpm
Weight	140kg (308lb) dry
Top speed	155mph (249kph)

■ LEFT *The Agusta firm's gear-cog logo became synonymous with success.*

■ RIGHT *Count Domenico Agusta strikes a pose with team riders John Surtees, Umberto Masetti, Carlo Ubbiali, Carlo Bandirola, Angelo Copeta, Remo Venturi, Luigi Taveri and Tito Forconi in 1956.*

in 1952 Englishman Cecil Sandford won MV's first world title in the 125cc class. In the smaller Grand Prix categories the firm's star rider was Italian ace Carlo Ubbiali, who won five 125cc championships for MV between 1955 and 1960, plus three more on a 250.

But it was in the bigger classes that MV was most successful. The design of MV's first twin-cam 500cc four of 1950 owed much to Gilera, for whom both chief engineer Piero Remor and team manager Arturo Magni had worked. Early bikes featured shaft final drive and a gearlever on each side of the engine, but after poor results a more conventional layout was adopted. John Surtees won MV's first 500cc championship in 1956 and went on to take three more, often winning with ease after the rival factories' withdrawal from racing in 1957. Gary Hocking and Mike Hailwood continued the run, then Giacomo Agostini took over with seven straight championships between 1966 and 1971, using a fine-handling three-cylinder machine.

MV had little serious opposition for long periods during the 1960s, but the so-called "Gallarate fire engines" were increasingly tested by the Japanese two-stroke challenge in the early 1970s. New four-valves-per-cylinder fours were built for both the 350 and 500cc classes, the smaller bike allowing Agostini to win his sixth consecutive 350cc title in 1973. Phil Read used the new 500, which produced 102bhp at 14,000rpm, to take the championship in 1973 and 1974, averaging 130mph (209kph) in winning the Belgian Grand Prix. Ironically it was Agostini, now on a two-stroke Yamaha, who finally ended the Italian firm's domination in 1975.

■ LEFT *Giacomo Agostini, who won 14 world titles for MV, takes "Ago's leap" en route to victory in the 1970 Senior TT.*

■ BELOW *This SOHC, single-cylinder racer, built by MV in the mid-1950s, was capable of over 90mph (145kph).*

MV AGUSTA

■ MV AGUSTA 750 SPORT

Despite producing many successful small-capacity roadsters throughout the 1950s and 1960s – bikes with names like the Pullman, the Turismo Rapido and the Raid – MV was slow to capitalize on its racing success with a four-cylinder street bike. Even when a DOHC MV four did reach the road in 1966 it was not a race-replica but an

MV AGUSTA 750 SPORT (1973)	
Engine	Aircooled 8-valve DOHC transverse four
Capacity	743cc (65 x 56mm)
Power	69bhp @ 7900rpm
Weight	230kg (506lb) dry
Top speed	120mph (192kph)

ugly, hump-tanked 600cc shaft-drive tourer designed at the insistence of the firm's autocratic owner Domenico Agusta, who did not want the production bike to be raced, for fear of devaluing his factory team's hard-won reputation.

The expensive 600 Four was a flop, and in 1970 MV belatedly released a much racier and more exciting roadster called the 750 Sport. This was all that

MV's racing fans had dreamt of. The big, four-cylinder engine had gear drive to twin overhead cams and produced 69bhp. The racy chassis featured clip-on handlebars, a sculpted fuel tank, humped seat and huge Grimeca four-leading-shoe front brake. The Sport was beautiful, expensive and fast, though its 120mph (192kph) top speed did not match MV's claims. Despite too much

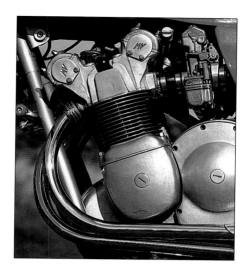

■ LEFT *MV's race-derived four, with gear drive to twin cams, was powerful but very expensive to produce.*

■ RIGHT *The last four-cylinder MV was the 750S America of 1975, here fitted with a handlebar fairing.*

weight and the retained shaft drive it handled reasonably well, and the howl from its four shiny megaphone exhausts was gloriously evocative of the Gallarate bikes that still dominated Grand Prix racing.

In subsequent years the Sport was updated with disc brakes, more power and a full fairing. And in 1975 came the 750S America, built for the US market with new, angular styling and a 789cc, 75bhp engine that pushed its top speed towards 130mph (209kph). Like the Sport, the America was an exotic and hugely desirable superbike, but it was no more commercially successful than its predecessor. Glamorous as the fours were, their intricate, competition-derived engine design and low-volume, hand-built construction meant that MVs were not profitable even at the huge

■ RIGHT *Its rarity has made MV's ugly 600cc tourer hugely valuable, but it was a sales disaster back in 1966.*

prices they commanded.

Far from making money for MV, the big roadsters merely added to the firm's problems. Domenico Agusta had died of a heart attack in 1971. His brother Corradino, who had taken over, could not match the passion with which Domenico had run MV's motorcycle division, by then a loss-making part of

the Agusta helicopter firm. By 1977 the Agusta family had lost control of much of the MV business, and was powerless to prevent motorcycle production being halted. Bikes remained on sale until stocks ran out, and in early 1980 MV closed. The name was bought by Cagiva, who could be planning MV's comeback with a three-cylinder Superbike.

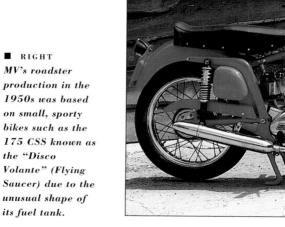

■ RIGHT *MV's roadster production in the 1950s was based on small, sporty bikes such as the 175 CSS known as the "Disco Volante" (Flying Saucer) due to the unusual shape of its fuel tank.*

MuZ

■ MuZ SKORPION SPORT

The original company, MZ, was founded after the Second World War at the former DKW factory at Zschopau in East Germany, after former DKW personnel had relocated in the West. The firm was

MuZ SKORPION SPORT (1994)	
Engine	Aircooled 2-valve SOHC single
Capacity	660cc (100 x 84mm)
Power	48bhp @ 6500rpm
Weight	174kg (383lb) dry
Top speed	105mph (168kph)

very successful in off-road competition in the 1960s, winning a string of honours in the International Six Days Enduro. But it was in road racing that MZ had the biggest impact, due to the powerful two-strokes developed by their engineer Walter Kaaden. Star rider Ernst Degner was on the verge of winning the 125cc world championship in 1961 when he defected, taking MZ's

secrets to Suzuki. Degner ended up second that year, and MZ never won the title.

Until quite recently, MZ's roadsters were predominantly single-cylinder two-strokes of moderate performance and curious, old-fashioned styling. Bikes such as the ES250/2 Trophy and TS250/1 Supa Five of the 1970s, and the later but only slightly better looking

■ LEFT *The former MZ firm had a strong tradition in off-road events such as the International Six Days Enduro.*

■ BELOW *MZ roadsters such as the 250cc Supa Five were popular for their price and practicality, but not their looks.*

■ BELOW *Ernst Degner (right), who later went to Suzuki, discusses two-stroke tuning with Walter Kaaden.*

ETZ250, provided cheap, reliable motorcycling for large numbers of riders, mainly in Eastern Europe.

After German reunification MZ fell into financial trouble, but resurfaced in 1994 with new management, a new name – MuZ – and a stylish new single-cylinder roadster, the Skorpion. Designed by British consultants Seymour Powell and powered by the aircooled, four-stroke engine from Yamaha's XTZ660 trail bike, the Skorpion was a neat and reasonably quick roadster, with a 105mph (168kph) top speed and good handling. Although MuZ remained in a difficult financial position, the Skorpion's arrival gave hope for a more prosperous future.

OTHER MAKES

■ NER-A-CAR

The name of this unusually designed machine of the 1920s was doubly apt, because it was designed by an American called Carl Neracher with the intention of being a bike that was as near a car as possible. His long, low creation was built first in Syracuse, New York state and then in Britain, initially with a 221cc two-stroke engine and later with a 350cc four-stroke single. Although civilized and very stable, thanks partly to its innovative hub-centre steering, the Ner-a-Car was not a commercial success. Production began in 1921 at the improbably high rate of 150 per day, and lasted only until 1926.

■ ABOVE *New Imperial's fast and handsome 500cc V-twin set records and won many races in the mid-1930s.*

■ NEW IMPERIAL

Birmingham firm New Imperial was notable in the early 1930s for pioneering unit construction of engine and gearbox on bikes including the Unit Minor 150 and Unit Super 250. Sporting successes included Ginger Wood's 102.2mph (164.4kph) average for an hour at Brooklands in 1934 on a 500cc V-twin, and Bob Foster's win in the 1936 Lightweight TT. The factory was bought by Jack Sangster, owner of Ariel and Triumph, and production did not restart after the Second World War.

■ ABOVE *The Ner-a-Car was stable and civilized, but even in the 1920s most riders preferred sportier bikes.*

NORTON

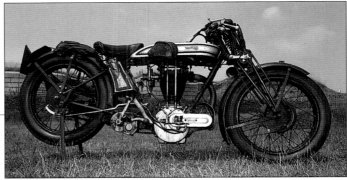

■ LEFT *This Model 19, from 1926, was finished in Norton's silver-and-black colours.*

■ NORTON CS1

James Lansdowne Norton built his first motorcycle in 1902, and soon gained a reputation for rapid racing bikes and strong, reliable roadsters. In 1907 Rem Fowler used a Peugeot-engined Norton to win the twin-cylinder class of the first Isle of Man TT. A year later, Norton introduced both single and twin-cylinder engines of its own construction. Early models included the 490cc 16H, a high-performance roadster, and the 633cc long-stroke Big 4, which was named after its 4bhp rating and was popular for pulling sidecars. But James Norton was a better engineer than businessman, and the firm went into liquidation in 1913.

Norton Motors Ltd was formed shortly afterwards under joint directorship of

■ LEFT *The right of the CS1's engine shows the bevel-driven overhead cam that gave the CamShaft 1 its name.*

■ BELOW *This 1927 works CS1 is pictured at Brooklands.*

NORTON CS1 (1927)

Engine	Aircooled 2-valve SOHC single
Capacity	490cc (79 x 100mm)
Power	20bhp approx
Weight	145kg (319lb) wet
Top speed	80mph (128kph)

A SENIOR T.T. WINNER

ROLAND DAVIES

OTHER MAKES

■ NIMBUS

Throughout its existence from 1919 to closure in the late 1950s, Danish firm Nimbus concentrated solely on bikes with a 750cc, aircooled in-line four-cylinder engine and shaft final drive. Early models had inlet-over-exhaust valve operation; later bikes used a redesigned, SOHC motor producing 22bhp. Nimbus's military fours were much-used by the Danish armed forces, but the civilian models were not exported in great numbers.

■ ABOVE *The 1934 Nimbus was one of the first to use the Danish firm's new SOHC in-line-four engine, which was introduced in that year.*

■ NORMAN

In the 1950s Norman, a small firm from Kent, was as notable for its displays at London's annual bike show as for its modest range of small capacity two-strokes. Villiers-engined roadsters such as the TS Uni-Twin and the B3 were competent and reliable, but performance was only moderate and the factory was closed in 1962.

■ ABOVE *This scene of a victorious Norton from the early 1930s celebrates the firm's long run of wins in the Senior TT.*

■ LEFT *Norton's key figures James "Pa" Norton and tuner "Wizard" O'Donovan, pose with rider Rex Judd.*

■ ABOVE *One of Norman's last and best roadsters was the B4 Sports of 1961, powered by a 250cc, twin-cylinder Villiers two-stroke engine.*

James Norton and Bob Shelley, whose brother-in-law Dan "Wizard" O'Donovan was a top racer and tuner. Based at Brooklands, O'Donovan developed the 490cc Norton single to produce the Brooklands Special or BS, which was sold with a certificate confirming that it had exceeded 75mph (120kph) at the Surrey track. The BS was the world's first production racing bike, and was also built in Brooklands Road Special (BRS) form, timed at 70mph (112kph). The chassis that O'Donovan used to test the BS and BRS engines at Brooklands was later restored, became known as "Old Miracle", and was ridden in classic

events for many years.

In the early 1920s Norton converted the single-cylinder engine to overhead valve operation, producing the Model 18 roadster. The PHV single won the Senior TT in 1924, a year before "Pa" Norton died, aged 56, following a long-standing heart problem. In 1927 the firm from Bracebridge Street, Birmingham introduced another technical advance with the CS1, which featured an overhead camshaft. The CS1 was immediately successful in racing, being ridden to victory by the great Stanley Woods and others, and a year later was released as a super-sports roadster.

NORTON

■ BELOW *The McCandless brothers'*
Featherbed frame gave the Manx, pictured
here in 1955, superb handling.

■ BOTTOM *Classically simple, its lasting*
success made the Manx the definitive
British racing single.

■ NORTON 500cc MANX

The 1930s were great years for Norton, who won every Senior and Junior TT race but two between 1931 and 1938. Led by team manager, tuner and former rider Joe Craig, the firm more than lived up to the "Unapproachable Norton" slogan that had been coined years earlier. Norton's sporting single during the 1930s was the International. The firm's Isle of Man success led to the racing version of this model, produced to individual orders at Norton's Bracebridge Street factory, being given the name Manx.

The most famous version of the Manx was created in 1950, when the works racebike, which had used a twin-camshaft engine since 1937, was

NORTON 500cc MANX (1962)	
Engine	Aircooled 4-valve DOHC single
Capacity	498cc (86 x 85.8mm)
Power	54bhp @ 7200rpm
Weight	140kg (308lb) dry
Top speed	140mph (225kph)

redesigned using an innovative tubular steel chassis devised by Irish racing brothers Rex and Cromie McCandless. During testing at Silverstone, Norton works rider Harold Daniell inadvertently christened the frame with his comment that the new bike felt as though he was riding a feather bed. Geoff Duke went on

to win both 500 and 350cc world titles on the fine-handling Featherbed Manx in 1951, retaining the 350 championship in 1952.

Although it was eventually overcome by the more powerful four-cylinder 500s of Gilera and MV Agusta, the Manx took numerous famous victories in

subsequent years, many by private riders on production bikes after Norton's factory team had been disbanded in 1955. A Manx ridden by Godfrey Nash won the Yugoslavian Grand Prix as late as 1969, and in the 1980s the single found a new lease of life with the rise in popularity of classic racing.

The success of Triumph's Speed Twin and its derivatives led Norton to introduce its own parallel twin, the 500cc Model 7 Dominator, in 1949. Designed by Bert Hopwood, the Dominator produced 29bhp, managed about 90mph (145kph), was reliable and handled well, though the initial model's brakes were poor. In 1952 Norton combined the twin-cylinder powerplant with the Featherbed frame made famous by the Manx single, to produce the Dominator 88. This was the bike that first earned the reputation for fine handling that Norton twins retained for many years.

The first Norton twin whose engine truly matched its chassis was the Dominator 650SS, which was launched in 1962 with an uprated, 49bhp motor in a Featherbed frame. With paintwork in

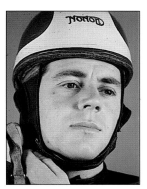

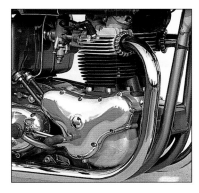

■ LEFT *A 600cc parallel-twin engine and Featherbed frame made the "Dommie 99" a winner.*

■ FAR LEFT *Geoff Duke won three world championships on Norton's factory singles.*

Norton's traditional silver the 650SS was a handsome bike, and it was fast, torquey and stable too. But the 650SS and later 750cc Atlas did not sell particularly well, partly due to relatively low production levels and high prices. That did not help the always difficult financial situation at Norton. In 1953 the firm had been bought by AMC, owners of AJS and Matchless, and in 1963 production was moved to AMC's factory in south London.

■ LEFT *Among the best Norton twins was the powerful and stylish 650SS, pictured here in 1966 form.*

NORTON

■ NORTON COMMANDO 750cc FASTBACK

The Norton Commando was one of the best and most famous parallel twins of them all. It was released in 1968, created massive interest — not least due to the striking styling that earned it the Fastback name — and sold well despite a backdrop of Norton's mounting financial problems. Powered by the 745cc engine from the 750 Atlas model, the Commando produced 58bhp and weighed a respectable 190kg (418lb). Its 115mph (185kph) plus performance was well-controlled by a chassis that again upheld Norton's reputation for handling and roadholding.

The Commando chassis was also notable for the way it controlled the

■ LEFT *Its blend of smoothness and traditional Norton handling made the Commando ideal for hard riding.*

■ BELOW *The Commando motor's vibration was controlled by Norton's Isolastic mounting system.*

■ BOTTOM *The Fastback Commando was a very stylish bike.*

NORTON COMMANDO 750cc FASTBACK (1968)	
Engine	Aircooled 4-valve OHV pushrod parallel twin
Capacity	745cc (73 x 89mm)
Power	58bhp @ 6800rpm
Weight	190kg (418lb) dry
Top speed	117mph (187kph)

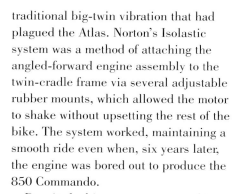

■ FAR LEFT TOP *Peter Williams won the Formula 750 TT for Norton in 1973.*

■ FAR LEFT BELOW *The Classic was the first Norton rotary to go on sale to the public.*

■ BELOW *The F1 sportster (left) was inspired by Steve Spray's 1989 racebike.*

traditional big-twin vibration that had plagued the Atlas. Norton's Isolastic system was a method of attaching the angled-forward engine assembly to the twin-cradle frame via several adjustable rubber mounts, which allowed the motor to shake without upsetting the rest of the bike. The system worked, maintaining a smooth ride even when, six years later, the engine was bored out to produce the 850 Commando.

Despite lacking power compared to most of its circuit rivals, the Commando was raced with some success in the early 1970s. Norton's Formula 750 racer used an innovative steel monocoque frame that helped give advantages in weight and aerodynamics. The bike was developed and ridden by Peter Williams, who won the 1973 Formula 750 TT on it. A road-going replica was also produced, but such rearguard actions were not enough to save Norton, which by now was part of the Norton Villiers Triumph group that had been struggling for years. NVT duly went into liquidation, and the last Commandos were built in 1978.

Norton's name did not disappear altogether, however, and between 1977 and 1987 the company continued low

key development of a rotary-engined bike that was used by several British police forces. Eventually Norton, now based at Shenstone in Staffordshire, produced a limited edition civilian roadster called the Classic, powered by a 588cc twin-chamber rotary engine. The touring Commander followed, and public interest in Norton snowballed when enthusiastic workers built an alloy-framed rotary racer that won two national championships in 1989.

A race-replica sportster, the F1, followed a year later, combining good

looks with 145mph (233kph) speed and sure-footed handling. The F1, however, had some rough edges, and its low-volume production kept prices up and profits down. By the mid-1990s Norton's promising recovery had foundered, several former directors had been accused of financial irregularities, and hundreds of shareholders had lost money invested in the company. Production of rotaries was then abandoned by the new Canadian owners, and Norton's future as a motorcycle manufacturer remained in doubt.

N S U

■ NSU 250cc SUPERMAX

German firm NSU started off by producing knitting machines, before expanding
to build bicycles and then, in 1901, its
first motorbike. The first machines used
a combination of a Swiss-made 1.5bhp

NSU SUPERMAX (1955)	
Engine	Aircooled 2-valve SOHC single
Capacity	247cc (69 x 66mm)
Power	18bhp @ 6500rpm
Weight	164kg (361lb) dry
Top speed	75mph (120kph)

■ LEFT *NSU's
250cc Supermax
(left) and 125cc
Superfox singles
shared an SOHC
single-cylinder
engine layout.*

■ BELOW *The
Supermax was one
of the most
sophisticated bikes
of the 1950s, but
its price limited
export sales.*

■ BELOW *The Supermax's fuel cap celebrated NSU's Grand Prix success.*

■ BOTTOM *Werner Haas, pictured on the superb Rennmax parallel twin, won both 250 and 125cc titles in 1953.*

Zedel engine in a bicycle frame; two years later NSU produced its own single and V-twin engines. Production grew, and in 1929 Norton's designer Walter Moore was hired to create NSU's first overhead-camshaft model. In fact, the 500SS was so similar to Norton's CS1 that Norton workers claimed NSU stood for Norton Spares Used.

NSU was one of the world's leading manufacturers before the Second World War, and afterwards introduced innovative bikes including the 250cc Max. This featured an SOHC single-cylinder engine, pressed-steel frame and leading-link forks. The Max's most famous descendent was the Supermax, introduced in 1955, which provided smooth, reliable 75mph (120kph) performance, stable handling and excellent braking. It was beautifully engineered and constructed, traditional assets which led Honda to base several bikes on NSUs. But the Supermax and its 125cc stablemate the Superfox were too expensive to sell in large numbers, and in the early 1960s NSU abandoned bikes to concentrate on car production.

OTHER MAKES

■ **OK-SUPREME**

After beginning volume production in 1911, Birmingham-based OK concentrated on two-strokes, notably a bike called the Junior. The firm became OK-Supreme in 1927, the year before Frank Longman scored its only TT win. Its best-known bike was the early 1930s single, built in 250 and 350cc form, that was known as the Lighthouse after the glass inspection plate in its camshaft tower. The cheap and reliable 250cc Flying Cloud was popular in the late 1930s, but the firm built only a few grass track bikes after the Second World War.

■ ABOVE *Legendary rider and tuner Bill Lacey with a record-breaking OK-Supreme on the Brooklands banking.*

■ **OSSA**

Founded by Manuel Giro in the late 1940s, Ossa developed a reputation for trials, enduro and trail machines, mostly with two-stroke engines. The Barcelona firm built numerous small capacity roadsters and made an impact in road racing with Santiago Herrero, who won several 250cc Grands Prix on a single-cylinder two-stroke in the late 1960s. Sadly, Herrero was killed at the Isle of Man TT in 1970, after which Ossa quit Grand Prix racing. During the 1970s the

NSU's 250cc Rennmax made a brief but memorable impact on Grand Prix racing in the early 1950s. The powerful Rennmax, a DOHC parallel twin with a large-diameter steel spine frame, was in a class of its own when winning the world championship for Werner Haas in

■ ABOVE *Over's Euro Twin, powered by Yamaha's TDM850 parallel twin motor, was fast, stylish and expensive.*

firm built successful enduro bikes and the rapid twin-cylinder two-stroke Yankee 500 roadster. But industrial problems and falling sales led to closure of the factory in 1984, after which some bikes were built as Ossamotos by a workers' co-operative.

■ **OVER**

The small firm run by Japanese engineer Kensei Sato has built several exotic and expensive specials in recent years, many using the oval-section tubular aluminium frames that have become an Over trademark. Among the best was the Euro Twin, powered by Yamaha's TDM850 engine.

■ ABOVE *Santiago Herrero cranks Ossa's rapid 250cc single through a bend at Brands Hatch in 1969.*

1953 and 1954. NSU retired from Grand Prix racing after that season but continued to sell single-cylinder Sportmax racers, based on the road-going Max. Hermann-Peter Müller used one to win NSU's third consecutive 250cc championship in 1955.

PANTHER

■ LEFT *For solo use the Model 100 sloper was efficient, with a top speed of 70mph (112kph) and fair handling.*

■ PANTHER MODEL 100S

A big single-cylinder Panther was the definitive bike for pulling a sidecar in the 1940s and 1950s, when an "outfit" was often the main means of transport for a family unable to afford a car. Although not particularly powerful, the long-stroke Panther motor produced plenty of useful low-down torque that

■ BELOW *A Model 100S was typically fitted with a sidecar such as this 1957 bike's Watsonian Avon single-seater.*

made it ideal for sidecar use. The Yorkshire firm, originally known as Phelon and Moore (P&M), had been building "slopers", named after their single, angled-forward cylinder, since 1904. Panther also built Villiers-engined two-strokes until the 1930s, and recommended two-stroke production in the 1950s with models including the 324cc Model 45 Sports.

The firm's most famous sloper was the Model 100, which was strong, slow-revving and reliable. The original 598cc

overhead-valve motor, with its twin exhaust ports, was introduced in 1928, and was relatively little changed by 1957 when the Model 100S Deluxe was produced. When fitted with a Watsonian sidecar it gave undramatic but efficient and fairly smooth performance. In 1960 the firm estimated that 90 per cent of Model 100s were attached to sidecars. That left Panther vulnerable when the attraction of three wheels faded, and production ended in the late 1960s.

PANTHER MODEL 100S (1957)

Engine	Aircooled 2-valve OHV pushrod single
Capacity	598cc (87 x 100mm)
Power	23bhp @ 5300rpm
Weight	193kg (425lb) dry
Top speed	68mph (109kph)

OTHER MAKES

■ PARILLA

Italian engineer Giovanni Parrilla built his first bike in 1946, and became well known for fast and stylish roadsters and racers, mostly single-cylinder four-strokes with capacities of between 125 and 250cc. Parillas – the spelling was changed for simplicity – were raced with fair success in the 1950s, but Giovanni later turned to go-kart engines, and the factory closed in 1967.

■ ABOVE *A neat 250cc single-cylinder Parilla, built in 1961, being ridden on the Isle of Man circuit in 1992.*

■ PATON

Giuseppe Pattoni was a former sidecar racer and Grand Prix mechanic until Mondial's retirement in 1957. The remarkable Italian engineer then began designing and building bikes to compete in racing's most glamorous class. From four-stroke parallel twins of the 1960s to recent two-stroke V-fours, green-finished Patons have been a familiar sight in 500cc Grands Prix for over 30 years.

■ PEUGEOT

A leading marque during France's great era of motorcycle production around the turn of the century, Peugeot was successful in racing and powered the Norton on which Rem Fowler won the first Isle of Man TT in 1907. As early as 1913 Peugeot built a 500cc parallel twin racebike with double overhead cams and four-valve cylinder heads. Peugeot dominated racing in the early 1920s but abandoned competition in 1926. Production in recent years has concentrated on mopeds.

■ PGO

Founded in 1964, Taiwanese firm PGO is a large-volume manufacturer of scooters.

■ ABOVE *PGO's 1600cc V-twin prototype sportsbike caused plenty of interest at the Milan Show in 1991.*

In 1991, PGO hinted at a possible future move into the large-capacity market by revealing the V2 1600, a prototype sportsbike powered by a 1596cc V-twin engine.

■ PIAGGIO

Best known for scooters and mopeds, Italian giant Piaggio is the largest motorcycle manufacturer in Europe and the third biggest in the world. As well as own-brand bikes such as the sophisticated Hexagon and Sfera scooters, Piaggio also owns Vespa and once-mighty Gilera.

■ ABOVE *Piaggio's Hexagon 125cc scooter provided comfort and weather-protection with a fair turn of speed.*

■ ABOVE *In 1911, the Pierce Arrow was one of several American bikes with an in-line four-cylinder engine.*

■ PIERCE

In 1909, American car manufacturer Pierce introduced an in-line four owing much to the design of the Belgian-made FN, but production of the Pierce Arrow lasted only a few years.

■ PÜCH

Austria's oldest bike manufacturer began production in 1903. In 1923 the firm introduced a 220cc two-stroke with a split-single engine layout that was still being built well into the 1960s. Later bikes have included trials and motocross machines, some with 500cc Rotax engines, but recent production has concentrated wholly on mopeds.

■ ABOVE *In the early 1960s, Püch built some competent roadsters such as this 125cc machine from 1962.*

■ QUANTEL-COSWORTH

Perhaps the ultimate British twin, the unique Quantel-Cosworth on which Roger Marshall won at Daytona in 1988 was powered by an 823cc, watercooled, DOHC parallel twin engine that formed a stressed member of an innovative alloy chassis.

■ QUASAR

The radical Quasar, with its feet-first riding position and distinctive bodywork that incorporated a roof, was first built in 1976 by British engineer Malcolm Newell. The original Quasar was powered by a 40bhp Reliant car engine, and despite being long and heavy it combined effortless 100mph (160kph) cruising ability with very good handling. Newell's numerous later developments included the 160mph (257kph) Phasar which was powered by Kawasaki's six-cylinder Z1300 unit, but this machine was built in only tiny numbers.

ROYAL ENFIELD

ROYAL ENFIELD 750cc INTERCEPTOR

Throughout most of its long existence Royal Enfield was one of Britain's larger manufacturers, without matching either the production levels or the glamour of giants such as BSA and Triumph. The firm from Redditch, near Birmingham, began, like many others, as a bicycle

ROYAL ENFIELD INTERCEPTOR (1965)	
Engine	Aircooled 4-valve OHV pushrod parallel twin
Capacity	736cc (71 x 93mm)
Power	53bhp @ 6000rpm
Weight	193kg (425lb) wet
Top speed	105mph (168kph)

■ ABOVE *Royal Enfield's name, little heard of in more recent years, was a very familiar sight in the 1950s and 1960s.*

■ LEFT *The Interceptor went round corners well, despite being a tall bike with rather soft front forks.*

manufacturer before producing its first motorcycles in 1901. By the 1930s Enfield had adopted the Bullet name for a range of 250, 350 and 500cc four-stroke singles. After the Second World War the company introduced a redesigned Bullet single that was successful on the road and in trials, and is now built in India.

Royal Enfield followed the trend for parallel twins in 1948, with a softly-tuned 500cc roadster. Five years later the engine was enlarged to 692cc to power the Meteor, the biggest parallel twin on the market. The sportier Super Meteor led in 1958 to the Constellation, which was later sold with Royal Enfield's innovative Airflow full fairing.

Biggest and best of the twins was the Interceptor, which was released in 1962 with a 736cc engine producing 53bhp. Created partly to supply the American export market's demand for cubic inches, the Interceptor combined impressive mid-range torque and reasonable smoothness with various failings one of which was a feeble front brake. In the mid-1960s Royal Enfield suffered severe financial problems. Interceptor production moved briefly to the West Country before ending in 1968.

■ LEFT *This high-handlebarred Interceptor, built for the US market in 1965, was a handsome and powerful bike.*

OTHER MAKES

■ RALEIGH

Nottingham-based Raleigh started as, and
remains, a bicycle manufacturer, but
between 1899 and 1933 the firm tried its
hand at building some high-quality
motorcycles. Raleigh's four-stroke single
was popular in the early 1920s. It came in
350cc sports or touring form, or bored out
to 400cc for sidecar use.

■ RICKMAN

After making a name with chassis, Don
and Derek Rickman moved into road
racing using Triumph Bonneville engines.
The early 1970s Rickman Interceptor
combined Royal Enfield's engine with a
frame of nickel-plated Reynolds 531
tubing. Rickman's later fully-faired Café
Racer housed a four-cylinder motor from
Honda or Kawasaki, after which the firm
concentrated on bike accessories.

■ ABOVE *When it produced this 350cc
single in 1926 Raleigh was a well-known
manufacturer of motorcycles.*

■ ABOVE *Rickman's Interceptor of 1970
was a fine-handling special, powered by
Royal Enfield's 736 parallel-twin.*

■ RENÉ GILLET

In the 1930s, René Gillet was well known
for its sturdy sidevalve V-twins of 750 and
1000cc capacity, which were well-suited
to sidecar use and became popular with

French armed forces and police. After the
Second World War the firm concentrated
on small two-strokes, and ceased
production in the late 1950s.

■ ROC

Serge Rosset's small ROC firm, based at
Annemasse in France, has established
itself as one of the world's leading racing
chassis specialists. In 1992, former ELF

and Yamaha France Grand Prix team
manager Rosset was, with Britain's Harris,
chosen by Yamaha to build privateer
chassis for the YZR500 V-four engine.
Even world champion Wayne Rainey's
works YZR used a ROC frame at times
during the following season. In 1994
Rosset revealed ROC's own prototype
Grand Prix 500cc V-four bike, called the
Moto Française GP1.

■ LEFT *Niall
Mackenzie was
the leading
500cc privateer
riding a ROC
Yamaha in
1992.*

RUDGE

■ RUDGE 500cc ULSTER

Two bicycle firms, Rudge and Whitworth, merged to form Rudge Whitworth and produced a 3.5bhp single-cylinder motorbike in 1909. Early innovations included a spring-up stand and a hinged rear mudguard to aid wheel removal, but it was a gearing system that led to the firm's first famous model – the Rudge Multi. This used an ingenious system of

RUDGE ULSTER (1930)

Engine	Aircooled 4-valve OHV pushrod single
Capacity	499cc (85 x 88mm)
Power	30bhp approx
Weight	131kg (290lb) dry
Top speed	100mph (160kph)

■ ABOVE *Graham Walker's 1928 Ulster Grand Prix win led to Rudge's 500cc four-valve single being called the Ulster.*

■ BELOW *The Ulster had further success with Wal Handley's Senior TT win in 1930.*

pulleys to maintain the tension of the final drive belt, while allowing the rider to select from no fewer than 21 gear ratios. The Multi was a big success, winning the 1914 Senior TT and remaining in production for nine more years.

Rudge was a leading exponent of four-valve cylinder heads in the mid-1920s, producing the 500cc single on which Graham Walker – the firm's sales manager – sped to victory in the 1928 Ulster Grand Prix.

The sportiest of Rudge's three models was renamed the Ulster in recognition. It used the firm's celebrated linked braking system, whereby the foot-pedal operated both front and rear drums, with the hand lever also working the front brake. Rudge had more racing success in the 1930s, but hit financial trouble and ceased production in 1939.

■ RIGHT *The Rudge Multi, with its long vertical gearlever on the left of the tank, gave a wide choice of ratios.*

OTHER MAKES

■ RUKUO

Japanese firm Rukuo built copies of Harley-Davidson sidevalve V-twins under licence in the 1930s and 1940s, but was one of the many firms that did not survive the sharp contraction of the Japanese industry that followed.

■ RUMI

The Bergamo-based Rumi family has been prominent in the motorcycle world since the early 1950s, when their firm built a rapid 125cc two-stroke twin that was raced with some success. In recent years the Rumi family has been involved in various projects including running a factory-backed Honda team in the World Superbike series, and producing a fine-handling aluminium-framed sportsbike, the RMS650, powered by Honda's single-cylinder NX650 engine.

■ ABOVE *Rumi's RMS650 sportster held a 650cc single-cylinder Honda engine in an aluminium twin-spar frame.*

☙ SCOTT

■ SCOTT SQUIRREL

Alfred Scott built some of the most advanced and distinctive bikes of motorcycling's early years. In 1909 he created a 333cc two-stroke parallel twin featuring the novelties of a kick start, foot-change two-speed gearbox and telescopic front forks. Shortly afterwards Scott adopted full watercooling and enlarged the engine to 486 and 534cc, adding performance that was put to good use in 1912 and 1913, when the

two-strokes won consecutive Senior TTs. The following year saw the start of the legendary Scott Trial, held in the Yorkshire dales near the factory.

Alfred Scott left the company after the First World War to build the three-wheeled Scott Sociable car. He died in 1923, only a year after the firm introduced the Squirrel range, and expanded with a variety of capacities, and names such as Super Squirrel, Sports Squirrel and Flying Squirrel. A typical mid-1920s Squirrel was powered by a 596cc engine with a three-speed,

hand-change gearbox. With a top speed of about 70mph (112kph), good handling and unique looks and sound, the Scotts won many followers.

The Squirrels could be temperamental, however, and prices were quite high. Later models, with conventionally shaped tanks, were heavier and less competitive, and production declined in the 1930s. In 1950 the firm was bought by Birmingham-based Scott fanatic Matt Holder, who continued developing and selling Squirrel motorcycles in small numbers right up until 1978.

SCOTT SQUIRREL (1925)	
Engine	Watercooled two-stroke parallel twin
Capacity	596cc (74.6 x 68.25mm)
Power	25bhp @ 5000rpm
Weight	115kg (253lb) wet
Top speed	70mph (112kph)

OTHER MAKES

■ SANGLAS

Founded in Barcelona in 1942, Sanglas differed from other Spanish firms by ignoring racing in favour of simple, low-revving four-stroke singles, which were popular with civilians and police for many years. In the 1960s, the firm also built two-strokes, known as Rovenas, using engines from Villiers and Zündapp. In the late 1970s Sanglas became involved with Yamaha, initially by using the XS400 twin engine in a roadster called the 400Y. The bike was reasonably successful but in 1981 the Spanish firm was taken over by Yamaha, and shortly afterwards the Sanglas name was dropped altogether.

■ SEELEY

Former sidecar Grand Prix racer Colin Seeley acquired rights to the Matchless G50 and AJS 7R singles in the late 1960s, and developed both the engine and a new chassis, producing the Seeley G50 racer — highly successful in classic racing in recent years — and the Condor roadster. He also developed many other frame kits and specials, including a stylish café racer based on Honda's CB750 four.

■ SEGALE

Italian chassis specialist Luigi Segale has built many high quality specials over the last two decades, around engines ranging from Kawasaki Z1000 fours to Honda 650cc singles, many using his trademark frame layout of narrow-gauge steel tubes and aluminium side-plates. In 1993, Segale produced the rapid and ultra-light SR900R, powered by Honda's four-cylinder CBR900RR motor.

■ SILK

In the early 1970s George Silk, a former Scott apprentice, developed a roadster based on the familiar watercooled, two-stroke parallel twin format. The Silk 700S used a 653cc engine that produced 47bhp, housed in a tubular steel frame made by Spondon Engineering. Although top speed was only 110mph (177kph), the Silk was smooth, light and handled well. Small production levels led to high prices and problems with suppliers, however, and the last bikes were built in 1979.

■ LEFT *A typical Sanglas roadster of the 1970s was a sturdy, efficient but unglamorous 500cc single.*

■ LEFT *The Seeley G50, powered by a single-cylinder Matchless engine, has starred in 500cc classic racing.*

■ LEFT *The Segale SR900R weighed even less than the standard CBR900RR, but cost a great deal more.*

■ LEFT *The stylish 700S owed its two-stroke parallel twin engine layout to its creator George Silk's love of Scotts.*

■ LEFT *The S7
was comfortable,
but had too much
weight, poor brakes
and only mediocre
handling.*

🏍 SUNBEAM

■ **SUNBEAM S8**

Quality and attention to detail were
characteristics for which Sunbeam's
early motorcycles became known,
following the Wolverhampton firm's
introduction of its first model, a 350cc
single, in 1912. Like Sunbeam's earlier
bicycles, the single had a fully-enclosed
drive chain that earned it the nickname

■ BELOW *The S8
was lighter and
faster than the S7,
but it was still not
successful enough
to save Sunbeam.*

SUNBEAM S8 (1949)	
Engine	Aircooled 4-valve SOHC tandem twin
Capacity	487cc (70 x 63.5mm)
Power	26bhp @ 5800rpm
Weight	182kg (400lb) dry
Top speed	85mph (136kph)

"Little Oil Bath". The 3.5bhp single,
introduced a year later, sold well, was
raced successfully and established
Sunbeam's colours of black with gold
lining. Development engineer George
Dance set several records on Sunbeams,
and the single scored two Senior TT
wins in the early 1920s.

Sales declined in the 1930s, and
Sunbeam was sold first to AMC and
then, in 1943, to BSA. After the Second
World War, BSA attempted to capitalize

on Sunbeam's reputation as the
gentleman's motor bicycle by building a
sophisticated roadster. The S7, released
in 1947, was powered by a 487cc four-
stroke tandem twin engine with shaft
final drive. It had a big, heavy chassis
which incorporated fat balloon tyres.
The S7 was underpowered, initially
vibrated terribly and handled poorly. It
was also one of the most expensive bikes
on the market, and unsurprisingly, was
not a commercial success.

■ **LEFT**
Alec Bennet won two TTs on black-and-gold Sunbeams similar to this 350cc model 2 from 1924.

In 1949 Sunbeam introduced the uprated S7 De Luxe, and also produced a sportier version of the twin, the S8. This featured new styling, a louder exhaust system, less weight, front forks similar to those of BSA's A10, and conventional wheels and tyres. With a top speed of about 85mph (136kph) the S8 was faster, and handled better than its predecessor. But further development was minimal, sales remained low and Sunbeam production finally ground to a halt in 1956.

OTHER MAKES

■ SINGER

The most notable design from early British firm Singer was a 222cc four-stroke single-cylinder engine which, together with its fuel tank and carburettor, was housed within a wheel. Singer bought the design in 1900 and used it, both as the rear wheel of a solo and the front wheel of a tricycle, for the next few years. The company also produced more conventional bikes before giving up to concentrate on building cars after the First World War.

■ SPONDON

Named after the Derbyshire town in which it is based, chassis specialist firm Spondon Engineering was founded by Bob Stevenson and Stuart Tiller in 1969. Several early Spondons used Yamaha two-stroke racing engines such as the 125cc AS1, TZ250 and 750cc OW31. Spondon has built frames for roadsters including the Silk and Norton's F1, and produced

numerous specials powered by Japanese fours, from Suzuki's GS1000 to Kawasaki's ZZ-R1100.

■ **ABOVE** *Many Sun roadsters were simple, single-cylinder two-strokes such as this 197cc model from 1956.*

■ **RIGHT** *Norton's rotary racebike, like the later F1 roadster, featured a Spondon twin-spar aluminium frame.*

■ SUN

Typical of the numerous British firms producing modest Villiers-engined two-strokes in the 1950s, Birmingham-based company Sun had a history that included the production of a rotary disc-valve two-stroke racer in the 1920s. Later roadsters such as the 250cc Overlander twin of 1957 were remarkable for the generous weather protection they offered. That wasn't enough to make them popular though, and Sun ceased motorcycle production a few years later.

SUZUKI

■ **SUZUKI T20 SUPER SIX**
Michio Suzuki set up a business manufacturing silk looms in 1909, and ran it until the Second World War. In 1952, problems in the silk loom industry led Suzuki to develop and sell a 36cc two-stroke engine, named the Power Free, which clipped to a bicycle frame. An improved, 60cc version called the Diamond Free followed one year later, and in May 1954 the revived Suzuki firm launched its first complete bike, a 90cc four-stroke single named the Colleda. Entered in that year's Mount Fuji hill-climb, it triumphed over 85 rivals.

Through the late 1950s and early 60s, Suzuki concentrated on small-capacity

■ LEFT *Suzuki entered the bike business with the Power Free, a 36cc engine that clipped to a bicycle.*

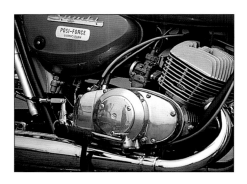

SUZUKI T20 SUPER SIX (1966)	
Engine	Aircooled two-stroke parallel twin
Capacity	247cc (54 x 54mm)
Power	29bhp @ 7500rpm
Weight	138kg (304lb) dry
Top speed	95mph (152kph)

■ ABOVE *The Super Six got its name from the two-stroke parallel twin engine's six-speed gearbox.*

■ LEFT *Attractive styling combined with performance and good handling to make the Super Six popular.*

■ OPPOSITE RIGHT *The GT500 parallel twin of the early 1970s combined 110mph (177kph) top speed with only mediocre handling.*

■ OPPOSITE LEFT *Suzuki's first complete bikes were the 90 and 125cc Colleda two-strokes of the mid-1950s.*

■ RIGHT *Although it was too big and heavy to handle really well, the GT750 proved a good sports-tourer.*

■ BELOW *The GT750's rather bulbous styling made little attempt to disguise its weight.*

two-strokes, in particular on the firm's first purpose-built competition machine, the 125cc Colleda RB of 1959. They included numerous cheap commuter bikes and the sportier, 250cc T10 of 1963 – the company's first export success. But it was a new generation 250 twin, the T20 Super Six – the X6 in America – that put Suzuki on the map when it was launched in 1966.

The name referred to the two-stroke's six-speed gearbox; an even more impressive – but slightly optimistic – number was the claimed top speed of 100mph (160kph). The Super Six's all-new engine produced 29bhp and incorporated a sophisticated Posi-Force lubrication system. Other classy features included Suzuki's first twin-cradle frame, which gave good handling in conjunction with light weight. True top speed was somewhere between 90 and 100mph (144-160kph) – enough anyway to make the Super Six a big hit.

In 1967, Suzuki entered the big bike market with an enlarged two-stroke parallel twin, the T500, which was known as the Titan in America and the Cobra in Britain. Although it was simple and handled rather poorly, the 46bhp T500 was reliable, economical and fast, with a top speed of 110mph (177kph). The twin remained in production for the

next ten years, gaining a disc front brake, electronic ignition, fresh styling and the name GT500 along the way.

Suzuki's first true superbike was the GT750, the big, watercooled three-cylinder two-stroke that became known as the Kettle in Britain and the Water Buffalo in America, following its introduction in 1971. The softly-tuned 738cc engine produced 67bhp, giving the triple a top speed of 115mph (185kph) to go with its generous mid-range torque. Although smooth, quiet and comfortable, the Suzuki was also big and ponderous. It couldn't match the acceleration or excitement of rivals such as Kawasaki's 750cc H1, but its all-round ability kept the GT750 popular for most of the 1970s.

SUZUKI

■ LEFT *The GS1000 combined raw power with the best handling yet from a Japanese Superbike.*

■ SUZUKI GS1000

The GS1000 was a landmark motorcycle not just for Suzuki but for the whole Japanese industry. When it was launched in 1978, the GS outperformed Kawasaki's legendary Z1, its direct rival, in almost every area. More importantly, here at last was a big four-cylinder machine whose chassis was a match for its motor. Japan had been building great powerplants for years, but the GS was the first open-class super-bike that handled really well.

The GS1000's format was conventional, closely based on that of the GS750 introduced a year earlier. The

■ BELOW *Suzuki based the GS1000's four-cylinder motor on Kawasaki's proven DOHC, eight-valve format.*

SUZUKI GS1000 (1978)	
Engine	Aircooled 8-valve DOHC transverse four
Capacity	997cc (70 x 64.8mm)
Power	87bhp @ 8000rpm
Weight	242kg (532lb) dry
Top speed	135mph (216kph)

■ RIGHT *The GS1000's rather ordinary styling disguised the fact that this was an exceptional motorcycle.*

■ BELOW *Wes Cooley won the US Superbike championship for Suzuki in 1980 on a Yoshimura-tuned GS1000S.*

■ BOTTOM *The stunning Katana 1100 of 1982, styled by Anglo-German firm Target Design, was as fast as it looked.*

■ BELOW *Suzuki's first big four-stroke roadster was the fast and sophisticated GS750 four, introduced in 1977.*

aircooled, 997cc engine used twin cams and eight valves to produce 87bhp. The chassis incorporated a rigid tubular steel frame, sophisticated, adjustable suspension parts, wide tyres and twin front disc brakes. Styling was clean and pleasant, if a bit bland.

There was certainly nothing ordinary about the Suzuki's performance, which combined fearsome acceleration with a top speed of 135mph (216 kph). Mid-range power delivery was equally strong, and the GS was comfortable and reliable too. Better still, the bike was rock-steady in a straight line, remaining stable even at cornering speeds that left most rivals wallowing in its wake. The GS1000's only failing was a certain lack of charisma. It was a hugely impressive machine that emphasized Suzuki's arrival as a leading superbike producer.

In 1977, just a year before unleashing the GS1000, Suzuki had released its first big four-cylinder bike in the shape of the GS750 – and scored an immediate success. With a maximum output of 68bhp on tap, the twin-cam GS750 whirred smoothly to over 120mph

(193kph), cruised at 90mph (144kph) and outperformed rivals such as Honda's CB750 and Yamaha's XS750. It handled acceptably, establishing a reputation that would be enhanced by future models. Fast, refined and reliable, the GS750 four represented the start of great things for Suzuki.

The 16-valve GSX1100 that replaced the 8-valve GS1000 in 1980 was an

even faster and more competent bike marred by ugly, angular looks. Two years later Suzuki revamped it to produce the stunning GSX1100S Katana, whose radical combination of nose fairing, low handlebars, humped fuel tank and combined seat/sidepanels gave a superbly raw, aggressive image. The aircooled four-cylinder engine was tuned to produce 111bhp, giving the Katana – named after a Samurai warrior's ceremonial sword – a top speed of more than 140mph (225kph). Handling was excellent despite 250kg (551lb) of weight, and the Suzuki's style and speed combined with a reasonable price to make it a big success.

SUZUKI

■ SUZUKI GSX-R750

The arrival of Suzuki's GSX-R750 in 1985 had a huge impact on the design of supersports motorcycles. This was the first true Japanese race-replica, startlingly close to being simply Suzuki's works endurance bike in road-legal form. The GSX-R was searingly fast, outrageously light and utterly singleminded. No other mass-produced four came close to matching its uniquely aggressive, race-bred image.

Every component of the GSX-R was designed for high performance and low weight. That included the 16-valve,

■ LEFT *The original GSX-R750's ultra-light chassis gave superb cornering but occasional high-speed instability.*

■ OPPOSITE *Early GSX-Rs held an oilcooled 16-valve motor in an aluminium frame.*

■ BELOW *Heavily based on Suzuki's works endurance motorcycles, the first GSX-R750 was a genuine race-replica.*

four-cylinder engine, which was oil-cooled, had a cam cover made from lightweight magnesium, and produced 100bhp at 10,500rpm. The Suzuki's aluminium frame weighed half as much as

the steel frame of the previous GSX750, and held stout 41mm diameter front forks. A racy twin-headlamp fairing, foam-backed clocks, clip-on bars and rearset footrests completed the package.

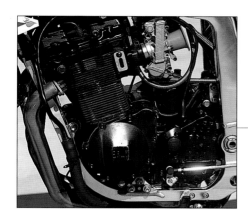

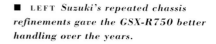

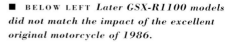

SUZUKI GSX-R750 (1985)	
Engine	Oilcooled 16-valve DOHC transverse four
Capacity	749cc (70 x 48.7mm)
Power	100bhp @ 10,500rpm
Weight	176kg (387lb) dry
Top speed	145mph (233kph)

Performance lived up to all expectations. Acceleration was flat below 7000rpm, after which the GSX-R raced towards 145mph (233kph) with a muted scream from its four-into-one exhaust system. Handling and braking were exceptional, aided by the remarkably low weight of 176kg (387lb). The GSX-R750 was instantly successful both on the racetrack and in the showrooms, and its format was hastily followed by other manufacturers to create the modern brand of sporting superbike.

A year after triggering the sportsbike revolution with the GSX-R750, Suzuki produced a bigger version that brought a new dimension to two-wheeled performance. The GSX-R1100 of 1986 added mid-range power and even more outright speed to the smaller model's assets of light weight, handling and racetrack style. Its 125bhp oilcooled engine provided a 155mph (249kph) top speed, plus instant acceleration at the twist of the throttle; its lightweight aluminium-framed chassis gave unmatched open-class handling. Unfortunately for Suzuki, a 1989 redesign, the 1100K, combined fresh

■ ABOVE *Hervé Moineau led Suzuki's works endurance team to many wins.*

■ BELOW *The 1994 model GSX-R750 had a watercooled, 116bhp powerplant.*

styling with a modified chassis that ruined the big GSX-R's handling. Frequent further revamps through the 1990s restored some poise and added even more power, but the GSX-R1100 never regained its performance lead.

In contrast to its problems with the GSX-R1100, Suzuki used a process of repeated refinement to keep the GSX-R750 popular, even when its impact in racing had dimmed. The first major revision was the 750J model of 1988 – known as the Slingshot after its carburettors – which was heavier but featured new styling, uprated chassis parts and a more powerful engine. In 1992 the GSX-R gained a watercooled motor with a peak output of 116bhp, the highest yet. A stiffer frame, revised chassis geometry and upside-down forks meant that the GSX-R750W shared almost no components with the original model. It had also gained a fair amount of weight along the way. But in spirit the GSX-R750 had not changed at all.

■ BELOW LEFT *Early RG500s housed the watercooled square-four engine in a tubular steel frame.*

■ BOTTOM *Barry Sheene's championship-winning RG500 was run by the British-based Texaco Heron team.*

SUZUKI

■ SUZUKI RG500

Suzuki's first move into international racing was at the Isle of Man TT in 1960, with a 125cc team including Mitsuo Itoh, who would later become the firm's racing chief. Results were modest but the experience proved vital. The team stayed at the same hotel as MZ rider Ernst Degner – who in 1961 defected from East Germany, bringing the secrets of MZ's powerful two-strokes to Suzuki. Degner won the Japanese firm's first world championship in 1962, in the new 50cc class. New Zealander Hugh Anderson and Germany's Hans-Georg Anscheidt added five more titles in the following six seasons on Suzuki's peaky little 50cc machines, and Anderson went on to win the 125cc championship in 1963 and 1965.

SUZUKI RG500 (1976)	
Engine	Watercooled rotary disc-valve two-stroke square four
Capacity	495cc (54 x 54mm)
Power	114bhp @ 11,000rpm
Weight	125kg (275lb) dry
Top speed	170mph (272kph)

Success in the prestigious 500cc class was eventually achieved with the legendary square-four RG500, which not only won four world championships but was favoured by privateer racers for over a decade. The RG's layout was developed from that of the short-lived 250cc RZ63 square-four of the mid-1960s, whose habit of seizing at high speed earned it the name "Whispering Death". The RG500 was first raced in 1974 by riders including rising British star Barry Sheene. After initial problems had been solved, its watercooled, disc-valve two-stroke engine proved to be powerful and reliable.

In 1976 the RG500, redesigned with new 54 x 54mm engine dimensions and with its output increased to 114bhp at 11,000 rpm, took Sheene to his and

■ RIGHT AND
BELOW *Barry
Sheene's glamour
and showmanship
were as important
to Suzuki as his
riding ability.*

■ RIGHT *Kevin
Schwantz won the 1993
title on the RGV500.*

■ BELOW RIGHT *Schwantz won two
Grands Prix on the RGV500 in 1988, but
winning the title took another five years.*

five Grand Prix wins were matched by
five crashes that left him second in the
championship.

In 1992 Suzuki followed Honda's lead
in revising the RGV, whose cylinders
were by now spaced at 70 degrees, with
a big bang firing order that made the
170bhp V-four more rideable. Injuries
ruined that season for Schwantz, but in
1993 his matured but still aggressive
riding, coupled with the Suzuki's speed,
reliability and traditional fine handling,
finally earned the Texan the right to
replace his familiar No. 34 plate with
the champion's No. 1.

Suzuki's first 500cc championship. RG
riders also filled the next five places.
Sheene retained the title for the Heron
Suzuki team in 1977, and Italians Marco
Lucchinelli and Franco Uncini won the
championship on Team Gallina RG500s
in 1981 and 1982. By then, the engine
had become a stepped-four, producing
124bhp, and the frame tubes were
aluminium instead of the original steel.

In 1987 the RG500 was replaced by
an all-new V-four, the RGV500, and
Suzuki increased its racing involvement
with a full factory-backed team. That
season saw some promising Grand Prix
rides from young American star Kevin
Schwantz, beginning a long association
with Suzuki. The following five seasons
would ultimately prove frustrating,
particularly in 1990 when Schwantz's

TRIUMPH

■ **TRIUMPH SPEED TWIN**

Triumph, one of Britain's oldest and
most famous manufacturers, was
founded by two Germans. Siegfried
Bettmann sold bicycles under his own
name in the 1880s before changing his
firm's name to Triumph. In 1902, in
partnership with Mauritz Schulte,
Bettmann fitted a Belgian 2.25bhp
Minerva engine into a bicycle to
produce the first Triumph motorcycle.

TRIUMPH SPEED TWIN (1937)	
Engine	Aircooled 4-valve OHV pushrod parallel twin
Capacity	498cc (63 x 80mm)
Power	29bhp @ 6000rpm
Weight	166kg (365lb) dry
Top speed	90mph (145kph)

Three years later the Coventry firm had
designed and built its own 3bhp engine,
and soon manufactured a range of bikes
whose reliability earned the nickname
"Trusty Triumph".

Triumph enhanced its reputation with
the 500cc four-stroke single Model H,
which was built in large numbers before,
during and after the First World War.
More innovative was the Model R,
whose four-valve cylinder head layout,
designed by Harry Ricardo, would be
perfected by Honda 40 years later.
Triumph's most popular bike of the
1920s was the 500cc sidevalve Model P,

which was produced at the impressive
rate of 1000 per week. But the company
hit financial problems and in 1936 was
sold to Ariel owner Jack Sangster, who

■ LEFT *Triumph's logo was a familiar sight in the 1950s.*

■ RIGHT *Early models, like this 1912 single, inspired the nickname "Trusty Triumph".*

■ BELOW *The 650cc Thunderbird, seen here in 1956 form, was another big hit for Triumph.*

appointed 35-year-old Edward Turner as chief designer and general manager.

Turner quickly showed an inspired touch, revamping Triumph's slow-selling line of 250, 350 and 500cc singles with better finish, extra performance and new names – Tiger 70, 80 and 90. They were immediately successful, and were followed in 1937 by Turner's master-piece, the 500cc Speed Twin. This was an all-new parallel twin, a brave move considering that singles had dominated the market for several decades, and that Triumph's own 650cc Model 6/1 of four years earlier had sold poorly.

The Speed Twin produced 29bhp, had lively acceleration and a respectable top speed of 90mph (145kph), and was far smoother than most comparable singles. It was also neatly styled and compact, as the motor slotted into the familiar Tiger 90 frame. At 166kg (365lb) it was slightly lighter than the single, and was only slightly more expensive. The Speed Twin was an immediate success, marking a turning point in Triumph's fortunes and inspiring the rival manufacturers to build parallel twins of their own.

A year after the Speed Twin, in 1938, Triumph released the Tiger 100 – a sportier, 33bhp version that on a good day really was capable of touching the magic 100mph (160kph). Both models were revised slightly and continued to sell well after the Second World War. In 1950, largely to satisfy the important American export market, Triumph enlarged the engine to 650cc to produce the 6T Thunderbird. The "T-bird" was another success, its handling and acceleration more than satisfying the demands of a speed-hungry motor-cycling fraternity.

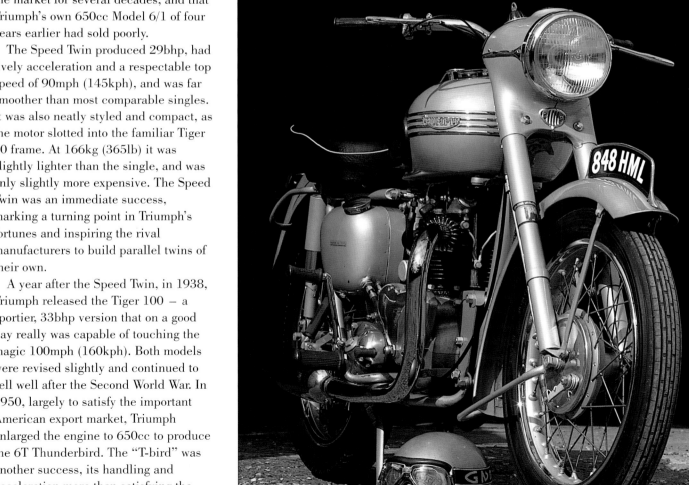

TRIUMPH

■ TRIUMPH T120 BONNEVILLE

The most famous Triumph of all was the Bonneville, which was released as a sporty 650cc twin in 1959. The original T120 Bonneville was basically the existing Tiger 110, fitted with optional splayed inlet ports and twin Amal carburettors. Its name came from the Bonneville salt flats in Utah, where a

TRIUMPH T120 BONNEVILLE (1961)	
Engine	Aircooled 4-valve OHV pushrod parallel twin
Capacity	649cc (71 x 82mm)
Power	46bhp @ 6500rpm
Weight	183kg (403lb) dry
Top speed	110mph (177kph)

■ BOTTOM *This neat 650cc Bonnie was built in 1970, the year before the oil-in-frame chassis was introduced.*

streamlined Triumph ridden by Johnny Allen had been timed at 214mph (344kph) in 1956. Although the FIM refused to ratify the speed as a world record, on a technicality, the ensuing row gave Triumph valuable publicity.

Initially the Bonneville was styled like the Tiger with a headlamp nacelle, swept-back touring handlebars and heavy mudguards. Peak output was 46bhp at 6500rpm, which was too much for the wobble-prone original chassis. In 1960 the T120 was revamped with a

new twin-cradle frame and forks, a separate headlamp, a new seat and sportier mudguards. Combining genuine 110mph (177kph) performance with mid-range punch, reasonable smoothness, adequate handling and good looks, the resultant "Bonnie" was a popular roadburner.

The Bonneville was regularly updated over the next decade, notably with the adoption of a unit-construction engine and gearbox in 1963. In 1971 the twin gained a new oil-in-frame chassis, which was much criticized until lowered a year

■ BELOW *Its 649cc, pushrod-operated parallel twin engine kept the Bonneville on top throughout the 1960s.*

■ ABOVE *The tuned Thruxton Bonneville was named after the British circuit where the T120 scored many production wins.*

■ LEFT *In 1977 Triumph produced the limited edition Silver Jubilee Bonneville.*

later. By 1972, it was estimated that 250,000 Bonnevilles had been built. Many were raced with success. In the Isle of Man, John Hartle won the production TT in 1967, and Malcolm Uphill set the first production 100mph (160kph) lap two years later.

In 1973 Triumph increased capacity to 744cc to produce the T140 Bonneville, which was more flexible, if no faster and less smooth. But parent company Norton Villiers Triumph was losing money, and rumours of imminent closure of the Meriden factory led to an 18-month sit-in, after which production was restarted by a workers' co-operative. Triumph struggled on, and fortunes improved enough to allow introduction of electric-start and eight-valve variations of the twin in the early 1980s. But low sales and rising debts finally led to the company going into liquidation in 1983, after which it was bought by current owner John Bloor. The Bonneville's final fling came when it was built under licence in Devon, by parts specialist Racing Spares, between 1985 and 1988.

OTHER MAKES

■ TRITON

The archetypal special of the 1960s was the Triton, the blend of parallel twin Triumph engine and Norton Featherbed frame that was loved by rockers and café racers. The man who did most to make the model famous was Dave Degens, the London-based racer/engineer

who won the Barcelona 24-hour endurance race on one in 1970. Degens' firm, Dresda Engineering, built numerous Tritons in the 1960s, and was still producing near-identical machines 30 years later. A less common Triumph derivative was the Tribsa, which combined a similar powerplant with a BSA frame.

■ LEFT *A Dresda Triton built by racer/engineer Dave Degens was one of the ultimate café racers of the 1960s.*

TRIUMPH

■ LEFT *Despite superior handling, the T150 did not make the same impact as Honda's CB750 four.*

■ TRIUMPH T150 TRIDENT

Triumph's T150 Trident was arguably the world's finest roadster when it was released in 1969. The new 740cc, pushrod-operated three-cylinder engine produced a healthy 58bhp, sending the Trident racing to a top speed of 125mph (201kph) with a pleasant howl from its distinctively shaped ray-gun tailpipes. The Trident's unusual, angular styling was by no means to every rider's taste in 1969. But the triple was smooth, allowing relaxed 90mph (145kph) cruising for as long as the upright riding position and poor fuel economy would allow. Handling was good, too, thanks to

a modified version of the chassis used by Triumph's twins.

BSA had owned Triumph since 1951, and also built a version of the triple, the Rocket 3. This had similar styling, with the motor tilted forward in a single-downtube frame. But the struggling firm had taken too long to produce the

■ BELOW *The original Trident's angular styling was unpopular with many riders, particularly in America.*

triples, which had been under development for several years. Only a few months later, Honda released the four-cylinder CB750, with the added sophistication of an overhead-cam engine, electric starter and superior reliability. Neither Trident nor Rocket 3 came close to matching the CB750's impact.

TRIUMPH T150 TRIDENT (1969)

Engine	Aircooled 6-valve OHV pushrod transverse triple
Capacity	740cc (67 x 70mm)
Power	58bhp @ 7250rpm
Weight	213kg (468lb) dry
Top speed	125mph (201kph)

Triples were successful on the race circuit though, in particular "Slippery Sam", the Trident that won consecutive Production TTs between 1971 and 1975. Some of the best results came in America, where Gary Nixon had been AMA Grand National champion on Triumph twins in 1967 and 1968. The road-race triples used frames made by Rob North, with blue-and-white fairings for Triumph, and red-and-white for BSA. At Daytona in 1971, the triples took the first three places, Dick Mann winning on a BSA ahead of Triumph's Gene Romero, the reigning Grand National champion. Shortly afterwards, the triples were outpaced by Yamaha's two-strokes.

The most distinctive version of the triple was the Triumph X-75 Hurricane, a special built in limited numbers from 1972. The Hurricane was commissioned by Triumph's American distributor and designed by fairing and luggage specialist Craig Vetter. It combined a lower-geared version of the standard 740cc engine with longer front forks, a stylish tank/seat unit and a bold new three-silencer exhaust system, and was a predecessor of the modern Japanese factory customs.

In 1975, the basic triple was restyled and overhauled to produce the T160 Trident, which featured its engine angled forward in a new and improved frame. Numerous other modifications included an electric starter, rear disc brake and left-foot gearchange. Handsome styling, smooth power and excellent handling made the new Trident arguably the best British roadster so far, but it was not enough to save struggling Triumph, and production was short-lived.

■ TOP *The T160 Trident introduced in 1975 was both fast and stylish, but came too late to save Triumph.*

■ ABOVE LEFT *Triumph's works triples took riders including Paul Smart to many wins in the 1970s.*

■ ABOVE RIGHT *Meriden development rider and racer Percy Tait raced triples including the famous "Slippery Sam".*

■ LEFT *The lean looks of the X-75 Hurricane gained the American-designed factory special many admirers.*

TRIUMPH

■ TRIUMPH SPEED TRIPLE

The British motorcycle industry's decline seemed almost complete in 1983, when Triumph finally went into liquidation. But the name was bought by building multi-millionaire John Bloor, who spent the next eight years secretly developing a range of modern bikes in a purpose-built factory at Hinckley, near the old Meriden site. In 1991 Triumph released a range of six roadsters, powered by watercooled, DOHC three- and four-cylinder engines. Their unique modular design employed many identical components, reducing cost. Ironically, a series of modular designs

TRIUMPH SPEED TRIPLE (1994)	
Engine	Watercooled 12-valve DOHC transverse triple
Capacity	885cc (76 x 65mm)
Power	97bhp @ 9000rpm
Weight	209kg (460lb) dry
Top speed	130mph (209kph)

produced by BSA-Triumph's engineers in 1973 had not been adopted.

Base model was the unfaired Trident, which had a 749 or 885cc three-cylinder engine. The larger unit produced 98bhp with plenty of mid-range torque, giving lively acceleration towards a top speed of 130mph (209kph). Like the other bikes the Trident had a large-diameter steel spine frame, with Japanese suspension and brakes. Top of the range

■ OPPOSITE TOP *The 1991 model Daytona 1000 sportster (left) and Trophy 1200 shared many parts.*

■ OPPOSITE BOTTOM *The popular Speed Triple of 1994 combined a three-cylinder engine with aggressive, naked styling.*

■ LEFT *Designed largely for the American market, the Thunderbird retro-bike was a hit worldwide in 1995.*

■ FAR LEFT *The basic Triumph model has been the unfaired Trident triple.*

■ BELOW LEFT *The Daytona 1200 gave 146bhp performance in 1993.*

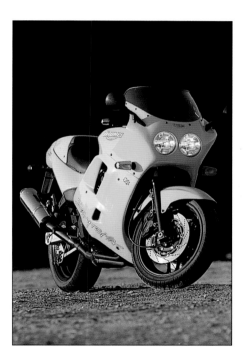

was the 1200 Trophy, whose 123bhp four-cylinder engine was effectively the triple with an extra pot. Smooth, well built and capable of over 150mph (241kph), the Trophy was a match for the best Japanese sports tourers.

Triumph was rapidly successful in Britain. Exports also took off, after a slow start in the important German market. Triumph soon learnt to concentrate on its traditional triples, and in 1994 produced its most inspired model yet. The Speed Triple retained the original 885cc engine and spine frame, gaining upmarket cycle parts including multi-adjustable suspension, bigger brakes and fat radial tyres. The Speed Triple was quick, responsive and agile; and its name, lean styling and low, clip-on handlebars brought to mind the 1960s' days of

burn-ups and twin-cylinder Triumphs.

Nostalgia played an even greater part in the model that Triumph developed to spearhead its delayed return to America in 1995. The Thunderbird incorporated traditional styling features such as a rounded fuel tank with mouth-organ badges, and peashooter silencers. Exaggerated cooling fins gave a new look to the 885cc triple engine, which was detuned to a modest 69bhp. Other features, including raised bars, wire wheels and a lower seat, also moved away from the modular concept.

The T-bird's style and smooth, torquey engine made it a hit. With the expanding Hinckley factory's annual production due to exceed 10,000 for the first time, John Bloor's huge investment seemed to be paying off.

OTHER MAKES

■ URAL

From a big factory in the Ural mountains, the firm of the same name has long produced 650cc flat-twins based on BMW designs of the early 1940s. Inevitably crude by modern standards, most of the 250,000 bikes built annually were sold in the former Soviet Union. British importer Neval produced custom versions including the Soviet Knight, which combined the original 32bhp pushrod motor and simple

steel-framed chassis with high handlebars, running lights and added chrome. Handling was heavy and sophistication lacking, but the Soviet Knight was cheap and cruised smoothly at 60mph (96kph) with a certain old-fashioned charm.

■ RIGHT *High bars and added chrome gave the Soviet Knight a touch of Harley-style glamour, without the expense.*

■ BELOW *The sporty Clubman Venom of the early 1960s (left) was uprated to produce the Thruxton in 1965.*

■ BOTTOM *Thruxton features included tuned motor, uprated front brake, silver paint finish and humped seat.*

VELOCETTE

■ VELOCETTE VENOM THRUXTON

From the 1930s until its demise in 1971, Velocette was best known for its large-capacity four-stroke singles, most of them with traditional black-and-gold finish and a distinctive fishtail silencer. The firm was founded in 1904 by German-born Johannes Gütgemann, who later changed his name to John

VELOCETTE VENOM THRUXTON (1965)	
Engine	Aircooled 2-valve OHV pushrod single
Capacity	499cc (86 x 86mm)
Power	40bhp @ 6200rpm
Weight	177kg (390lb) dry
Top speed	105mph (168kph)

Goodman, and was later run by his sons and grandson. Initially called Veloce Ltd, the company began by producing four-strokes. The first two-stroke, built in 1913, was called Velocette, after which the name was used for all of their subsequent models.

Velocette's racing involvement boosted development and prestige, although the expense was considerable. The Birmingham firm's first great bike was the overhead-cam 350cc single, designed by Percy Goodman, which won the 1926 Junior TT. Velocette's

■ BELOW LEFT
*The 350cc MAC of
the mid-1930s was
a hugely successful
machine.*

■ BELOW RIGHT
*Stanley Woods
powers his Velo to
Junior TT victory
in 1939.*

■ BOTTOM RIGHT
*Neglecting singles
to build the LE,
pictured in Mk.2
form from 1955,
proved disastrous
for Velocette.*

■ LEFT *The rapid 500cc parallel twin
Roarer of 1939 was halted by the War and
subsequent ban on supercharging.*

OTHER MAKES

■ **VAN VEEN**
Henk van Veen was the Dutch importer of German Kreidlers. He took over the firm's race effort and led the Van Veen Kreidlers to a string of 50cc world championships in the 1970s. An even more ambitious project was the Van Veen OCR1000, a luxurious rotary-engined superbike. Although fast and smooth, the OCR was more remarkable for being the world's most expensive roadster in the late 1970s, and production was perhaps understandably short-lived.

■ **VICTORIA**
Like BMW, fellow German firm Victoria built flat-twins in the 1920s. Best known model was the V35 Bergmeister of the 1950s, a 350cc V-twin whose early vibration problems required lengthy development. Later bikes included the revolutionary 197cc Swing of 1956, which featured push-button gearchanging. In 1958 Victoria joined DKW and Express to form the Zweirad Union, but sales were poor and production came to an end in 1966.

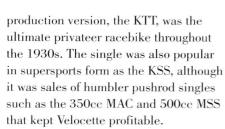
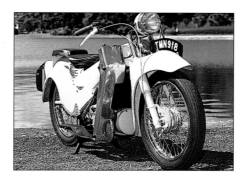

production version, the KTT, was the ultimate privateer racebike throughout the 1930s. The single was also popular in supersports form as the KSS, although it was sales of humbler pushrod singles such as the 350cc MAC and 500cc MSS that kept Velocette profitable.

After the Second World War, Velocette's racing success continued, notably with 350cc world championships for Freddie Frith and Bob Foster in 1949 and 1950. Best known roadsters were the 500cc Venom and 350cc Viper singles, which from 1960 were available in Clubmans trim with tuned engines and stiffer suspension. Fastest of all was the Venom Thruxton, released in 1965. Its tuned engine put out 40bhp and the chassis specification included alloy rims and a powerful twin-leading-shoe front brake. Typically hard to start, and rough at low speeds, the Thruxton – named after the Hampshire track used for long-distance production races – was a rapid street racer that could cruise at a respectable 90mph (145kph).

Velocette was also keen to produce less sporty bikes, and by 1949 almost all the singles had been dropped to make way for the revolutionary LE. This strange looking bike had legshields, a pressed-steel frame and a watercooled, flat-twin sidevalve engine, initially of 150cc. Although well built and reliable, the LE was also expensive. Even when uprated with a 192cc engine in 1951 the LE was popular only with the police, earning it the nickname "Noddy bike". The later Viceroy, a large 250cc scooter, proved even more disastrous, and Velocette went into liquidation in 1971.

■ ABOVE *The stylish and powerful Dutch-built Van Veen OCR1000 rotary was one of the most exotic Superbikes of the 1970s, but its inevitably high price limited sales.*

■ BELOW *Vincent's scroll logo, normally on a black background, adorned arguably the finest bikes of the 1950s.*

■ MIDDLE *The Black Shadow's 998cc V-twin engine featured tuned and polished internals plus black enamel finish.*

■ BOTTOM *Vincent's Series C Rapide combined thunderous performance with excellent handling and braking.*

VINCENT

■ VINCENT RAPIDE SERIES C

Fast, rugged and comfortable, Vincent's big V-twins were the ultimate high performance roadsters of their day. The firm was founded in 1928 by visionary engineer Philip Vincent, who as a schoolboy had designed the cantilever rear suspension system that all his bikes would use. Backed by his father, Vincent bought the defunct company HRD in an attempt to overcome market resistance to his first bikes, which used JAP single engines.

Vincent and Australian designer Phil Irving produced the Stevenage firm's first engine, a high camshaft 500cc single, in 1934. The resultant Meteor tourer and Comet sports singles were a success, the latter capable of an impressive 90mph (145kph). In 1936 Irving combined two Comet cylinders at 47 degrees to produce a 998cc, 45bhp V-twin. The Series A Rapide's 110mph (177kph) top speed

VINCENT RAPIDE SERIES C (1949)	
Engine	Aircooled 4-valve pushrod 50-degree V-twin
Capacity	998cc (84 x 90mm)
Power	45bhp @ 5200rpm
Weight	208kg (458lb) dry
Top speed	110mph (177kph)

made it the fastest production vehicle on the road, but the power led to transmission problems, and external oil lines led to the bike being nicknamed "the plumber's nightmare".

After the Second World War, Vincent introduced the Series B Rapide. This featured a redesigned 50-degree, unit-construction V-twin engine that was an integral part of the chassis, taking the place of the previous tubular frame. As

■ RIGHT *The Series A Rapide's 110mph (177kph) top speed made it the world's fastest roadster in the late 1930s.*

■ BELOW RIGHT *Only about 200 of the dramatic, fully enclosed Series D models were built, before production ended in 1955.*

OTHER MAKES

■ WANDERER

German firm Wanderer was founded in 1902 and built numerous singles and twins, some of which were used by the Germans in the First World War. Janecek of Prague built the Wanderer under licence, and in 1929 became the sole manufacturer as Janecek-Wanderer, later shortening the name to Jawa.

■ ABOVE *Wanderer produced this attractive little belt-drive V-twin, rated at 3.25bhp, in 1911.*

■ WASP

Chassis specialist Wasp began building off-road competition frames in 1968. The Wiltshire, England, firm's successful involvement in sidecar motocross led to production of its own 1000cc parallel twin engine in the early 1980s.

■ WERNER

The Russian-born, Paris-based Werner brothers, Michel and Eugene, were among motorcycling's greatest pioneers. Their first 217cc single, produced from 1898 onwards, was light and practical, and sold well. But the Werners are chiefly remembered for the innovative 1901-model New Werner whose layout, with the engine set low in a diamond-style bicycle frame, greatly improved handling and set the pattern for years to come.

well as reaching an effortless 100mph (160kph) at just 4600rpm, the mighty Rapide handled well and braked hard, thanks to twin drums on each wheel. In 1949 Vincent introduced the Series C Rapide, with Girdraulic forks replacing the previous Brampton girders.

The ultimate V-twin was the Black Shadow, introduced a year earlier, which was powered by a tuned, 55bhp black-finished engine. Top speed was a remarkable 120mph (193kph) plus, recorded on a speedometer calibrated to 150mph (241kph). That speed was achieved in the same year at Bonneville when Rollie Free, riding a tuned V-twin, stripped to swimming trunks and shoes to set a world record for unsupercharged bikes at 150.313mph (241.898kph). Other legendary Vincents were Gunga Din, Nero and the supercharged Super Nero, on which George Brown set speed records and won many races.

In 1955 Vincent introduced the Series D models, the Black Knight and tuned Black Prince. Despite Vincent's traditional high prices, the motorcycles were by then being sold at a loss, and production ceased at the end of the year. Hopes that the name would be revived came 40 years later, when American Bernard Li revealed plans for a traditionally styled but modern 1500cc V-twin roadster to be called the Vincent Black Eagle.

■ ABOVE *Rollie Free stripped to just a pair of bathing trunks to top 150mph (241kph) at Bonneville in 1948.*

■ ABOVE *The less sporty of Vincent's early 500cc singles was the Meteor, seen here in 1938 form.*

YAMAHA

■ YAMAHA 350cc YR5

Torakusu Yamaha trained as a clockmaker before, in 1897, founding Nippon Gakki, which grew into one of the world's largest musical instrument manufacturers. In 1955, Nippon Gakki established the Yamaha company to build motorbikes, using machinery that had made aircraft propellers in the Second World War. The first bike was a 125cc two-stroke single called the YA-1 or Red Dragonfly, based on a German DKW. The twin-cylinder YD-1 followed in 1957 and Yamaha began establishing a reputation for quick, light and reliable two-strokes, many of which featured the company's tuning fork logo on the tank.

■ **ABOVE LEFT** *Good handling combined with brisk acceleration and competitive price to ensure the YR5's success.*

■ **MIDDLE LEFT** *Victory in the 1955 Asama road race helped the YA-1's reputation.*

■ **BELOW** *The shape of the YR5, and the RD350, was echoed in many smaller Yamahas.*

■ LEFT *Phil Read heads for victory in the 250cc TT in 1971, the year he won his fourth world title for Yamaha.*

■ RIGHT *Future Grand Prix star Niall Mackenzie heads a typically frenzied battle in a RD350 Pro-Am race in 1983.*

YAMAHA 350cc YR5 (1970)	
Engine	Aircooled reed-valve two-stroke parallel twin
Capacity	347cc (64 x 54mm)
Power	36bhp @ 7000rpm
Weight	150kg (330lb) wet
Top speed	95mph (152kph)

■ ABOVE *Yamaha's first four-stroke roadster, the XS-1 of 1969, copied British bikes with its 650cc parallel twin engine.*

In the 1960s, Yamaha's successful series of 250cc YDS models led to the first 350cc twin, the YR1. In 1970, the firm released the neatly styled YR5, its aircooled parallel twin engine producing a maximum of 36bhp, which was enough to send the lightweight Yamaha screaming to 95mph (152kph). Handling and braking were good, reliability was excellent, price was competitive and the YR5 became hugely popular. Notable successors included the six-speed RD350 of 1974; the angular, 100mph (160kph) RD400 of 1976; the watercooled, single-shock RD350LC of 1981; and the legendary 1983 model YPVS or Power Valve, whose exhaust power valve improved mid-range performance and helped produce a claimed 53bhp, over 50 per cent up on the YR5's output. The fully-faired RD350LC F2 that followed was still being built, in Brazil, in the mid-1990s.

Yamaha's first period of Grand Prix success came in the 1960s, in the smaller classes. Phil Read won the 250cc title in 1964 on the parallel twin RD56 – the first time it had been won by a two-stroke – and retained it the following season. For 1967, Yamaha built a 35bhp, 16,000rpm V-four on which Bill Ivy won that year's 125cc title. Following Honda's retirement from racing, Yamaha intended to share the 1968 championships between team-mates Read and Ivy. But Read, with the 125cc crown safe, controversially refused to play that game and went on to take the 250cc title too.

Yamaha's first four-stroke roadster was the 650cc XS-1 of 1969, a British-style parallel twin that was capable of 105mph (168kph). In America the twin was competitively priced and was a success, particularly when updated to produce a series of XS650 models. The last of these, the US-market Heritage Special cruiser, brought the XS into the early 1980s, by which time production had soared well into six figures.

■ RIGHT *The fast and popular RD350LC Power Valve was available with or without a fairing in the late 1980s.*

YAMAHA

■ YAMAHA FZR1000

The bike that brought Yamaha to the forefront of superbike design was the four-cylinder FZR1000, which many riders regarded as the best Japanese sportster in the years following its launch in 1987. Its powerplant was a watercooled, 989cc engine whose angled-forward cylinder layout and DOHC, 20-valve cylinder head format had been introduced on the FZ750 two years earlier. The FZR's peak output of 125bhp matched that of Suzuki's GSX-R1100, class leader at the time.

Yamaha's Genesis factory racebike provided inspiration for the FZR's chassis, which centred on a rigid aluminium twin-spar Deltabox frame. Cycle parts included stout 41mm forks, a 17-inch front wheel and low-profile radial tyres. The motor was more than impressive, pulling smoothly from low revs until the FZR was hurtling towards its top speed of 160mph (257kph), with its rider crouching behind an efficient

twin-headlamp fairing. Handling and braking were also excellent, and the Yamaha rapidly became hugely popular.

Numerous updates in subsequent years succeeded in retaining the FZR's cutting edge – notably in 1989 when Yamaha enlarged the motor to 1002cc and added an electronically operated exhaust valve whose acronym led to the bike being universally known as the EXUP. The system

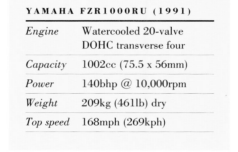

YAMAHA FZR1000RU (1991)	
Engine	Watercooled 20-valve DOHC transverse four
Capacity	1002cc (75.5 x 56mm)
Power	140bhp @ 10,000rpm
Weight	209kg (461lb) dry
Top speed	168mph (269kph)

added useful mid-range performance; peak power was also increased, to 140bhp. A comprehensively revamped chassis provided improved handling to match, making the EXUP the pick of the Japanese Superbikes. Two years later the package was further improved with the FZR1000RU, featuring sharper styling and upside-down front forks.

In marked contrast to the light and agile FZR1000, Yamaha's first big four, the 1978 model XS1100, was a Japanese Superbike of the old school – a large, powerful, aircooled engine in a heavy chassis that was barely capable of keeping it under control. The 1101cc twin-cam motor produced a maximum of 95bhp and was particularly memorable for its huge reserves of mid-range

■ BELOW *By the early 1990s the FZR1000 had been overtaken by faster sportsbikes, but still remained a fine machine.*

■ LEFT *The FZR1000's torquey, 140bhp engine meant that wheelies were only a twist of the throttle away.*

■ RIGHT *The powerful and fine-handling FZ750 of 1985 did not attract the sales that it deserved.*

torque, which gave effortless acceleration to a top speed of 135mph (217kph). The XS was also smooth, comfortable and well-equipped. But the shaft-drive Yamaha's bulk and 270kg (595lb) of weight made for ponderous handling and instability at high speed, which severely limited its appeal.

Although Yamaha's FJ1100 was billed as a pure sportsbike when it was launched in 1984, the aircooled four quickly found its niche as a smooth, comfortable and effortlessly fast sports-tourer. It looked good, handled well, had a protective fairing and a 150mph (241kph) top speed, and most of all its broad powerband gave instant acceler-ation from almost any engine speed. That was even truer of the FJ1200, created in 1986 by enlarging the 16-valve engine to 1188cc. In the 1990s Yamaha intro-duced further refinements, including a rubber-mounted engine and anti-lock brakes, that kept the FJ popular after over ten years in production.

■ RIGHT *Few rival sports-tourers have approached the FJ1200's blend of speed and long-distance comfort.*

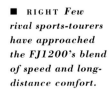

YAMAHA

■ YAMAHA YZR500

Yamaha's YZR has been the dominant 500cc Grand Prix bike of the modern era, winning six world championships between 1984 and 1993, and also providing the basis for the ROC and Harris-framed privateer V-fours of recent seasons. The Japanese factory's experience with 500cc V-fours began with Kenny Roberts' disc-valve OW61

YAMAHA YZR500 (1991)	
Engine	Watercooled 80-degree V-four crankcase reed-valve two-stroke
Capacity	498cc (56 x 50.6mm)
Power	165bhp @ 12,500rpm
Weight	130kg (286lb) dry
Top speed	190mph (304kph)

■ ABOVE *Eddie Lawson won the 1986 Dutch TT on the way to the second of his three world titles on the YZR500.*

■ LEFT *Six world titles in the decade following its introduction emphasized the YZR500's impact on Grand Prix racing.*

■ LEFT *Wayne Rainey (17) took over from Eddie Lawson (3) to win a hat-trick of titles for Yamaha.*

OTHER MAKES

■ ZENITH

A leading marque in the early years of the century, Zenith was best known for the popular Gradua with its adjustable gearing, operated by a long, so-called coffee grinder hand lever. Zenith built Villiers and JAP-engined singles in the 1930s, but production effectively ended at the start of the Second World War.

■ ZÜNDAPP

One of the major German firms for many years, Zündapp was founded in 1917 initially to make gun parts. Successful bikes included numerous flat-twins such as the KS750, much used by German troops in the Second World War, and the sporty 1951 model KS601, known as the Green Elephant. Zündapp thrived in the 1960s and 1970s, producing successful off-road competition bikes and two-stroke roadsters. But sales fell dramatically in the early 1980s. Stefan Dörflinger won the 80cc world title for Zündapp in 1984, but the firm went into liquidation the following year.

of 1982. The YZR, with its crankcase reed-valve induction system, was introduced as the OW81 model in 1984. Its engine used twin crankshafts geared together, the layout actually more accurately resembling a W4. This format has also been adopted by Suzuki and Cagiva, leaving only Honda's NSR as a true V-four.

The YZR's output has risen gradually over the years, to a figure of over 180bhp from the recent big bang unit. Chassis layout has remained typical of a Grand Prix 500, based around a thick twin-spar aluminium frame, with suspension generally provided by Öhlins, the Swedish specialist firm owned by Yamaha. In many seasons the YZR has not been the fastest bike in a straight line, but it has been tractable, reliable and a good all-rounder, capable

of winning at any circuit, especially at the hands of strars like Californians Eddie Lawson and Wayne Rainey, both of whom rode it to three world championships.

Arguably the greatest racebikes of the 1970s were Yamaha's TZs, from the TZ250 twin to the TZ750 four. After winning its first race in 700cc form in 1974, the four dominated Formula 750 racing for the rest of the decade. Powerful and fast yet impressively reliable, the TZ750 won four F750 titles and was still capable of taking Graeme Crosby to Daytona victory in 1982. Agostini won Yamaha's first 500cc world championship on a straight four in 1975, ending MV's four-stroke domination. Most successful of all was Kenny Roberts, who rode the four to a hat-trick of titles between 1978 and 1980.

■ ABOVE *Frenchman Christian Sarron won the 250cc world championship on Yamaha's TZ twin in 1984..*

■ RIGHT AND INSET RIGHT *Kenny Roberts won world titles with Yamaha as a rider and, more recently, as a manager.*

✦ INDEX